THE
1930s

Other books in this series:

THE
1930s

Louise I. Gerdes, *Book Editor*

David L. Bender, *Publisher*
Bruno Leone, *Executive Editor*
Bonnie Szumski, *Series Editor*
David M. Haugen, *Managing Editor*

Greenhaven Press, Inc., San Diego, California

AMERICA'S DECADES

Every effort has been made to trace the owners of copyrighted material. The articles in this volume may have been edited for content, length, and/or reading level. The titles have been changed to enhance the editorial purpose.

No part of this book may be reproduced or used in any form or by any means, electrical, mechanical, or otherwise, including, but not limited to, photocopy, recording, or any information storage and retrieval system, without prior written permission from the publisher.

Library of Congress Cataloging-in-Publication Data

The 1930s / Louise I. Gerdes, book editor.
    p.   cm. — (America's decades)
  Includes bibliographical references and index.
  ISBN 0-7377-0300-8 (lib. bdg. : alk. paper) —
  ISBN 0-7377-0299-0 (pbk. : alk. paper)
    1. United States—Civilization—1918–1945. 2. Nineteen
thirties. I. Gerdes, Louise I. II. Series

E169.1 .A1129 2000
973.91—dc21
                                                99-047626
                                                      CIP

Cover photo: (top) AP/Wide World, Jesse Owens at a medal ceremony at the 1936 Berlin Olympics; (bottom) PhotoDisc
Library of Congress, 20, 73, 92, 179
Franklin D. Roosevelt Library, 121
National Archives, 166

©2000 by Greenhaven Press, Inc.
P.O. Box 289009, San Diego, CA 92198-9009

Printed in the U.S.A.

Contents

Chapter 2: The Great Depression and the New Deal

ity for both courage and cowardice in the people who participated.

Chapter 5: Entertainment, Expression, and Escape in the Thirties

United States should not become involved in world politics. However, between 1937 and 1940, President Roosevelt urged Congress to prepare the military and took a firmer stand against German and Japanese aggression.

Foreword

In his book *The American Century*, historian Harold Evans maintains that the history of the twentieth century has been dominated by the rise of the United States as a global power: "The British dominated the nineteenth century, and the Chinese may cast a long shadow on the twenty-first, but the twentieth century belongs to the United States." In a 1998 interview he summarized his sweeping hypothesis this way: "At the beginning of the century the number of free democratic nations in the world was very limited. Now, at the end of the century, democracy is ascendant around the globe, and America has played the major part in making that happen."

As the new century dawns, historians are eager to appraise the past one hundred years. Evans's book is just one of many attempts to assess the historical impact that the United States has had in the past century. Although not all historians agree with Evans's characterization of the twentieth century as "America's century," no one disputes his basic observation that "in only the second century of its existence the United States became the world's leading economic, military and cultural power." For most of the twentieth century the United States has played an increasingly larger role in shaping world events. The Greenhaven Press America's Decades series is designed to help readers develop a better understanding of America and Americans during this important time.

Each volume in the ten-volume series provides an in-depth examination of the time period. In compiling each volume, editors have striven to cover not only the defining events of the decade—in both the domestic and international arenas—but also the cultural, intellectual, and technological trends that affected people's everyday lives.

Essays in the America's Decades series have been chosen for their concise, accessible, and engaging presentation of the facts. Each selection is preceded by a summary of the article's content. A comprehensive index and an annotated table of contents also aid readers in quickly locating material of interest. Each volume begins with an introductory essay that presents the broader themes of each decade. Several research aids are also present, including an extensive bibliography and a timeline that provides an at-a-glance overview of each decade.

Each volume in the Greenhaven Press America's Decades series serves as an informative introduction to a specific period in U.S. history. Together, the volumes comprise a detailed overview of twentieth century American history and serve as a valuable resource for students conducting research on this fascinating time period.

Introduction: The Rise of the Common Man

The decade of the 1930s is bound on one side by the stock market crash of October 29, 1929, and on the other by the bombing of Pearl Harbor on December 7, 1941. The decade was dominated by the gravest economic crisis the country had ever faced. In fact, for many Americans the Great Depression and the 1930s have become nearly synonymous. Americans would come to see themselves and their government in a whole new way. During the 1930s Americans who had enjoyed an unprecedented era of personal freedom and independence came to realize that only by working together under the strong leadership of the government could they combat the Great Depression. Technological developments in film, radio, and television not only helped provide escapist entertainment but also brought Americans together like never before, creating a national identity and the beginnings of an American consumer culture.

The 1920s: A Decade of Self-Determination

In the 1920s the nation's productivity and economic growth had achieved unprecedented prosperity. The gross national product rose an average of 5 percent per year, and industrial output increased by more than 60 percent for the decade. Unemployment seldom exceeded 2 percent, and the annual income rose significantly from $520 to $681. Purchasing power increased, and millions of people enjoyed improved living standards. Consumers chose from new and affordable products such as automobiles, radios, phonographs, washing machines, vacuum cleaners, telephones, and sewing machines.

During the twenties, Americans held steadfastly to the belief that prosperity came from individual determination—the foundation of American society. Americans believed in the self-made man who could start at rock bottom and rise to the top. People who were not born to privilege could change their circumstances by working hard.

The self-made man of the twenties could achieve his dreams with the support of a free-market economy that was motivated by self-interest. According to this philosophy, individuals were free to seek their own occupations, to enter any business, and to act as they saw fit to improve their economic welfare. Competition regulated the economy, determining not only the prices of goods and services but also wage rates. Economists of the time believed that the economy should be self-regulating: Any fluctuations in production, employment, and consumption would correct themselves. Since self-interest motivated and drove the economy and competition served to regulate it, a policy of laissez-faire (or no government intervention) prevailed, and the government kept its hands off the economic activities of individuals and business and restricted its role to acting as an umpire in economic disputes.

Unfortunately, in many cases self-interest translated into greed and abuse of economic liberty, and competition failed to guarantee a free market. Certain individuals and firms began interfering with the economic freedom of others. For example, large firms exploited small firms, monopolies controlled markets, public utilities exploited consumers, and competing employers pushed wages down. Despite the wealth of prosperous Americans, most Americans were still poor. Despite the unfailing belief that the prosperity would continue, business had already begun to slow, and unemployment was increasing. Farmers had been overproducing crops at reduced value, and many who had been caught up in the frenzy of purchasing farm mortgage options were hopelessly in debt. When the stock market crashed on October 29, 1929, the individual stock speculator looked for someone to blame, but looking back at the crash, economist John Kenneth Galbraith explains,

> No one was responsible for the great Wall Street crash. No one engineered the speculation that preceded it. Both were

the product of the free choice and decision of hundreds of thousands of individuals. The latter were not led to the slaughter. They were impelled to it by the seminal lunacy which has always seized people who are seized in turn with the notion that they can become very rich.[1]

The dreams of many self-made men of the twenties crashed along with the stock market.

Herbert Hoover's Progressive Individualism

Herbert Hoover had assumed the presidency shortly before the stock market crashed. Hoover was a self-made million-aire and, according to historian Louis W. Liebovich, em-bodied the nineteenth-century hero: "the boy who rose from humble beginnings to become a successful business-man through independence, hard work, and determination. . . . Hoover represented everything most Americans hoped for—power, success, and wealth mixed with decency and compassion, not flash and conspicuous consumption."[2]

Hoover's reaction to the stock market crash, then, was not surprising: Hoover encouraged optimism, arguing that pessimism would discourage investment and limit produc-tion. Although Hoover formed several conferences and commissions to study the nation's economic problems, he believed the government's role was merely to advise. His-torian Roger Biles summarizes Hoover's philosophy: "Hoover saw only failure in the heavy hand of coercive government, believing that America's history ratified the reliance of individual effort."[3]

Some authorities claim that the government's inaction turned the recession into a prolonged depression. Hoover did respond, however, with some government action: The Reconstruction Finance Corporation, for example, was the first government intervention in a peacetime economy, and the Emergency Relief and Construction Act was the first time a government assumed responsibility for relief. Nev-ertheless, most historians argue that it was too little too late, and although Hoover continued to sanction the cre-ation of government agencies, their role was to remain advisory alone. While later generations have treated Hoover more kindly, his contemporaries condemned his performance. Unfortunately, the problem was without a solution. When historians and economists look back at the Great Depression, most conclude that there was no solution. As Geoffrey Perrett writes, "What made the Depression so appalling a human tragedy was that it could be overcome only by an event as awesome, as terrifying, and as irresistible as the Depression itself. And that was the Second World War."[4]

Although economists now generally agree no solution to the nation's economic problems existed, when the economy failed, the American people blamed Hoover. People named the communities of makeshift shacks erected at the outskirts of urban centers where displaced families were forced to live "Hoovervilles." Hoover had become the symbol of complacency and inaction. "People were starving because of Herbert Hoover. . . . My Mother was out of work because of Herbert Hoover. Men were killing themselves because of Herbert Hoover, and their fatherless children were being packed away into orphanages . . . because of Herbert Hoover."[5] Hoover's reputation as a nineteenth-century hero had unraveled.

The Economic Decline

By the winter of 1932–1933, industrial output had practically ground to a halt while prices and interest rates fell. In December 1933 unemployment was at 24.9 percent. In 1934 the national income was $10 billion less than in 1931, just above half the 1929 level. Instead of recovering from this downturn, as economists predicted, the economy slipped deeper and deeper into a prolonged depression, and economists could not explain or offer a way out of the continuing depression.

Agriculture was one of the areas hardest hit by the Great Depression. Farm prices plummeted in reaction to the stock market crash. Farmers had huge surpluses, but consumers could not afford to buy their crops. The drop in farm income meant that many farmers could no longer meet mortgage payments, and they watched helplessly as their homes and farms were foreclosed and auctioned off. Compounding these problems, the 1930s brought serious drought, making farming even more difficult in the dust storms that choked the Midwest. This, in turn, fueled a steady stream of migrants to the Pacific Northwest and California.

Urban families were also struggling. At its peak in 1933, unemployment affected between 12 and 15 million American workers; during the rest of the decade, the number of unemployed hovered around 8 million. At times 25 percent of the workforce was out of a job. People learned to get by with less, and they even got used to hunger. As historian Susan Ware remarks,

> One persistent irony of the Depression was the vast economic dislocation: want in the midst of plenty. While crops rotted in the fields because farmers did not have enough money to harvest them, people starved in the cities. People wore threadbare clothing, while bales of cotton stood unsold in southern commercial centers. Thousands of shoe workers were laid off, while people walked the streets in cardboard shoes.[6]

Looking to the Government for Help

American life had changed dramatically, and unfortunately for Herbert Hoover, the impact of these changes was realized during his presidency. When Americans began to lose their jobs, charity alone was insufficient to care for the people, and whole communities came apart. The rugged individualism that made America great was now believed to be the source of the nation's economic woes. Overcome with despair, many Americans reluctantly discarded their deeply held belief in self-reliance and turned finally to the federal government as a last resort.

Unfortunately, these Americans looked to a government unfamiliar with the role of savior. No previous president had been asked to assume responsibility for managing the American economy. In the twenties, Americans expected the government to play only a minor role in their lives. This same government was now asked to create jobs, support farmers, protect investments, and ensure the security of the future of its citizens. A government that had once focused primarily on foreign affairs was expected to protect American citizens from a domestic enemy more unfamiliar than any foreign foe it had ever faced.

The Modern Presidency

While the economic depression damaged Hoover and the Republicans, Franklin Delano Roosevelt's bold efforts to combat the depression while governor of New York enhanced his reputation. In 1932 Roosevelt was nominated the Democratic Party candidate for president. He broke with tradition and flew to Chicago to accept the nomination in person, where he pledged "a New Deal" for the American people. He then campaigned energetically, calling for government intervention in the economy to provide relief, recovery, and reform. His activist approach and personal charm helped to defeat Hoover by 7 million votes in November 1932.

Although millions of people had seen Roosevelt, most Americans did not think of him as handicapped. Roosevelt was, however, a polio paraplegic who used a wheelchair for mobility. Roosevelt had to be pulled to a standing position and lifted in and out of cars and up and down stairs. Americans did not want to think of their president as crippled, particularly when the country itself was crippled by the Great Depression. Knowing this, Roosevelt disguised the extent of his disability through a series of complex strategies designed to make him appear able-bodied in public. Roosevelt was aware of the skill required to deceive the American people and once remarked to the great Orson Welles, "Orson, you and I are the two best actors in America!"[7]

The contrast between Herbert Hoover and Franklin Delano Roosevelt represents the change in American attitudes from the 1920s. Unlike Hoover, Roosevelt never personally experienced poverty. He was born in Hyde Park, New York, to wealth and social position. Despite Hoover's experience, principles, and efficiency, Americans were looking for a leader, and Hoover did not have the skills for dealing with people and the flair for politics that came naturally to Roosevelt. Americans no longer wanted an efficient bureaucrat as president; they needed a strong paternal figure to lead them out of the depression.

Franklin D. Roosevelt

If America wanted a president who would give the government an active role in their lives, they got it. Arguably no president before or since has pushed the role of the executive branch to its limits like Roosevelt, who took on his paternal role openly and with the support of the people. Roosevelt made his objectives clear in his first inaugural address on Saturday, March 4, 1933:

> It is to be hoped that the normal balance of executive and legislative authority may be wholly adequate to meet the unprecedented task before us. But it may be that an unprecedented demand and need for undeclared action may call for temporary departure from that normal balance of public procedure . . . and in the event that the national emergency is still critical, I shall not evade the clear course of duty that will then confront me. I shall ask the Congress for the one remaining instrument to meet the crisis—broad Executive power to wage a war against the emergency, as great as the power that would be given me if we were in fact invaded by a foreign foe. . . . We do not distrust the future of essential democracy. The people of the United States have not failed. In their need they have registered a man-

date that they want direct, vigorous action. They have asked for discipline and direction under leadership. They have made me the present instrument of their wishes. In the spirit of the gift I take it.[8]

A New Deal for America

Once in office, Roosevelt moved quickly to address the enormous need for the three R's: relief, recovery, and reform. During his first eight days in office, Roosevelt took immediate action to initiate his New Deal for the American people. To halt depositor panics, he temporarily closed the nation's banks until examiners ruled them sound. Shortly thereafter, three of every four banks reopened. Because Roosevelt said so, people concluded that the banks were safe, and they began to deposit the cash they had stashed under mattresses. One of Roosevelt's top aides, Raymond Moley, maintained that "capitalism was saved in eight days."[9]

In a special session of Congress, during what became known as the first one hundred days, Roosevelt worked to pass recovery legislation that set up agencies such as the Agricultural Adjustment Administration to support farm prices and the Civilian Conservation Corps to employ young men. Other agencies helped business and labor, insured bank deposits, regulated the stock market, subsidized home and farm mortgage payments, and aided the unemployed. The National Recovery Act encouraged business leaders to work together to create codes that would control wages and prices. These measures revived confidence in the economy. Banks reopened and direct relief saved millions of Americans from starvation. But the New Deal measures also involved government directly in areas of social and economic life as never before and resulted in greatly increased spending and unbalanced budgets, which led to criticism of Roosevelt's programs. However, the nation-at-large supported Roosevelt, electing additional Democrats to state legislatures and governorships in the midterm elections.

Another flurry of New Deal legislation followed in

1935, including the establishment of the Works Projects Administration (WPA) that put 3.5 million jobless Americans to work on roads, parks, and buildings. Moreover, the WPA provided jobs not only for laborers but also artists, writers, musicians, and authors. In the past the arts had always been supported by private funding, and many believed the government had no business supporting them. On the one side, some people did not consider singing, acting, or painting to be work, which made it difficult to find support for these programs. Artists, too, were concerned, as historian Robert S. McElvaine suggests, "that as Washington began paying the pianist it would want to call the tune. Even if there were no conscious interference—and who could be sure there would not be?—the possibility that bureaucracy would stifle creativity was omnipresent."[10]

Also enacted in 1935, the Social Security Act provided unemployment compensation and a program of old-age and survivors' benefits that continues today. On June 8, 1934, President Roosevelt created the Committee on Economic Security to study the problem, and the congressional report that followed included a detailed legislative proposal. Although the act did not achieve all the aspirations of those who supported it, it did provide disability coverage, medical benefits, aid to dependent children, and grants to the states to provide medical care.

Facing Domestic and Foreign Foes

After his overwhelming victory in the election of 1936, Roosevelt took on the critics of the New Deal: namely, the Supreme Court that had declared much of his legislation unconstitutional. In 1937 he proposed to add new justices to the Supreme Court, but critics said he was "packing" the Court and undermining the separation of powers. Congress defeated his proposal, but the Court began to decide in favor of New Deal legislation. These setbacks, coupled with the recession that occurred midway through his second term, represented the low point in Roosevelt's presidential career.

Although Roosevelt's New Deal would not cure America's economic woes, its reforms would endure, from Social Security and accessible home mortgages to cheap electricity and a supervised stock market. Journalist Lewis Lord writes of Roosevelt, "Long before political scientists concluded he had created the modem presidency, long before economists decided he had saved capitalism, long before historians ranked him beside Washington and Lincoln as 'great,' a man who couldn't walk put America on its feet."[11] Nevertheless, by the end of the decade, New Deal reform legislation diminished, and the ills of the depression would not fully abate until the nation mobilized for war. Only during the massive spending necessary for World War II would unemployment finally slip below 15 percent.

Many Americans extended their philosophy of self-reliance to U.S. foreign policy. Isolationists believed that America should tend to its own affairs. However, when Adolf Hitler attacked Poland in September 1939, Roosevelt stated that although the nation was neutral, he did not expect America to remain inactive in the face of Nazi aggression. Accordingly, he tried to make American aid available to Britain, France, and China and to obtain an amendment of the Neutrality Acts, which rendered such assistance difficult. He also took measures to build up the armed forces in the face of isolationist opposition.

With the fall of France in 1940, the American mood and Roosevelt's policy changed dramatically. Congress enacted a draft for military service, and Roosevelt signed a lend-lease bill in March 1941 to furnish aid to nations at war with Germany and Italy. Although neutral in the war and still at peace, America was becoming the arsenal of democracy as its factories began producing as they had in the years before the Great Depression.

Helping America's Youth

As First Lady, Eleanor Roosevelt, too, broke with the past. She initiated weekly press conferences with female reporters, lectured throughout the country, and had her own radio program and syndicated newspaper column, "My Day." She served as Franklin's eyes and ears and became a major voice in his administration on issues concerning America's youth, the underprivileged, and racial minorities. In fact, President Harry S. Truman once called her "the First Lady of the World." Many of her ideas were incorporated into the New Deal Social Welfare Program.

The New Deal did have a better record than the previous administration in helping America's youth. The National Recovery Act of 1934 and the Fair Labor Standards Act of 1938 banned exploitative child labor. More than 2 million students worked on National Youth Administration projects between 1936 and 1943, and 12.9 percent of high school jobs were given to minorities. The Federal Emergency Relief Administration's (FERA) college aid program of 1934 funded work-study jobs. The Civilian Conservation Corps funded another 2.6 million needy youths, and the Social Security Administration's Aid to Dependent Children provided impoverished boys and girls with support. New Deal money also funded a free school lunch program and the construction of new schools. Furthermore, FERA funded teacher salaries, thus preventing four thousand school closings. Not only did the Roosevelt administration's New Deal set a precedent for federal programs that support youth and education but also paved the way for reforms well into the 1960s.

The Politics of Labor

While Eleanor Roosevelt fought for America's youth, minorities, and the underprivileged, the president, along with his other efforts, worked to protect the rights of working people. Although the well-to-do despised Franklin Roosevelt, American workers loved him. Journalist Lewis Lord notes, "A reporter quizzed a North Carolina millworker about his enthusiasm for the president: Didn't he realize that FDR's crackpot notions would wreck America? The worker didn't know that, but he did know this: 'Roosevelt is the only man we ever had in the White House who would understand that my boss is a son of a bitch.'"[12]

Prior to the Great Depression, labor was poorly organized. If organized at all, the unions were "company unions," always under the watchful eye of employers. The government took little interest in labor relations and maintained a "hands-off" approach to business. Hoover's philosophy of progressive individualism relied on the belief that benevolent employers led grateful workers into prosperity. When Hoover's system failed, many of the unemployed began to look at radical solutions such as communism and socialism, but most chose to wait, hoping the New Deal administration would offer some relief.

Roosevelt's first response to the industrial crisis was the National Industrial Recovery Act (NIRA) of 1933, which seemed to favor business more than labor. The act encouraged businesses to meet together and set codes of conduct to eliminate excessive competition. Ironically, United Mine Workers President John L. Lewis took hold of Section 7a, which dictated that every industry-wide code must allow workers the right to organize unions and bargain collectively, and he told miners that the president wanted them to join a union, although this was never Roosevelt's intention. Lewis and his followers organized hundreds of thousands of miners. By the end of 1933, the American Federation of Labor had added more than a half million members.

NIRA was no panacea for workers because the act provided no means of enforcement, which forced workers to take alternative action. In 1934 more than 1.5 million American workers went on strike, including San Francisco longshoremen who brought the city's waterfront to a standstill. When the police intervened, open fighting led to the deaths of two strikers. Two weeks later, two other striking teamsters were killed in Minneapolis.

When the Supreme Court declared NIRA unconstitutional in 1935, however, Roosevelt remained committed to labor, recognizing its importance in the reform of the nation's economic system. Roosevelt now turned to New York senator Robert F. Wagner and his proposed legislation that would create a National Labor Relations Board (NLRB). The Wagner bill prohibited unfair labor practices and empowered the NLRB to investigate and punish lawbreakers. The NLRB would oversee employee elections to choose unions and to make sure that employers negotiated solely with unions properly elected by workers. Although opposed by business, the National Labor Relations Act became law in the summer of 1935.

The Sit-Down Strike

In this same year, automobile workers organized the United Automobile Workers of America (UAW). General Motors (GM) would not recognize the UAW as a bargaining representative, so the battles between workers and GM management began. At GM's Fisher Body Plant in Cleveland, which made bodies for the nations biggest-selling cars, the workers were angered because the plant manager refused to discuss reductions in the piecework rate. On December 28, 1936, the UAW representative walked down the line banging on the machines with a wrench and shouting "Sit down! Sit down!" The workers shut off the machines and sat down. They would not leave. Two days later, hearing that GM was moving work to factories without strong unions, workers in Flint, Michigan, also began a sit-down strike. Within a week, for the time being at least, GM was out of the automaking business.

The sit-down strike was more effective than the picket line because employers could replace striking employees who walked the picket line, but if the workers stayed in the plant, management could not replace them with other workers. During negotiations, relations between the striking employees and management remained relatively amicable. On January 11th, however, Flint's uneasy truce was shattered when plant guards barred delivery of evening meals to the one hundred men occupying the plant and a GM official turned off the heat. Both sides called in reinforcements. Union toughs from Detroit headed for Flint while the police headed for the plant. Strikers seized the gate, and the police fired tear gas. When the wind shifted, the police retreated under a hail of parts and debris thrown by the strikers. A few officers fired their pistols, and several workers were wounded, one seriously.

To support the striking workers, the Women's Auxiliary organized a first aid station, provided child care, and collected food and money for strikers and their families. An offshoot of the auxiliary called the Emergency Brigade actually picketed the auto plant to divert management while workers seized another plant. The brigade smashed the plant's windows when they heard the strikers had been gassed. These women wore red hats called tams, armbands, and political buttons, some showing support for President Roosevelt.

When Michigan governor Frank Murphy ordered the National Guard into Flint to keep the peace, hostilities ceased. However, when GM went to court obtaining an injunction ordering the workers out, workers seized the engine plant in Flint. Infuriated that GM's rivals were building cars and GM was not, management agreed to recognize the UAW. After forty-four days, the strike was over on March 12, 1937. The success of the UAW inspired others, and unions continued to grow. While unions provided American workers with strength in unity, the radio, knowing no geographic boundaries, gathered people together and gave them a national identity.

The Golden Age of Radio

Listeners came from urban and rural communities, from every age, culture, and class. Radio was truly the first modern mass medium. It brought the world into American homes, and it did so with immediacy. Radio allowed the nation to be part of an event the moment it occurred— whether it was celebrating the return of America's new hero, Charles A. Lindbergh, after his flight to Paris on June 11, 1927, or listening in horror as the zeppelin *Hindenburg* burst into flames while making its final approach into Lakehurst, New Jersey, on May 6, 1937. Americans no longer had to read of current events in newspapers. The radio brought these events into their homes, and it did so in a manner that newspapers could not replicate, enabling listeners to experience these events as they happened.

Radio was a fledgling media in the 1920s, and Americans were so awed by the radio that they would listen to almost anything, but by the end of the decade and during the Great Depression, the radio grew in popularity. The American audience wanted more than inspirational and educational programming, and broadcasters began to offer comedy, variety, and popular music. Vaudevillian performers like the Marx Brothers, George Burns, Gracie Allen, and Jack Benny provided escape from the economic trials of the American people. Comedies like *Amos 'n' Andy* were so popular that sponsors began to see the commercial potential of radio, and by the early thirties radio was financed by commercial sponsors. Radio advertising revenues rose from $40 million in 1930 to $112 million in 1935.

Ironically, although the thirties were a period of widespread economic hardship, it was a time when radio helped create a national consumer culture. The radio sold Americans products they never knew they needed. The radio soap opera was one of the most creative vehicles of mass consumption. Advertisers began to recognize that women purchased the majority of household consumer goods. While most American families listened to evening radio broadcasts, during the day, housewives remained at home. Cooking and household advice broadcasts, however, were insufficient to sustain the interest of housewives, and the soap opera was born. Shows like *Painted Dreams, Ma Perkins,* and *Today's Children* not only provided serial entertainment but also sold products for Montgomery Ward, Procter and Gamble, and Pillsbury.

In 1923 an estimated 400,000 American households had a radio; by the mid-thirties over 19 million households had radio sets. Because whole families would listen to each radio, the potential for influence grew exponentially. Americans were not truly aware of the potential power of this medium until the end of the decade, when 6 million listeners heard Orson Welles's infamous broadcast of *War of the Worlds,* H.G. Wells's science-fiction tale of Martian invasion. Many Americans thought the Martian invasion was real, setting off panic in the New York City area.

The radio personalized events for the listener. People did not have to read about Roosevelt's plans to rejuvenate the economy; they heard it from the man himself. On his eighth day in office, Roosevelt spoke from the White House and told a national radio audience why closing the banks was necessary. He did it so well, political satirist Will Rogers remarked, that even bankers could understand it. These "fireside chats" represented a bond across the airwaves between the people and their leader. For the first time in history, one person with a microphone could speak to many, influence them, and perhaps change their lives. But Roosevelt was not the only world leader who used the radio to communicate to his people. Adolf Hitler would use radio as an instrument of propaganda and, by the end of the decade, people all over the world would learn the power of radio. Just how the U.S. government should use the radio during World War II was a subject of debate throughout Roosevelt's administration.

Radio not only made possible the mass marketing of products such as Ivory Snow, Lucky Strikes cigarettes, and Jell-O to the American people but the mass marketing of music as well. When Prohibition ended in 1933, jazz emerged from the underground speakeasies and forbidden nightclubs. Record companies that were struggling during the depression were purchased by the radio networks: the Radio Corporation of America (RCA) purchased Victor records and the Columbia Broadcasting System (CBS) purchased Columbia records, which gave radio control over what music was heard or withheld from the public. The radio networks discovered how popular big-band jazz was among young audiences and how readily these young people would attend concerts, buy record albums, and listen to concerts on the radio. The marketing of jazz began.

The jazz style created by the big dance band came to be

known as swing, and the commercial dance band with leaders like Benny Goodman, Tommy Dorsey, Artie Shaw, Glenn Miller, Duke Ellington, and Cab Calloway were most popular among young audiences.

The Birth of Television

At the decade's end, RCA introduced a new form of technology to the American people at the New York World's Fair in Flushing Meadows, Queens. RCA's display of television sets was one of the most popular attractions at the fair, attracting more than 20 million Americans. At this time RCA also began the nation's first schedule of television programs by televising the fair's opening day. The first television audience watching these events not only saw New York's Mayor Fiorello LaGuardia but also their president, Franklin D. Roosevelt, who was the first president to appear live on television.

Sales of television sets in 1939 were minimal, however. Although RCA continued televising programs to serve their small audience, television needed a bigger audience to survive. RCA needed to sell more televisions. In the fall of 1939, RCA launched an aggressive campaign to sell televisions in Newburgh, New York. The company stocked appliance and department stores in the city with new sets, lowered the sales price by a third, and ran weekly advertisements in the local newspapers. For a down payment of just twenty-nine dollars and fifty cents and terms less than five dollars a week, you could own your own television receiver—"the Greatest Christmas Thrill of Your Life."[13] The strategy worked, and in a few weeks two hundred television sets had been sold, followed by four hundred more sets in the months immediately following the campaign. Nevertheless, not until the late forties would television truly compete with radio as the most influential American media.

Providing Escapist Entertainment

During the Great Depression movies were a vital form of popular culture. Eighty million customers went to the movies each week to escape their daily troubles. While some studios used the new sound technology to develop film subjects that had been successful in the twenties, such as the horror film and the gangster movie, others created new styles, such as the screwball comedy and the backstage musical. To deal with the financial setbacks of the depression, some studios turned to double-feature programming to entice people to the movie theaters and introduced the concept of producing B pictures—low-budget films with formulaic plots and lesser-known stars.

In the thirties the giant studios held nearly complete control over the careers of their employees and assembled their own roster of creators, performers, and technicians who worked so closely together over the years that the movies of each studio had their own "look": the elaborate musical production numbers of Warner Brothers, the ominous lighting of Universal's horror films, and the special effects of Radio-Keith-Orpheum (RKO).

Not only did the studios have control over production, but they had control over distribution and exhibition, a function that was crucial to their power. The studios owned chains of theaters across the country. Metro-Goldwyn-Mayer, Twentieth Century–Fox, Paramount Pictures, Warner Brothers, and RKO produced more than fifty features a year for their theaters. The smaller of the eight major studios—Universal, Columbia Pictures, and United Artists—had to have their films shown in the theaters of the other five.

Censoring Hollywood

The eight major studios formed the Motion Picture Producers and Distributors of America (MPPDA), the trade organization that self-censored the content of the films produced. The MPPDA hired Will H. Hays, postmaster general and former national chairman of the Republican Party to represent Hollywood. Known as a pillar of morality, Hays managed to placate a growing group of citizens who feared the freer morality of Hollywood and encouraged censorship. However, as a result of the threat of a boycott and government intervention, the MPPDA adopted a Motion Picture Production Code in 1930, which contained very specific restrictions.

Of particular concern to some Americans during this period of censorship and regulation was the influence of the gangster films. The film industry's love affair with members of criminal gangs was only natural as they were colorful, violent, and charismatic, and millions of law-abiding Americans followed their law-breaking activities. Between 1930 and 1933, gangsters were without doubt the American cinema's most conspicuous heroes. The dominant image of the movie gangster was formed primarily by the two charismatic stars who successfully played the gangster character: Edward G. Robinson and James Cagney. Robinson was best known for his role as Caesar Enrico Bandello in *Little Caesar* (1930) and Cagney for his performance as Tom Powers in *Public Enemy* (1931).

As the decade wore on, Hollywood producers discovered that the best way to exploit the crime genre's popularity and satisfy the censors at the same time was to turn the gangster character into a law enforcement officer. The gangster icon was transformed into a federal government man (G-man) drafted into the war on rising crime. By the mid-thirties, in patriotic films like *G-men* (1935), starring James Cagney, and *Special Agent* (1935), starring George Brent, Warner started to offer idealized portraits of policemen and the Federal Bureau of Investigation (FBI) rather than of gangsters and criminals. Edward G. Robinson, too, was enlisted as a crusading cop infiltrating a gang led by a vicious Humphrey Bogart in *Bullets or Ballots* (1936).

Emerging Forms and New Technology

Another popular movie form that came out of Hollywood during the thirties was the backstage musical. Movies like *42nd Street* (1933) had story lines that involved romantic and business conflicts that revolved around the creation of musical productions. These films culminated in elaborate musical spectacles using cinematic techniques to create special effects impossible on a stage. For example, overhead cameras would film a chorus line of dancers as they formed kaleidoscopic patterns.

Fred Astaire and Ginger Rogers danced their way through a series of films as professional dancers, which made it possible for them to break into song and dance in settings outside the musical theater. In *Shall We Dance* (1937), Astaire, returning from Paris on board the *Queen Anne,* wanders into the engine room to sing and dance with the black crew, and in another scene Rogers and Astaire perform a shipboard number while walking their dogs.

The horror film was the particular specialty of Universal Studios. Having mastered lighting techniques originated in Germany, movies like *Frankenstein* and *Dracula,* both released in 1931, created archetypal figures who flourished in desolate landscapes. The demonic scientist Frankenstein defies the conventions of society in his quest for knowledge and is punished by his own creation for his arrogance. The Frankenstein monster, played by Boris Karloff, aroused sympathy as an outcast of society. Karloff's portrayal was so successful the studio produced spin-offs of the original, including *The Bride of Frankenstein* (1935) and *The Son of Frankenstein* (1939).

The "screwball" comedy combined intellectual sophistication with slapstick behavior. These films tended to include one or both of two important ingredients: class or sex role manipulation and wacky, oddball behavior, either by a daffy, lovestruck, and well-meaning character, usually female, or by a character who goes temporarily insane, usually male. Carole Lombard was this film form's brightest star. In *My Man Godfrey* (1936), she is an immature rich girl who rescues hobo William Powell from the city dump and proceeds to fall in love with him. In Howard Hawk's *Bringing Up Baby* (1938), Cary Grant, playing a bookish paleontologist, is pursued by Katharine Hepburn, an heiress. In the film Grant is forced to wear women's clothing, dig up dog bones, sing to a pet leopard, and is thrown in jail. While some film historians argue that such films served merely as escapist entertainment, others assert that the societal role manipulations reflected ways Americans were dealing with the changing world.

Walt Disney seized upon technology that transformed the whole motion picture industry. Utilizing the three-color Technicolor process, Disney developed the cartoon shorts that he called *Silly Symphonies* (1929–1939). Disney also created the first feature-length cartoon, *Snow White and the Seven Dwarfs* (1937), which was actually an animated musical. The first to use stereophonic sound, Disney also created the feature-length cartoon *Fantasia* (1940), an animated ballet that ranges from the romantic *Nutcracker Suite* to the horrific *Night on Bald Mountain.*

The live-action features of the thirties were expensive to make but made a lot for the studios that produced them. Films like *Mutiny on the Bounty* (1935), *Captain Blood* (1935), and *The Adventures of Robin Hood* (1938) were taken from literature, drama, or history and created a spectacular illusion for the audience. According to film historian Jack C. Ellis,

> The resources needed for that sort of film making—the carefully assembled and developed character players, along with the stars, the museum-like collections of props, the set construction and special effects departments—have all passed away with the older big-studio system itself. They don't make pictures like that the way they used to; or, when they do, the exceptions only prove the rule.[14]

America's Favorite Pastime

Like most businesses, major league baseball felt the effects of the Great Depression. Attendance fell to 6.3 million in 1933, and the salaries of players were slashed from the average salary of seventy-five hundred dollars in 1929 to six thousand dollars in 1933. Suffering clubs were forced to sell players to more successful clubs, which worsened attendance even further. The clubs had to find new ways to improve their financial condition. One solution was the introduction of night baseball. Another source of revenue was the sale of the rights to broadcast accounts of games to radio. By 1939 radio income was 7.3 percent of club revenue. Sale of the broadcast of the World Series, shared by all major league clubs, also fetched higher prices.

Although the fans worshiped baseball heroes in the twenties, the baseball heroes of the thirties had to be more than mere men. According to baseball fan Robert T. Smith, "Heroes had to be of truly heroic size: not men who owed allegiance to a team, a private ethic, . . . but men who faced a whole world of enemies, with a town, a county, or even half a nation at their backs."[15]

The 1930s continued the record-breaking career of Babe Ruth. When Ruth's career ended in 1935, new sluggers like Hank Greenberg, Ted Williams, and Joe DiMaggio continued the excitement. "Joltin'" Joe DiMaggio was a center fielder from California who played for the New York Yankees in the thirties. To many, DiMaggio appeared to be more than a mere mortal. He played like a machine, often playing while injured and, unlike Babe Ruth, showed little emotion, which, unfortunately for the press, made him a rather unexciting story. DiMaggio set new hitting records and was as great in the outfield as he was at bat—he seemed to speed effortlessly to the ball. He helped the Yankees win ten American League championships and nine World Series titles.

The Yankees produced another greater-than-life hero in Lou Gehrig, who did not miss a ball game for fourteen years, recording an amazing playing streak of 2,130 games. Sometimes called "the Iron Horse," Gehrig was a five-time league leader for runs batted in, a three-time home run champion, and four-time winner of the Most Valuable Player Award. Stricken with a rare type of paralysis that now bears his name, Gehrig retired from baseball on July 4, 1939. Gehrig told a stadium full of Yankee fans, "For the past two weeks you have been reading about the bad break I got. Yet today I consider myself the luckiest man on the face of the earth."

The Legacy of the 1930s

Few historians or economists would dispute that the 1930s represented a remarkable change in the way Americans saw themselves. Once powerless employees recognized that they had strength in unity, crying "Sit down! Sit down!" The radio brought the world into American homes and not only did Americans begin to listen as a nation, they also began to consume as a nation. With the widespread deprivation brought on by the Great Depression, rugged individualism had to make way for government intervention, and the influence of the government in the lives of the American people begun in the 1930s remains today: educational subsidies, endowments for the arts, public utilities, selective service, welfare, and more. From decisions on the future of Social Security to an increase in the minimum wage, economists and politicians continue to refer to the Roosevelt administration's New Deal legislation when making economic policy decisions. Although Americans continue to debate the role the government should play in the lives of its citizens, few historians doubt Roosevelt's commitment to the American people during the 1930s and his desire to keep his first inaugural promise, "This great nation will endure as it has endured, will revive and will prosper."[16] Soon after the next decade began, Roosevelt would keep his promise.

1. John Kenneth Galbraith, *The Great Crash: 1929*. New York: Time, 1962, p. 4.

2. Louis W. Liebovich, *Bylines in Despair: Herbert Hoover, the Great Depression, and the U.S. News Media*. Westport, CT: Praeger, 1994, p. xiii.

3. Roger Biles, *A New Deal for the American People*. DeKalb: Northern Illinois University Press, 1991, p. 16.

4. Geoffrey Perrett, *America in the Twenties: A History*. New York: Simon & Schuster, 1982, pp. 490–91.

5. Quoted in Thomas R. Pegram, *Battling Demon Rum: The Struggle for a Dry America, 1800–1933*. Chicago: Ivan R. Dee, 1998, p. 182.

6. Susan Ware, *Holding Their Own: American Women in the 1930s*. New York: Twayne, 1982, p. xiii.

7. Quoted in Hugh Gallagher, "The Politics of Polio," *Social Education*, September 1996, p. 265.

8. Franklin D. Roosevelt, first inaugural address, Saturday, March 3, 1933. Taken from the Avalon Project at the Yale Law School: Documents in Law, History, and Diplomacy, available at www.yale.edu/lawweb/ avalon/avalon.htm.

9. Quoted in Lewis Lord, "The Rise of the Common Man," *U.S. News & World Report*, October 25, 1993, p. 10.

10. Robert S. McElvaine, *The Great Depression: America, 1929–1941.* New York: Times Books, 1984, p. 269.

11. Lord, "The Rise of the Common Man," p. 10.

12. Lord, "The Rise of the Common Man," p. 10.

13. Jim von Schilling, "Sixty Years Ago: October 1939," *Television Archives.* http://ccs.compubell.com/~mweinber/newburgh.html.

14. Jack C. Ellis, *A History of Film.* Englewood Cliffs, NJ: Prentice-Hall, 1985, p. 198.

15. Robert T. Smith, *Baseball: A Historical Narrative of the Game, the Men Who Have Played It, and Its Place in American Life.* New York: Simon & Schuster, 1947, p. 310.

16. Franklin D. Roosevelt, first inaugural address, Saturday, March 4, 1933.

CHAPTER 1

Signs of Change

AMERICA'S DECADES

1929: A Year of Transition

Joe Alex Morris

Although life changed for most Americans when the stock market crashed on October 24, 1929, many Americans responded with courage, innovation, and even humor, writes the late author and journalist Joe Alex Morris. In the following review of the events of December 1929, Morris tells of lost fortunes and shattered lives, but he also relates stories of creativity and discovery. For example, a retired man who lost his investments in the crash was forced back into the business world; however, Morris reveals, he regained his fortune, returned to school, and eventually became a college president. With the support of business leaders, President Herbert Hoover was confident the economy would survive, and most Americans carried on with their lives. An American journalist and bureau chief for the *Los Angeles Times*, Morris was killed while covering the revolution in Iran during an uprising in Tehran in 1979.

The Roaring Twenties didn't end with a bang, but neither did they end with a whimper. In retrospect, it might seem that when bleak December 1929 brought a close to that fabulous decade the American people would have been justified in feeling that the end of their world had arrived. But it was not that way at all.

America was not only a powerful industrial nation; it

Excerpted from *What a Year!* by Joe Alex Morris. Copyright ©1956 by Joe Alex Morris, renewed 1984 by Joe Alex Morris. Reprinted with permission from HarperCollins Publishers, Inc.

was a young industrial nation. The factories were still there. The coal and iron were still there; the food and the people were still there. What had happened was that big and foolish America had been on a year-long binge; a real, hell-raising binge like Saturday night at the county fair. It had listened happily to the deceptive pitch of the barkers in fancy vests at the entrances to the sideshow tents and had been lured onto the roller coaster by an enticing dame called Lady Luck. Naturally, in the cold gray dawn of December 1929, America woke up with a supercolossal hangover that was all wool and a yard wide. It was painful and it made a guy feel foolish. There wasn't any use reaching for your pocketbook because you knew it was gone. But this was another day. It was time to mutter "Never again!" and to get back on the job. The headache would go away. The shaking hand would steady. Boy! Will you mix me a bicarb, please?—and say! just put it on the tab until payday, will you? Yeah, I'm a little rocky this morning. But come to think of it—we had a helluva time while it lasted!

The Lighter Side of the Crash

After the first shock had worn off, most Americans were able to enjoy the many jokes and wisecracks that grew out of the market collapse and the confusion attending it. Eddie Cantor [a popular radio comedian], who had been planning to live on his investments, wrote a book called *Caught Short! A Saga of Wailing Wall Street* that had everybody in stitches. He described himself as a comedian, author, statistician and victim, and dated his tome 1929 A.C., meaning "After the Crash." Almost everybody got a good laugh out of the story of one speculator whose margin account was exhausted and who was sold out twice in one day by his rattled broker.

Groucho Marx [a popular comic actor and comedian], according to a tale related by Margaret Case Harriman [an actress who worked with Marx], had invested in a number of stocks on the advice of friends. When the crash came, he seized his list of investments and rushed to the office of his attorney, Morris Ernst, for advice. Ernst checked the list over and discovered that most of Groucho's stocks had taken a nose dive.

"Where did you get this recommendation?" he asked Groucho, pointing to a stock that had dropped fifty points or so.

"That one was suggested by my friend, [businessman and statesman] Bernard Baruch."

"What about this one—down from 122 to 58?" Ernst continued.

"Well, that was on the recommendation of Gerard Swope."

At last Ernst found one item on the list that had not suffered disaster. It was a stock that had lost only one point in the crash.

"Where on earth," he exclaimed, "did you get *that* tip?"

"Oh, *that*," Groucho replied. "I got that one from a wardrobe woman in the Shubert Theater in Chicago."

There also were some unusual tales drifting back from foreign lands, especially from France where many American artists, writers and loafers had more or less settled down to live on their paper profits. A large percentage of these expatriates suddenly found themselves broke after the crash and unable to buy even a third-class passage back to the United States. Some of them went to work and others sold their furniture and clothes. One enterprising group of Americans who had been living high in Paris, France, organized a parade of their sports automobiles down the Champs Elysées, each car marked with a "for sale" sign and a price that the owner intended to use to pay his way back home. In a dispatch from Constantinople, an American correspondent reported what Turkish newspapers were saying about the aftermath of the crash in New York. One Constantinople newspaper informed the Turks that New Yorkers were in grave distress and living mainly on bread, cheese and cabbage, being unable to afford anything else. They had no table linen, the story added, although it failed to make clear whether the linen had been seized by creditors or was being held by the laundries pending payment of overdue bills. As a result, most New Yorkers were said to be eating off old newspapers and not a few, presumably evicted from apartments, were living on the roofs of sky-scrapers. This was so amusing that the *New York Times* printed the story on its front page.

A few gags and exaggerations were also dreamed up by New Yorkers for their own amusement, including some rather grim ones. There was, for example, the story of the midtown hotel clerk who asked each new arrival whether he wanted a room "for sleeping or for jumping." Another concerned the two men wiped out in the market, who had leaped hand-in-hand from a high roof. They had held a joint stock account.

Changing Lifestyles

An ability to laugh, however, did not mean that all was lightness and fun. Many thousands of men and women who had happily retired to live—some meagerly, some in great comfort—on their investments now discovered that they had to go back to work. Some of them never were able to find jobs. Some of them made new fortunes. In Indiana, a prominent manufacturer who had retired in order to complete his interrupted college education saw his invest-ments so depleted by the Wall Street collapse that he had to return to business. Two years later he had restored his fi-nances, again returned to school and later became a college president, which had been his goal for years.

Alexander Woollcott's biographer estimated that the New York critic had about a hundred thousand dollars spread thinly on margin in September 1929, but found himself seven thousand in debt in December. Woollcott au-daciously raised his prices for contributions to magazines, became perhaps the highest-priced book reviewer in his-tory and was soon back on his financial feet. "In the empty, silly, noisy years which immediately preceded the Wall Street crash," he wrote later, "I used to get hot tips on the market from big shots. I suppose they rather fancied them-

Stock Market Suicide?

Although the suicide rate following the collapse of the stock market on October 24, 1929, was less than the suicide rate for the same period in 1928, many suicides were still blamed on the crash, as the following article found in the New York Sunday News *suggests. The news article also points out that James J. Riordan was a close friend of Alfred E. Smith, the Democratic candidate who was defeated by Herbert Hoover in the 1928 presidential election.*

The suicide of James J. Riordan, president of the County Trust Company, financial backer of the Democratic Party, and close friend of former Gov. Alfred E. Smith, was revealed early yesterday afternoon—almost 24 hours after Riordan shot himself.

The banker, who was 47, was a victim of the stock market. He died with a bullet through his right temple in his bedroom at the home of his sister, Mrs. Margaret Murray, at 21 West 12th Street, where he lived, on Friday afternoon. . . .

Both Mrs. Murray and Mrs. [Molly] Geagan, [the maid], told the medical examiner that Riordan had been depressed and in poor health for about 3 weeks and that for several days he was not in a normal mental state.

The banker is reported to have suffered heavily in the collapse of Radio shares. Radio dropped to 35½ on Friday, a loss of 14½ points. . . .

News of the suicide broke like a bomb yesterday at the National Democratic Club during a luncheon given by the Democratic Union attended by Gov. Franklin D. Roosevelt, Lieut. Gov. Herbert Lehman and John F. Curry, sachem of Tammany Hall.

The luncheon was postponed and the guests, all friends of Riordan's, left the table and divided into little knots, discussing the tragedy. Gov. Roosevelt, seemingly profoundly shocked, only murmured: 'This is terrible; this is terrible.'

New York Sunday News, November 10, 1929.

selves in the role of Maecenas [patrons of the arts], giving a financial lift to someone more literate (and therefore more incompetent and idiotic) than themselves. No good ever accrued from these tips except the potential benefit which anyone can experience by merely losing money."

A wealthy man who lived on a large estate near New York told his neighbors in November 1929 that he had lost four million dollars in the market crash. He fired three gardeners, five stablemen, the first and second butlers, the assistant chauffeur and various other employees, including the pastry cook. Then he gave his neighbors the impression that he was looking earnestly for a high window, suitable for jumping. While putting his affairs in order, however, he discovered that he had carelessly overlooked some three million dollars that was in safe investments. This prompted him to cease worrying about a high window, but he cautiously refused to rehire the discharged servants except for his beagle trainer.

Few were so lucky or so absent-minded. News dispatches from all over the country told of suicides which were—often inaccurately—blamed on the crash. Two brokers in Philadelphia, Pennsylvania, a grain dealer in Chicago, Illinois, a utilities president in Rochester, New York, a civil engineer in Scranton, Pennsylvania. And not a few in New York, including James J. Riordan, a man of considerable political influence and president of the County Trust Company, which, incidentally, was in sound condition. The fact that newspaper reporters naturally checked into all suicides to determine whether they could be linked in any way to the market tended at times to give the impression that Wall Street was a dangerous place to walk because of falling bodies. This false impression was exploded later by statistics showing that there were only forty-four suicides in all of Manhattan between mid-October and mid-November 1929, as compared to fifty-three in the same period of 1928. The same was generally true for the United States as a whole. There were, for instance, more suicides during the summer months of 1929 when the market was booming than during the months of the big crash.

The Hoover Business Conference

The first snow of the season had hardly covered the White House grounds when President Hoover began a series of conferences with industrial, financial, agricultural and labor leaders, designed to reassure the public as to the economic future of the nation. "Words are not of any great importance in times of economic disturbance," the President said. "It is action that counts." Sitting behind his big desk, smoking a cigar, Mr. Hoover took the position that there had been no business recession but that there was a threat of one. As to the market collapse, he believed that: "The long upward trend of fundamental progress gave rise to overoptimism as to profits, which translated itself into a wave of uncontrolled speculation in securities, resulting in the diversion of capital from business to the stock market, and the inevitable crash." By the first week in December 1929, he believed that "we have re-established confidence."

Most of the leaders who attended the White House conferences seemed to agree with him. Henry Ford snapped out the opinion that the market collapse was due to "a serious withdrawal of brains from business" and recommended "reducing prices to the level of actual value" as well as increasing wages. He told the President that he was going to boost wages. In general, the industrial leaders told the President that they would not cut wages if the unions would take a co-operative attitude. Other conferees promised the President to help in stabilizing economic conditions and devising means for increasing the nation's purchasing power. Thirty-five public utility officials, led by Owen D. Young, pledged almost two billion dollars to the President's program for stimulating industrial activity, particularly in regard to expansion and new construction.

Mr. Hoover also sent telegrams to the governors of all states urging them to inaugurate "energetic, yet prudent" public works programs to relieve unemployment. As Christmas approached, the President was hard at work and appeared to be making progress. The only sour note came one afternoon when a group of thirty-five young men and women appeared on Pennsylvania Avenue and began marching back and forth in front of the White House, carrying big placards that said:

DOWN WITH HOOVER

THE HOOVER BUSINESS

CONFERENCE IS A DECLARATION

OF WAR ON THE WORKING MASSES

They hadn't marched very long, however, before White House and city police appeared and arrested them on charges of parading without a permit. The paraders jeered and sang the Communist "Internationale" as they were led off to the police station. As soon as Mr. Hoover heard about the arrests he ordered the demonstrators released, saying that "the President considers that the misguided youths calling themselves Communists . . . should be released and sent to their parents. He does not believe any such discourtesy seriously injures the Republic and a night in jail is only doing them the favor of giving them a cheap martyrdom." To most Americans, this seemed a sensible way of dealing with such crackpot demonstrations.

The View from the Kremlin

The year 1929 was "the year of Mighty Change" in the opinion of Joseph V. Stalin, the Communist dictator of Soviet Russia. Stalin had been ill for some weeks but censorship concealed all details of his illness. There were frequent rumors that he was dying and at public ceremonies the people occasionally cried out for government officials to say whether the Man of Steel was sick or well. They got no replies, but at last Stalin himself appeared unexpectedly at a celebration in Moscow and was greeted by thunderous cheers. He was thin but his smile was benign. The dictator could well afford to smile. In 1929, he had succeeded in expelling from Russia his ancient enemy, Leon Trotsky. And then had come the gratifying news that the capitalistic nations had been shaken to the core by the Wall Street crash. Hailing "the year of Mighty Change," Stalin declared that "we are attacking capitalism all along the line and defeating it. Without foreign capital we are accomplishing the unprecedented feat of building up heavy industry in a backward country. . . . When we have industrialized the Soviet Union and set the peasants to driving tractors . . . we shall see which country can be called backward and which the vanguard of human progress."

As viewed from the towers of the Kremlin there seemed, indeed, to be a mighty change in the face of America in December of 1929. Yet the change was not easy to see if you were walking on Main Street in Sauk Center, Minnesota, on Bourbon Street in New Orleans, on Grant Street in Pittsburgh or on Fifth Avenue in New York. At the newly opened Fifth Avenue jewelry store of Black, Starr and Frost-Gorham, Inc., where the interior was sixteenth-century Italian Gothic, an exquisitely matched pearl necklace was confidently offered to Christmas shoppers for seven hundred thousand dollars.

Focusing on Other Interests

Christmas shopping in general was at a brisk pace and in volume exceeded the sales records of 1928, although it was noted that the greatest increases in buying were in chain stores featuring low-priced goods. In the Middle West retail sales were "considerably" higher than in the previous holiday season and one Chicago department store sold more than a million dollars' worth of goods in a single day despite a snowstorm. "Prosperity," said the New York *Herald Tribune*, "is still with us, though it is not hysterical prosperity." The *Herald Tribune*'s chart of a hundred stocks, which had shown an average of only 155 on November 14, 1929, was back up to 177 in early December as the market made a slight recovery. U.S. Steel, which had fallen to 150, was back to 171 by the end of the year; A.T.&T. was up from a low of 193 to 222; General Electric rose from a low of 168 to 243 and General Motors from 33 to 40.

"A general price rise ends 1929 stock trading, with Wall

Street moderately bullish for 1930," the *New York Times* reported.

In Chicago, Illinois, talk about the market collapse had given way to sharp argument over how to play bridge. There were two basic theories of contract bridge. One was known as the Vanderbilt convention, a bid of one club to oblige your partner to declare strength or weakness; the other was the new forcing system, in which the initial bidder, seeking a stronger indication of his partner's strength, bid two in any suit. In a big room on the mezzanine floor of the Drake Hotel, some three hundred leading American bridge players battled morning, afternoon and night for four days to decide who were the bridge champions of the nation. Prominent among half a dozen prize winners were Ely Culbertson and his wife, Josephine, proponents of the "forcing" system and perhaps the best-known bridge team in the United States.

In Philadelphia, Pennsylvania, the economic situation had failed to make any impression on the artistic temperament of the famed conductor of the Symphony Orchestra. Interrupting an audience that was applauding him, Leopold Stokowski declared: "This strange habit of beating the hands together is meaningless and, to me, very disturbing. We try to make sounds like music. Then you make this strange sound called clapping. I don't know where it originated but it must have been back in some dark forest in medieval times." He turned abruptly back to the orchestra and the audience delightedly clapped hands again.

A Time of Creativity and Discovery

In Hollywood, financial disaster was completely ignored by Warner Brothers who released a new motion picture called *Is Everybody Happy?* starring one of "jazz's first jazzbos," Ted Lewis. In New York, a five-foot rattlesnake was discovered crawling unhappily around a subway station and was killed by a policeman, who threw it in an ash can. At the University of Chicago, Dr. Sydney I. Falk announced discovery of *polymorphous streptococcus,* the germ that causes influenza. It looked like "a microscopic chain of unmatched beads which a child had strung." In New York, the American Birth Control League held its first general conference in five years under sponsorship of such well-known citizens as Mrs. Thomas Lamont, Mrs. Eleanor Roosevelt, Norman Thomas and Harry Emerson Fosdick. Mrs. Margaret Sanger, who had resigned as president in 1928, was replaced by Mrs. Frederick R. Jones, wife of an insurance economist. The League was informed that there were only twenty-nine centers in the United States, most of them under disguised names, where birth control information was made available. In the New York *Journal*, readers were urged to join in a new circulation-building stunt by writing a letter on "Why I want to go to Paris"—the winner, whether a man or a woman, to be taken to Paris personally by the star of a current motion picture, voluptuous Irene Bordoni.

One of the most remarkable results of the big crash, however, may have been the fact that John Davison Rockefeller, Jr., was left "holding the bag" in a huge New York real estate deal. Rockefeller, a violinist of some skill in his youth, and a number of other wealthy men had been interested for some time in efforts to build a new home for the Metropolitan Opera Company. They agreed that a real estate development with the opera house as its center would not only enhance the beauty of Fifth Avenue in the lower Fifties, but that the development could make the opera company self-supporting in the future. As the first step in this agreement, Rockefeller leased a rundown area bounded by Fifth Avenue, Forty-eighth Street, Sixth Avenue (later the Avenue of the Americas) and Fifty-first Street, paying a rental of over three million dollars a year under a lease which, with options, runs until 2015.

The lease was no sooner signed, however, than the Wall Street collapse frightened the sponsors of the development plan and they hastily took cover, leaving Rockefeller clutching a bag that contained some of the most expensive rock and 229 of the most dilapidated old brownstone houses—many of them harboring speakeasies—in New York City. Rockefeller made no attempt to get out from under a deal that would lose approximately four million dollars a year, including taxes of one million. But there was only one alternative open to him and that was to defy the Wall Street disaster by constructing a commercial office building development on the site. Ten years and $125 million later, Rockefeller Center's fourteen towering office buildings were a vast commercial center, one of the nation's most spectacular attractions for sight-seers and an impressive monument to the builder's faith in the future.

Between Two Worlds: America During the Hoover Years

Geoffrey Perrett

In the following excerpt taken from his book *America in the Twenties: A History*, Geoffrey Perrett argues that during the early years of Herbert Hoover's presidency (1928–1932), the west was still "wild," economies recovered without intervention, and people received help from close-knit communities rather than the government. However, Perrett writes, the depression forced Americans into the "modern" world where the government, particularly the presidency, was given the responsibility of overcoming economic and social problems. Americans expected Hoover to beat the depression, Perrett claims, and although he made significant efforts to restore the economy, only World War II would return the United States to prosperity.

The election of 1932 saw the victory of what soon became known as the New Deal coalition—western and southern, urban and rural, blacks, Catholics, and Jews. It set the shape of American political life for the next forty years, in which the Democratic party was, in effect, the "natural" party of government. It was the most epochal victory since the election of 1860, which brought Lincoln to power on a pledge to save the Union.

Franklin D. Roosevelt's campaign had, by way of contrast, made no monumental promises; merely the repeal of Prohibition and a 25 percent cut in federal spending. Nor did he win by holding a mirror up to nature in which the American people could see themselves as they were—harried, depressed, impoverished. What Roosevelt held up was a piece of blank canvas on which they could outline for themselves their desire for a different world.

Torn Between Centuries

Whatever the future really held was as much a mystery to Roosevelt as it was to everyone else. Yet no coup d'etat, no revolution, no civil war, could have marked a break with the past more clearly than this election. The voting booth is a blunt instrument. It offers crude choices, it gives crude replies. Political commentators and political scientists pore over most election results, looking for the meaning, like Roman haruspices sorting through the entrails of slaughtered sheep.

The meaning of the 1932 election, however, is plain: it marked the overt acceptance of the modern world, no matter what that involved. The Twenties was a no-man's land, torn between the nineteenth century and the twentieth. This split ran clear through American life. The frontier was cheek by jowl with the Machine Age. In 1926 a band of Apache Indians crossed the border into Arizona and attacked the ranch of Francisco Fimores, killing his wife and kidnaping his son. With an armed band of a dozen friends and neighbors, Fimores chased the Apaches deep into Mexico. Just as in the movies, the rescue party was ambushed and only one survived to tell the tale. In November 1929 a Union Pacific train was derailed in the middle of Wyoming. Out from the bushes came a nervous man with fair hair and a .38 revolver. He proceeded to hold up the passengers, took $800 from them, and galloped away. He lacked the style of Jesse James but the general approach was the same.

In a state such as South Dakota, many of the original white settlers were still alive in the Twenties. In Oklahoma, a state only since 1907, governors were regularly impeached, and frontier "justice" flourished. Orderly government involved habits not learned overnight.

The same split between two worlds, two centuries, prevailed in the realm of ideas. If there was one point on which all economists agreed, it was that economies had built-in elements that made them bob up like corks, no matter how far down they were dragged. This was certainly true of nineteenth-century economic orders. They did right themselves after a while with virtually no help from government. But a modern economy, with its complicated debt structure and its constant need for new long-term investment, is a different matter. Savings virtually disappeared in 1931, as people began struggling to pay off their debts. Result—investment virtually disappeared in 1932. And without new investment there could be no recovery. The modern economic order had come into existence almost unnoticed. But it was there, ticking away alongside outworn economic ideas.

The same was true of social values. Americans believed in self-help and the caring, close-knit community. Yet most people now depended on wages, and communities had come unraveled. Besides, pioneer America was both a young country and a country of the young. The Twenties saw the graying of America. The over-sixty-fives were the fastest-growing part of the population. In a wage-based economy provision had to be made for them. Recognition of that fact, however, was a long time in coming.

The Government Takes on a New Responsibility

The Depression made it impossible to continue the tug-of-war between two worlds that had given tension and form to the Twenties. Much of what we think of as the New Deal had been created by Herbert Hoover or anticipated by him before Roosevelt's election. In the Reconstruction Finance Corporation the government intervened directly in the peacetime economy for the first time; its creation marked the beginning of the mixed economy. In the Emergency Relief and Construction Act the federal government for the first time assumed responsibility for relief. By 1933 it was funding 80 percent of state and local relief spending. With the creation of the Federal Farm Board the federal government assumed responsibility for making up the incomes of farmers with taxpayers' money. The Federal Home Loan Banks made the federal government an active partner in promoting home ownership. The most important change, however, the one from which the others flowed, was the changed role of the presidency.

Hoover presided over a country that expected him to beat the Depression. No president had ever assumed responsibility for managing the American economy. The business of government since 1776 had been limited to war, diplomacy, and foreign trade. It was not expected to create prosperity. Even a president as committed to reform as Wilson was able, up to 1917, to do all his work in four or five hours a day.

Hoover assumed complete responsibility for overcoming the Depression. Alas, there was no solution to it. The banks were shaky, business paralyzed, farmers impoverished, charities inadequate, unions demoralized, cities and states broke, intellectuals misled, and all were looking to the federal government to play the role of the knight in shining armor. There was no escape, not even in escapism. In the movies made during the Depression local government is invariably shown as ineffective and corrupt, whereas the federal government is a benign, incorruptible deity. But there was no knight in shining armor. Had there been a way to beat the Depression, Hoover or Roosevelt would have found it.

A Problem Without a Solution

Hoover was described by Henry Stimson as being "capable of more prolonged and intense intellectual effort" than any president he knew, and Stimson served under every president from Teddy Roosevelt to Harry Truman. Roosevelt was pragmatic and flexible. In the Brain Trust he enjoyed the dedicated service of some of the most capable men ever brought into American government. But no twitching of the reins of power would ever conquer the Depression, and for one overriding reason: to restore demand on the scale required by government action would have first destroyed money and then would have destroyed the government. It would have had to borrow at least $20 billion a year for several years, at a time when the entire nation's income had fallen to $39 billion a year. Unable to borrow so much from so little, it would have had to run the printing presses until the money turned out was worth less than the paper used. Roosevelt, like Hoover, became a wound-dresser; he did, however, apply the bandages with greater flair.

Small doses of inflation could help to ease the agony and, here and there, put people back to work. In 1936 the bonus was paid, a $2.3 billion boost that fueled the mild upturn of 1937, followed by the downturn of 1938. What made the Depression so appalling a human tragedy was that it could be overcome only by an event as awesome, as terrifying, and as irresistible as the Depression itself. And that was the Second World War, a conflict that was not contrived, but part of the bedrock of the twentieth century. Only with the onset of the war was borrowing and spending on the scale required finally possible. A government can create money; it cannot create belief in it. Hoover could not overcome the Depression, nor could Roosevelt, nor could any man.

The important things that Hoover did were done because they had to be done, but Hoover, with one foot in the nineteenth century, hated having to do them. In trying to defeat the Depression he had created the modern presidency—the presidency of wildly inflated expectations: the "manager of the economy" presidency; the "toughest-job-in-the-world" presidency; the crisis-management presidency. When Hoover left office, William Allen White wrote a dispassionate farewell under the title, "Herbert Hoover—The Last of the Old Presidents or the First of the New?" The short answer is, "Both."

The Politics of Change: Herbert Hoover and Franklin D. Roosevelt

Wayne S. Cole

Herbert Hoover and Franklin D. Roosevelt personified the changing role of the federal government in the years between 1928 and 1945, writes historian Wayne S. Cole. In the following article, Cole contrasts the political life of these two men, examining differences in their background, personality, and political philosophy. Cole reveals that these differences made the transition between the administration of Hoover and Roosevelt difficult, and left Americans with the historical impression that Hoover was a "do nothing" president, while Roosevelt was remembered as a heroic figure.

P oor people seldom become kings or prime ministers or presidents. That eliminates many of us. Until the second half of the twentieth century no Catholic made it to the presidency. To this day no female, African-American, Asian-American, Native-American, Jew, or Muslim has ever been president of the United States. All that narrows the field considerably. But even among wealthy white male Christians there has been substantial variety among those rare individuals elevated to the presidency of the United States. Herbert Hoover and Franklin D. Roosevelt nicely illustrate that diversity in the first half of the twentieth century.

At their time, and in their separate ways, both Hoover and Roosevelt were seen as giants in public life. As a highly

Excerpted from the Introduction to *Herbert Hoover and Franklin D. Roosevelt: A Documentary History,* by Wayne S. Cole, edited by Timothy Walch and Dwight M. Miller, with a Foreword by John W. Carlin. Copyright ©1998 by The Herbert Hoover Library Association. Reprinted with the permission of Greenwood Publishing Group, Inc., Westport, CT.

successful international mining engineer, as Food Administrator during World War I, and as Secretary of Commerce in Republican presidential administrations during the prosperity decade of the 1920s, Herbert Hoover was a much respected model of administrative skill, statesmanship, professional integrity, and public service. He probably could have been elected president in 1920 if he had clearly made himself available. Handsome, personable, outgoing, and bearing the "Rough Rider's" famous name, Roosevelt was a bright light on the political scene early on. Even his courageous battle against the crippling effects of poliomyelitis in mid-life failed to check his skyrocketing career in public life for long. Hoover and Roosevelt were both tall, robust, and energetic—two very special men destined for distinguished roles in public life.

Two Men from Different Worlds

For all of that, however, Herbert Hoover and Franklin D. Roosevelt, their presidential administrations, and their places in history provide a study in contrasts. Some eight years older than Roosevelt, Hoover lived a much longer life. Born in 1874 into a modest Quaker family in the tiny village of West Branch in eastern Iowa, Hoover was an orphan before he reached his teens. Reared by a maternal uncle in a comfortable environment in the west coast state of Oregon, Hoover studied geology and engineering at the new Stanford University in California, graduating in 1895. Drawn into international mining enterprises, young Hoover quickly became a wealthy "self-made" mining entrepreneur with offices scattered all over the world.

Despite his parochial beginnings in the American middle west, Hoover's business and mining operations took him to the several continents and a wide range of cultures and economies. With the precision of an engineer, Hoover paid attention to detail and was an efficient "clean-desk" administrator. Getting things right was more his thing than pursuing a course that won political support or popular approval. Though he was not a pacifist, Hoover's Quaker religious background and beliefs did not place military solutions and values high in his scheme of things.

Hoover was a gentleman and treated others with courtesy and respect, but he was never a "glad hander," a "hail-fellow-well-met," or naturally outgoing. A bit shy, diffident, and "thin skinned," Hoover never delighted in the "rough-and-tumble" of politics and public life. He tended to become defensive and resentful in the face of public criticism. He was not naturally gregarious; he did not easily project warmth and charisma. His was an image of probity, character, decency, integrity, and responsibility. His reputation was never marred by any serious allegations of personal or financial scandal or corruption. His image served well until it was overwhelmed by the deluge that was the Great Depression of the 1930s.

In almost every respect, the patterns for Franklin Delano Roosevelt were different. Unlike Hoover, Roosevelt never personally experienced poverty or deprivation. Unlike Hoover, Roosevelt was born in Hyde Park, New York, to wealth and social position, with an almost aristocratic background. Though he was proud of China traders in his maternal ancestry, in his formative and young adult years Roosevelt's personal experiences were limited largely to the northeast in the United States and to western Europe in world affairs—a comparatively parochial pattern if viewed from the whole of the United States or from a truly world-wide multicultural perspective.

As an only child in that setting, Franklin was privileged and pampered in ways that Hoover never knew. Roosevelt's Episcopalian religious affiliation and beliefs were as shallow and unquestioning as Hoover's Quaker beliefs were deep and personal—and the comparative class perspectives of the two faiths extended into attitudes each of the two men carried with them in public life. Though not brilliant, Roosevelt performed creditably as a student in the best of America's elite schools: Groton, Harvard, and Columbia. Roosevelt's infidelity and unsatisfying family life contrasted with Hoover's comfortable and contented home life.

Personality, Politics, and Public Image

Roosevelt's personality and charm carried him so well that efficiency and mastery of detail never seemed as important or essential as they were to Hoover. At the same time, Roosevelt developed a feel for dealing with people and a talent for politics that Hoover never mastered and did not put high in his scale of values. Roosevelt's love of sailing, his early attachment to the big navy views of Captain Alfred Thayer Mahan, and his service as assistant secretary of the navy before and during World War I, gave him a regard for naval power and an awareness of the roles of power in international affairs that Hoover never commanded to the same degree.

Roosevelt's optimistic "can-do" style contrasted with Hoover's more pessimistic mein. Roosevelt's flexible, undoctrinaire approaches contrasted with Hoover's more rigidly doctrinaire and principled style. Roosevelt's casual administrative style contrasted with Hoover's efficient administrative performance. Roosevelt was decidedly a "loose constructionist" and envisaged a large positive role for the federal government in serving human needs at home and abroad; though Hoover conceded the necessity for government action to perform special functions, he had comparatively more confidence in private individual initiative and "voluntarism."

And Franklin D. Roosevelt's image of success, triumph, and inspiring accomplishment in peace and war contrasted with Hoover's image of ultimate defeat and failure. Herbert Hoover is remembered for the 1929 stock market crash early in his one term as president, for the depression that followed, and for his inability to end that depression and restore prosperity. In striking contrast, Franklin D. Roosevelt is remembered for his ebullient leadership as his New Deal extended relief to the needy, brought the economy out of the depression, restored prosperity, and reformed the flawed economy so it would be less likely to suffer economic disaster in the future. And he is remembered for leading the United States and its allies successfully through the most terrible war in human history toward victory over the most fearsome and evil enemy in recorded history.

Even Roosevelt's death at Warm Springs, Georgia, on April 12, 1945, from a massive cerebral hemorrhage (early in his fourth term as president) left an image of glorious triumph over adversity even in death. Those who wondered if the New Deal had really ended the depression, whether involvement in World War II was really necessary, and whether the consequences of Roosevelt's leadership methods were entirely laudatory, won little encouragement from professional historians and generally found it expedient to keep a low profile.

Though it was the Great Depression on the domestic scene in the United States that ruined Hoover's presidential administration, and though it was that same Great Depression in America that enabled Roosevelt and the Democrats to win the presidency in 1932, developments in foreign affairs and international relations played the largest roles in direct relations between Hoover and Roosevelt.

Developing Political Philosophies

World War I introduced the two men to each other as they played their separate roles in President Woodrow Wilson's conduct of America's participation in that Great War. International attempts to resolve the Great Depression on the world scene brought the two men to their most intense encounters—and highlighted their differences in dealing with those intractable problems. And their sharply differing approaches in 1939–1941 on America's policies toward the wars raging in Asia, Africa, and Europe put the two men on opposite sides in the tremendously important "Great Debate" on American foreign policies before the Japanese attack on Pearl Harbor, Hawaii.

Hoover's impressive performance in providing humanitarian relief to suffering people in Belgium from late 1914 to America's entry into the war in 1917, his role as Food Administrator in the Wilson administration during World

War I, his performance in providing food relief to millions of people in Russia and elsewhere after the war, and Roosevelt's important position as assistant secretary of the navy before, during, and after World War I, allowed the two men to meet for the first time, socialize with each other, and learn to respect each other's talents and potential in public life. Each used those wartime "contacts" with each other for incidental purposes in the 1920s when Hoover was Secretary of Commerce in the Republican administrations of Harding and Coolidge, and when Roosevelt was struggling to overcome the effects of polio and trying to build his political future in the Democratic party.

Their rising political fortunes on opposite sides of the political fence strained their relationship. In the elections of 1928 Hoover and the Republicans successfully triumphed over New York's Democratic Governor Al Smith's bid for the presidency. Smith had been Roosevelt's political patron and his choice for the presidency. Roosevelt's campaign for Smith included unfavorable evaluations of Hoover in comparison with Smith that troubled the sensitive Hoover. Though the election of 1928 brought Hoover to the presidency and crushed Smith, it also elevated Roosevelt to the governorship of New York State, a position that served as his springboard to the presidency four years later. And in 1932 the hard-fought campaigns between the badly pummeled Hoover and the confident challenge from Roosevelt left neither man with warm feelings toward the other.

An Uncomfortable Transition

The interregnum between the election on November 8, 1932, and the inauguration of Roosevelt on March 4, 1933, produced the most intense and ultimately unsatisfying personal encounters between the two men—and did so on what were essentially international issues. The Great Depression was not simply an American phenomenon; it was a worldwide disaster affecting governments and countless millions of people on every continent. German reparations owed to the Allies after World War I, Allied war debts owed to the United States, financial collapse in Germany and central Europe, fluctuating exchange rates disrupting both financial and trade relations, frustrated disarmament efforts, and consequent political disturbances and instability in countries throughout the world made the depression a truly international phenomenon. It desperately called for international solutions. Those acute international problems were given specific focus by the Lausanne agreements of 1932 in which the European governments attempted to link any adjustment of the reparations to comparable adjustments of the war debts, by the World Disarmament Conference that began its deliberations in Geneva early in 1932, and by the World Economic Conference scheduled to begin in London in 1933.

Hoover's long personal involvement in international economic activities and his heavy focus on international trade and investment during his years as Secretary of Commerce made him especially alert to the international dimensions of the Great Depression. The leading role of the United States in the world economy made its actions (and inactions) of vital importance for developments elsewhere. And with economies collapsing everywhere, leaders of other major countries almost desperately turned to the United States (and to President Hoover) for help and solutions. The very high tariff rates provided by the Smoot-Hawley Tariff of 1930 and the war debts owed to the United States provided focal points for those concerns abroad.

During the four months between Roosevelt's election in the fall of 1932 and his inauguration in the early spring of 1933, all those economic difficulties came together in alarmingly acute crises. There was no time to waste. But as a lame-duck president with a Congress controlled by his opponents, Hoover had little power to act effectively and, in any event, could not commit the United States beyond the end of his term. In desperation he sought the cooperation of president-elect Roosevelt to help cope with those crises. Given Roosevelt's identification both earlier and later with internationalism, one might have expected him to have responded helpfully. Not so!

Conflict over Foreign Affairs

For one thing, Roosevelt simply did not have the legal authority to make policy decisions or actions until he was sworn in as president on March 4, 1933. Furthermore, despite Roosevelt's earlier and later internationalism, his approach in 1932–1933 was that the problems of the depression had to be resolved first on the domestic scene before turning in time to international actions. That priority was consistent with directions encouraged by his Brains Trust advisers who had helped guide his presidential campaign and would help mold his early New Deal. Psychologically, it could be unwise to identify too closely with the failed policies of the defeated outgoing Hoover administration.

There was also a significant political dimension to FDR's approach. In 1932 Roosevelt had won his greatest following in the South and the West. To win enactment of his New Deal program, Roosevelt depended partly on support from western agrarian progressives—most of whom were Republicans politically and so-called "isolationists" in foreign affairs. To have cooperated with Hoover's internationalist approaches to the problem could have alienated those western progressives. And though President Hoover insisted that he was not attempting to influence the policies that Roosevelt might pursue after he took office, the cooperation that he sought from Roosevelt entailed international dimensions that may not have meshed comfortably with the approaches Roosevelt would implement in his early New Deal. Some around Roosevelt worried that the outgoing Hoover might trick the incoming president into sharing in his flawed approaches. As Republican Senator Hiram Johnson of California (himself a western agrarian progressive isolationist who supported much of FDR's early New Deal) warned Roosevelt: "beware of Greeks bearing gifts."

In response to President Hoover's pleas, the two men

and their close advisers met three times during the interim. They conducted the meetings courteously. Hoover displayed commanding knowledge of the international economic problems at issue. Both men agreed that reparations and war debts were separate matters that should not be linked as the European governments attempted to do through the Lausanne agreements. But Roosevelt insisted that he had no legal authority to share in decision-making until March 4. Whatever Roosevelt's impressions of the meetings may have been, the meetings did nothing to improve Hoover's image of Roosevelt. By the time of inaugural day on March 4, the two men were barely speaking to each other. The relations (if one can call them relations at all) never improved after that.

Hoover had not been a "do-nothing" president. He had taken more positive and vigorous federal government actions to contend with the economic difficulties and depression than any earlier president had ever initiated. Under his leadership Congress had enacted the Agricultural Marketing Act, had authorized formation of the Reconstruction Finance Corporation, and adopted the Home Loan Act. On his initiative, the Congress authorized and his administration negotiated a one-year moratorium on intergovernment debts (the Hoover Moratorium) designed to ease the international financial crises. But he saw the federal government's authority under the Constitution as decidedly limited and, in any event, saw a large responsibility and authority resting with state and local governments. And based on his personal experiences over the years, Hoover had confidence in voluntary cooperative initiatives from private associations and individuals. In the years that followed, Hoover continued to believe that his policies had been sound and, had politics not intruded, could have restored American prosperity in an environment of democracy and freedom.

The Changing Mood of America: The Repeal of Prohibition

Thomas R. Pegram

The repeal of the Eighteenth Amendment prohibiting the manufacture, sale, or transportation of intoxicating liquors reflected the changing social, cultural, political, and economic climate between 1926 and 1933, writes Thomas R. Pegram in the following excerpt from his book *Battling Demon Rum: The Struggle for a Dry America*. Pegram reveals that many Americans who believed that Prohibition would improve the social, economic, and moral condition in the United States, discovered that in many ways Prohibition was in fact a threat to society. For example, opponents claimed that Prohibition not only fostered crime, but the gunplay between federal officers and smugglers often resulted in the deaths of civilians. Moreover, the author suggests, attitudes toward drinking began to change, and opponents believed repeal would relieve the economic problems brought on by the depression. Pegram is a professor of history at Loyola College in Baltimore, Maryland.

B y the mid-1920s the weaknesses of national prohibition [of liquor] were well known. Most Americans nevertheless believed that prohibition, set into the granite of the United States Constitution, had become a permanent

Excerpted from *Battling Demon Rum*, by Thomas R. Pegram. Copyright ©1968 by Thomas R. Pegram. Reprinted with permission from Ivan R. Dee, Publisher.

fixture in the nation's public life. Even as vociferous a wet [an opposer of prohibition] as Clarence Darrow, the famed attorney and civil libertarian, acknowledged the seeming unassailability of prohibition. "Even to modify the Volstead Act [prohibiting the manufacture, sale, or transportation of liquor] would require a political revolution," he glumly conceded in 1924. "To repeal the Eighteenth Amendment is well-nigh inconceivable."

In 1929 Herbert Hoover became the first president during prohibition to commit himself to more stringent enforcement of the law. Just before he took office, Congress raised the maximum punishment for first-time violators of the Volstead Act to five years in prison and $10,000 in fines. Critics complained that the five federal penitentiaries were already overcrowded with liquor-law violators. In response, Hoover authorized the construction of six additional federal prisons, including Alcatraz in San Francisco Bay; by 1930 more than one-third of the 12,332 federal inmates were Volstead Act offenders. Also in 1930, the Prohibition Bureau was finally transferred to the Justice Department, with the expectation that it would function with greater efficiency. Nearly a decade after its adoption as the law of the land, it appeared that prohibition might actually be put to the test. Yet by the end of 1933 the 18th Amendment had been repealed, and national prohibition, once the shining goal of reform aspirations, slipped into popular memory as a laughable and embarrassing episode in misdirected zeal. A generation later the historian Richard Hofstadter dismissed it as a "pseudo-reform" perpetrated on the nation by the cranky remnants of the rural, evangelical culture of the nineteenth century.

A Time of Change

The popular repudiation of prohibition, which Hofstadter's biting judgment accurately reflected, was the product of social, cultural, political, and economic developments that between 1926 and 1933 came together with astonishing force. They did not significantly alter ethnic and working-class opposition to the dry laws [that prohibited liquor], which remained relatively constant throughout the 1920s. Instead, the depth of the repudiation stemmed from the erosion of middle-class support for prohibition. Americans who had demanded the suppression of the saloon at the turn of the century were troubled by the crime, corruption, and governmental incompetence that accompanied prohibition. Unlike the Progressive Era, when the argument against prohibition was left to representatives of the despised liquor trades or marginalized immigrant or working-class associations, by the late 1920s business leaders, professionals, and women's groups raised their voices in opposition to prohibition, primarily through the Association Against the Prohibition Amendment (AAPA) and the Women's Organization for National Prohibition Reform (WONPR).

The cultural significance of drinking had also shifted by the late 1920s, realigning middle-class attitudes toward prohibition. Despite the bureaucratic innovations of the Anti-Saloon League, a constellation of values formed in the Victorian Era—a culture of duty and denial, of faith in God and progress, that sought to protect the family and impose order on society—deeply influenced dry sentiment into the twentieth century. The pervasively secular consumer culture of the 1920s, with its emphasis on youth, self-fulfillment, and entertainment, overwhelmed the older middle-class culture that had celebrated prohibition as a necessary reform. Whereas saloons had offended middle-class sensibilities before prohibition, prohibition-era speakeasies furnished enjoyment and a hint of illegal adventure to the self-indulgent new middle class of the 1920s.

Even middle-class women's support for prohibition, a central article of faith in the dry movement, fractured in the 1920s. Observers on both sides of the liquor debate at the turn of the century had anticipated that women, once enfranchised, would form a powerful bloc of dry voters. But after women gained the vote in 1920, they demonstrated not unity of outlook but rather a variety of political opinions on prohibition as well as other public issues. The breakdown of traditional saloon culture in fact opened the way for women's participation in the new atmosphere of public drinking taking shape in speakeasies. When the repeal movement gained momentum after 1929, American women did not flock to the defense of prohibition.

The Politics of Prohibition

Alterations in middle-class culture help explain the extent of prohibition's vulnerability by the end of the twenties, but the startling suddenness of repeal was the result of political and economic events. After years of evasion by both Democrats and Republicans, the liquor issue crept back into national politics. Spurred by the 1928 presidential candidacy of Al Smith, a prominent opponent of the Volstead Act, Herbert Hoover's growing identification with prohibition after 1929, and intense internal debates in both parties, prohibition became an issue in the 1932 presidential election. The Democratic party forced its cautious candidate, Franklin D. Roosevelt, to embrace repeal while Hoover dragged a reluctant GOP into open support for the continuation of what Hoover had once described as "a great social and economic experiment"—this despite the critical assessment of prohibition issued in 1931 by Hoover's own special investigative body, the National Commission on Law Observance and Enforcement, popularly known as the Wickersham Commission.

Overshadowing Hoover's efforts to defend prohibition, and casting a pall on his hopes for reelection in 1932, was the enormous specter of the Great Depression. As the national economy crashed down around them, Americans came to view Hoover with disdain. The president's assurances of a quick return to prosperity and his futile appeal for voluntary cooperation to reverse the collapse of the banking system and industry generated a wave of popular resentment. In light of Hoover's inability to face the facts of economic disaster, his continued insistence on the viability of prohibition appeared foolish and trivial. On the other hand, assurances from wets that repeal of prohibition would restore jobs and tax dollars offered hope at a moment of desperate scarcity. Tangled in the wreckage of Hoover's reputation, and taking on the aspect of an unnecessary burden in a time of national emergency, prohibition was jettisoned in 1933 with unusual speed and few second thoughts.

The Changing Image of Prohibition

From its origins in the nineteenth century, temperance reform had developed as a forward-looking, optimistic social movement. Its proponents had been modernizers, those who looked forward to social, economic, and moral improvement. That image became badly tarnished in the 1920s as prohibition came to be labeled the creaky obsession of puritanical moralists, rural busybodies, and religious bigots. One of the most damaging blows to the reform image of prohibition was the dry enthusiasm exhibited by the hooded knights of the resurgent Ku Klux Klan. The Klan of the 1920s took its name from the terrorist band of Southern night riders that intimidated black voters and federal officials during Reconstruction; but the new KKK, founded in Georgia in 1915, appealed to a wider constituency of native-born white Protestants. . . .

If the violent images evoked by the hooded figures of the Ku Klux Klan undermined prohibition, violence of another sort accelerated popular frustration with the dry laws. Before the adoption of national prohibition, organized criminal enterprise in the United States was considered part of the seamy underside of saloon culture. As the numerous vice commissions that formed in Progressive Era cities discovered, an underworld of criminality, mainly gambling and prostitution, operated on the shadowy margins of saloon life. Prohibition offered young, energetic lieutenants within existing crime organizations opportunities to branch out into the profitable commerce in illegal liquor. Most of the leading criminal bootleggers, according to the historian Humbert Nelli, were ambitious Italian, Polish, or Jewish men in their twenties and early thirties whose youth and immigrant origins had restricted their rise within traditional criminal organizations. "Everybody calls me a racketeer," complained Al Capone of Chicago, the most notorious of the gangland bootleggers by his mid-twenties. "I call myself a businessman." For such men, supplying liquor to the estimated 219,000 speakeasies in prohibition America became a formula for social mobility.

Corruption and violence accompanied the rise of criminal bootlegging gangs. Gangsters hijacked cargoes of illegal liquor from their competitors, bribed police and public officials, and, most sensationally, engaged in bloody territorial battles. In Chicago alone between 1920 and 1930, almost 550 criminals died at the hands of their rivals; the police killed a few hundred more. Gang warfare in New York killed more than a thousand people. Such highly visible violence created public fears of a "prohibition crime wave." Statisticians cautioned that the murder rate, although climbing steadily since 1900, had made its biggest jump well before the coming of prohibition. Nevertheless a burst of violence in Chicago between 1926 and 1929, which included the murder of an assistant state's attorney, brutal criminal interference in elections, and the machine-gunning of seven rival bootleggers by Capone's men in the famous St. Valentine's Day Massacre, reinforced the popular linkage of prohibition with unbridled criminality. The celebrity status of gangland figures, magnified by the appearance in the early 1930s of gangster films featuring charismatic stars such as James Cagney and Edward G. Robinson as appealing criminal entrepreneurs, as well as the commonplace violation of the Volstead Act, furthered the impression that prohibition had brought a dangerous quality of lawlessness to American society.

Questioning the Enforcers

Opponents of prohibition also condemned the violence and incompetence with which the law was enforced. Critics claimed that gunplay between federal officers and smugglers resulted in more than a thousand deaths. (The government acknowledged 286 killings, including agents and civilians.) Incidents in which the undisciplined fire of Prohibition Bureau agents hurt or killed innocent bystanders, including several children and a United States senator, were widely publicized by the Association Against the Prohibition Amendment, which in 1929 gathered them together in a pamphlet entitled *Reforming America with a Shotgun.*

Other observers complained that dry lawmen abused their authority. After prohibition agents entered the lakeside property of Henry Joy, wealthy president of the Packard Motor Company, to shoot at smugglers and seize the modest alcoholic stock of his watchman, the businessman protested that "the people live in fear of unlawful search of their homes and their motor cars as they travel, and unlawful shootings and killings by the officers of the Treasury Department." By the late 1920s many prominent citizens had come to the conclusion that prohibition fostered a contempt for law and order both among those who defied the law and those entrusted to enforce it.

Changing Social Attitudes

Changing social mores further corroded respect for prohibition among the middle class. "It is safe to say that a significant change has taken place in the social attitude toward drinking," concluded the Wickersham Commission in 1931 after extensive investigation into the drinking habits of Americans. Although Americans as a whole were drinking less during prohibition, the context of drinking, especially middle-class drinking, had undergone a transformation since prohibition shut down the old-time saloon. An intersection of powerful social forces—an assertive youth movement, new patterns of sexual dynamics, and demands for leisure-time amusements spurred by an expanding consumer economy—broke down the saloon culture of male drinking and replaced it with a culture of youthful, recreational drinking which emphasized social contact between men and women.

One need not accept overdrawn portraits of a hedonistic Jazz Age to recognize the shift in values and behavior from

Victorian patterns to the recognizably modern emphasis on entertainment and personal fulfillment that became apparent during the 1920s. Social life was recast for working-class and middle-class Americans alike by automobiles, radio, and the movies. Before World War I, Roy Rosenzweig reports, movies began to compete with saloons as centers of working-class leisure. In the 1920s movies and public drinking became middle-class amusements, especially among the young. On college campuses, polls revealed, two of three students drank alcoholic beverages during prohibition. For some, carrying hip flasks and engaging in the occasional display of public drunkenness reflected the "smart," cosmopolitan outlook one found in the irreverent films of the period. More important was the fact, revealed by the historian Paula Fass, that by the mid-twenties college men and women drank together.

As the historian Mary Murphy has noted, "Drinking in the late nineteenth and early twentieth centuries was one of the most gender-segregated activities in the United States." Men drank in saloons; women, if they drank, did so at home. Prohibition helped alter that arrangement. Murphy found that in Butte, Montana, the closing of saloons opened up opportunities for women to enter "spaces that had once been reserved exclusively for men." Women—young and old, working class and middle class—manufactured and sold bootleg liquor. More remarkably, women in groups and in the company of young men were welcomed in the liquor-serving restaurants and nightclubs that had replaced the saloons.

From New York to Butte, the dismantling of the saloon-based drinking environment introduced new possibilities for social interaction in the clandestine drinking establishments that took their place. In some cities, interracial contact became far more common in speakeasies than had been the case in saloons. In New York, the historian George Chauncey reports, the city's gay subculture flourished in the shifting public space of prohibition nightclubs. Most common, however, was the development of what Murphy calls "a new heterosocial nightlife." Speakeasies as well as movie theaters and restaurants catered to the new custom of dating, defined

by Fass as a "ritual of sexual interaction" less binding than courting, its nineteenth-century predecessor. In the 1920s drinking and dating were meant to be entertaining and experimental. In that context, elders often preached control rather than abstinence. In a 1931 magazine article, one woman expressed the wish that her grandsons "know the difference between drinking like gentlemen and lapping it up like puppies." From such experiences was the legend born that drinking actually increased during prohibition. In reality, it was middle-class exposure to drinking that grew during the dry years.

The illegal activities of bootleggers like Al Capone (left) led to the eventual repeal of Prohibition.

Gathering Support for Repeal

By the late 1920s middle-class complaints that prohibition fostered crime, subverted respect for laws and government, and threatened society rather than purified it had grown powerful enough to sustain a movement among business and professional people against the 18th Amendment. Between 1928 and 1930, for example, opposition to prohibition among lawyers grew more pronounced. The bar associations of eight cities and three states called for an end to federal liquor controls. In 1929 a coalition of respected attorneys organized the Voluntary Committee of Lawyers (VCL) to combat national prohibition. After a quiet campaign by the VCL, an American Bar Association referendum in 1930 produced a two-to-one ratio in favor of repeal.

Two other significant organizations opposed to prohibition formed in 1929. One of them, a young men's association called the Crusaders (inspired, it was later claimed, by anger following the St. Valentine's Day Massacre), ultimately attracted nearly one million members but produced few tangible results. The other, the Women's Organization for National Prohibition Reform (WONPR), was both politically influential and symbolically important. Organized by Pauline Sabin, a socially prominent figure who was also influential in the Republican party, the WONPR offered a firm rebuttal to the claim that all American women stood behind national prohibition. Privately convinced that prohibition violated constitutional liberties and produced in the young "a total lack of respect for the Constitution and for the law," Sabin took dramatic public action after hearing WCTU president Ella Boole claim in 1928 to speak for the women of America.

Many of the leaders of the WONPR (including Sabin) were married to prominent, wealthy advocates of the anti-prohibition cause, sparking dry accusations that the WONPR was simply a glamorous front organization for male-dominated repeal groups. In the bitter yet picturesque language of onetime reformer Fletcher Dobyns, cynical wets, "in true Russian fashion, . . . ordered their wives and daughters into the trenches" to bring down prohibition. But research by David Kyvig, Kenneth Rose, and Caryn Neumann has established that the WONPR maintained an independent and effective political presence and attracted the allegiance of women from all social classes. By 1933 the WONPR, which did not demand dues from its supporters, claimed 1.5 million members. Although Kyvig, the chief authority on repeal organizations, cannot verify that figure, he concludes that the WONPR was still "by far the largest antiprohibition association."

The most influential group in the repeal coalition was the oldest, the Association Against the Prohibition Amendment (AAPA). The AAPA shaped popular anti-prohibition sentiment into effective action, worked closely with the other major repeal groups, and orchestrated the political campaign that ended national prohibition. Founded in 1918 by William Stayton, a former naval officer, to resist the adoption of the 18th Amendment, the AAPA grew into a significant force in the mid-1920s by attracting the support of prominent business leaders, most notably Pierre, Irénée, and Lammot du Pont of the giant chemical firm, and John J. Raskob, Pierre du Pont's associate at Du Pont and General Motors. Also involved were political figures such as James Wadsworth, former Republican senator from New York, and Maryland Democrat William Cabell Bruce. Although the AAPA expressed dismay at the reports of increased crime, violence, corruption, and excessive drinking associated with prohibition, Kyvig has shown that the core of its opposition to national prohibition was a conservative political conviction that the dry laws represented an unwarranted intrusion of national government into local and private affairs. . . .

The Politics of Repeal

Through the influence of the AAPA, repeal sentiment also made inroads into the party system. New York governor Al Smith, who had signed the repeal of the Empire State's prohibition enforcement act in 1923, had been denied the 1924 Democratic presidential nomination by the party's rural, dry wing and its old hero William Jennings Bryan. In 1928 Bryan was three years dead, and the charismatic Smith, a hero to urban, ethnic Democrats, received the party's nomination. Cautious as ever on the liquor question, the Democratic platform committed the party to enforcement of the 18th Amendment. Smith, however, made no secret of his belief that prohibition was a decision for state and local authorities, not the federal government. Doomed by his Catholicism and background in urban machine politics to failure in the 1928 election (five solidly Democratic Southern states voted for Hoover against Smith), Smith nevertheless began to tilt the Democratic party to the wet side of the prohibition debate, especially by appointing John J. Raskob, a former Republican, as chairman of the Democratic National Committee. Raskob, a member of the AAPA's governing board, worked with almost single-minded energy over the next four years to convert Democrats to an official endorsement of prohibition repeal.

The final drama of the prohibition decade was also taking shape in the Republican party. Urged on by its dry enthusiasts, the GOP platform moved beyond its usual vague homage to law and order and instead promised "vigorous enforcement" of prohibition. The Republican nominee, Herbert Hoover, had been somewhat circumspect on the subject of prohibition, at one point calling the dry reform "a moral failure and an economic success." Yet Hoover believed in the rule of law and displayed the progressive confidence in the public spirit. He therefore announced his opposition to repeal and promised to give prohibition a fair and complete trial. His position was enough to drive some prominent AAPA Republicans to support Smith. The liquor issue, in a modest way, had once again begun to reshuffle American political allegiances.

If Hoover had lost the 1928 election, which he won by more than six million votes, he would be a less prominent but more fondly remembered historical personality. As a noted engineer, a highly praised architect of American food aid to Europe after World War I, and a talented cabinet member standing above the general mediocrity and corruption of the Harding and Coolidge administrations, Hoover had forged a brilliant record of public service. The Great Depression destroyed it all. . . .

The Wickersham Commission

The depression made Hoover's resolution to enforce prohibition seem desperately misplaced. Adding significantly to that impression in 1931 were the conclusions of the Wickersham Commission. Upon taking office in 1929, Hoover had named eleven respected public figures, known as moderates on the subject of prohibition, to investigate the workings of the 18th Amendment as well as crime generally in the United States. The commission produced what is still the most exhaustive examination of prohibition ever undertaken, with devastating results for Hoover and the drys. The report documented the utter disorganization and inadequacy of prohibition enforcement and the widespread defiance of the law. Although the report concluded by opposing repeal of prohibition or modification of the Volstead Act to allow the sale of beer and light wines, the individual statements appended to the conclusion were far more critical of the dry status quo. Only one commissioner was steadfast in his support for the continuation of national prohibition. Most of the others supported modification of the dry laws, with a government-regulated liquor monopoly patterned after the Swedish system attracting the majority of enthusiasm. Two commissioners called for outright repeal of the 18th Amendment.

Hoover shook off the contradictions between the summary conclusions and the personal statements of the commissioners and declared that the report supported his own policy of more efficient enforcement. To most Americans, however, the Wickersham Commission report offered definitive evidence of prohibition's failure and Hoover's folly in pursuing the enforcement of a repudiated policy. Unhappily for Republicans, the GOP now carried a double burden as the party of depression *and* prohibition.

As the depression deepened, repeal sentiment gained momentum. AAPA publications began to stress the tax savings that would result from the end of prohibition and the return of federal levies on liquor. A national poll conducted by the *Literary Digest* in 1930 recorded 30.5 percent of its participants in favor of prohibition, 29 percent urging the legalization of wine and beer, and more than 40 percent backing outright repeal. In the same year Republican party platforms in five states and Democratic party platforms in fourteen states called for repeal. Both the American Legion and the Veterans of Foreign Wars endorsed repeal in 1931, while the American Federation of Labor began to move beyond its demand to amend the Volstead Act and explore the possibility of repeal. In 1932 the major repeal organizations, led by the AAPA, formed the United Repeal Council to help with the final push in the coming election.

Republicans in 1932 could not disentangle themselves from Hoover's ties to prohibition. Although Hoover himself came to realize that alterations in national prohibition were advisable, at the party's convention he refused to entertain the repeal initiatives of wet Republicans. Instead the party platform allowed for the possibility of a constitutional amendment open to popular ratification that would allow some autonomy on the part of the states while retaining federal control of prohibition. This last, confusing straddle on prohibition completed, the GOP forlornly prepared to go down to defeat, chained to its stubborn, taciturn leader.

The Democrats Support Repeal

Among Democrats the matter of repeal became part of an intricate struggle for control of the party before the 1932 convention. Following the 1928 election, Raskob used his position as party chairman to build an organization committed to the repeal of prohibition but also dedicated to the conservative, business-oriented, limited-government philosophy of the AAPA. The chief opponent of Raskob and the conservative Democratic coalition was New York governor Franklin D. Roosevelt, an adherent of the party's liberal, activist wing. Although Roosevelt had come out for repeal in 1930, that was in the context of New York state politics. As a cautious politician, FDR resisted efforts to commit the party and its candidate to repeal until public opinion overwhelmingly demanded it.

By the time of the 1932 convention, the party's prohibition plank became the centerpiece of a complex power struggle that pitted Roosevelt against Raskob, Al Smith, and the party conservatives. The conservatives hoped to use FDR's hesitancy to embrace repeal as a device to deny him the nomination. Once Roosevelt determined the depth of party support for repeal at the convention, however, he accepted the repeal plank, thereby disarming the conservatives and assuring his nomination for president. As Roosevelt cheerily declared his support for swift passage of a constitutional amendment to end national prohibition, Raskob and the AAPA conservatives must have realized that in winning the prohibition fight, they had lost their war for the Democratic party. By 1934 the remnants of the AAPA reorganized as the American Liberty League to wage a lonely and unpopular resistance to Roosevelt and the New Deal. To the very end, the liquor issue confounded those politicians who tried to control it.

Barriers to the repeal of the 18th Amendment fell away in the 1932 election. Roosevelt beat Hoover by more than seven million votes, a huge Democratic majority swept into Congress, and nine states voted to repeal their own prohibition enforcement laws. Before the new administration took office, Congress passed a repeal amendment specifying that special state conventions, not sitting legislatures, ratify the amendment, thus assuring popular control of the repeal process. The Voluntary Committee of Lawyers stepped forward with a formula for electing convention delegates that was immediately adopted by the states. One month after Roosevelt was inaugurated in 1933, the Volstead Act was amended so as to legalize 3.2 percent alcohol beer.

The dizzying pace continued as popular elections to select ratification convention delegates in the states produced majorities of 70 percent or higher in favor of repeal. Repeal of the 18th Amendment became official on December 5, 1933, after the Utah convention became the thirty-sixth state gathering to ratify the 21st Amendment. Prohibition—a powerful influence in the public life of Americans for nearly a century—disappeared thereafter as a national political issue.

CHAPTER 2

The Great Depression and the New Deal

Causes of the Great Depression

Adrian A. Paradis

In the concise summary that follows, Adrian A. Paradis explores the primary factors that contributed to the Great Depression in the United States. American business was slowing, unemployment was increasing, and farmers were overproducing crops at reduced value before the stock market crash on October 24, 1929, Paradis writes. Most Americans were already poor, so when holding companies crumbled, investment trusts collapsed, and banks closed, the author explains, prosperous Americans lost the wealth that could have helped keep the economy from crumbling. Moreover, despite warnings from politicians who suggested restraint, the author claims, politicians who were profiting from the economic boom of the twenties did not want to disturb the status quo. Paradis has drawn upon his own experience during the depression, and his employment as a corporate executive when writing *The Hungry Years: The Story of the Great American Depression*, from which the following article is taken.

The depression [in the United States] was part of a world-wide collapse brought on by World War I, a war which gave rise to nationalism and the erecting of high tariff walls that restricted international trade.

Most countries experienced no strong recovery follow-

Excerpted from *The Hungry Years: The Story of the Great American Depression*, by Adrian A. Paradis (Philadelphia, PA: Chilton, 1967). Copyright ©1967 by Adrian A. Paradis. Reprinted with permission from the author.

ing the war. Germany, for instance, was required to pay such heavy reparations to the Allies after the peace treaty was signed that her recovery was impeded and she could not resume normal trading with her prewar customers. The Communist revolution of 1919 practically isolated Russia from other nations and eliminated her from the world marketplace.

There was unrest in many places as revolution and the threat of revolution added to uncertainty and endangered American investments abroad. Depression had come to other nations before October, 1929, when our [stock] market crashed. Some of the countries which had already felt an economic recession were Australia, Bolivia, Brazil, Belgium, Germany, and India, while another half-dozen nations were already experiencing the effects of the first stages of recession.

No two economists or historians agree on all the causes responsible for those disastrous years, but there has been fairly general agreement that the following factors contributed to the calamity in the United States.

The stock market did not crash until October 24, 1929, but looking back we can see that the prosperous New Era, as the late nineteen-twenties were popularly called, began to lose its head of steam some time before Black Thursday. . . .

Stores had built up such large inventories of goods that they stopped ordering from the factories. When the market crash came, with many people losing all their savings and extra spending money, the demand dropped for goods which had piled up in stores and warehouses. Adding to the problem was the growing number of unemployed, whose purchasing stopped except for absolute necessities. Farmers too, millions of them, had little money and had been unable to do any buying for years. Little wonder the economy was in trouble!

The Plight of the Farmers

While the rest of the nation was enjoying Coolidge prosperity in the New Era, many farmers were living in privation, hopelessly in debt, and mortgaged with no possibility of ever regaining title to their property. Seemingly, no one was concerned.

"Farmers have never made money. I don't believe we can do much about it," President Calvin Coolidge told the chairman of the Farm Loan Board. In 1925–1926, farmers' cash receipts were only 40 per cent above the 1921 depression low point, but this proved to be the high point of the decade and thereafter income fell off. When Congress was asked to protect the farmer from foreign competition, as the protective tariff had shielded the manufacturer, there was little sympathetic response. Twice President Coolidge vetoed legislation that would have provided relief for destitute farmers. . . .

Many farmers remained in business, and those who gradually tried to farm more efficiently through the use of machines found that, although they could produce at less cost, they were soon creating for themselves and other farmers a new problem—overproduction.

In 1926, the corn crop increased over the previous year's production by six hundred million bushels but decreased in value by three hundred million dollars! The same thing happened to other farm products. Thus the depressed condition of the majority of our farmers proved such a drag on the economy that eventually it became one of the forces that helped turn our prosperity into depression.

The old-fashioned virtue of thrift gave place to the new cult of installment buying. Americans discovered that it was now possible to heed the call of the hucksters because a man's purchasing ability was no longer limited by the size of his bank balance. The way was open for new sales promotions and campaigns that helped to broaden markets, step up industrial production, and give business new vitality.

Prosperity was not shared by everyone, however. We have already noted the farmers' plight. Textiles, lumber, and leather were among industries which seemed to have slumped into a continuous state of depression. Even during the boom years the average number of unemployed ran to a million and a half, and neither wage earners nor salaried workers were becoming rich. After 1923, real wages remained practically stationary, and unemployment caused by technological advances increased each year.

Wealth Concentrated in the Hands of a Few

The tragic fact was that most Americans were really poor. Six out of every ten families had incomes of less than $2,000 a year, a sum which permitted them to buy only the most basic necessities of life. Only three out of every hundred families had incomes of over $10,000 a year, and it was this small group of wealthy individuals who provided much of the money needed for investments in new plants. They spent most of their money on food, rent, and clothing, and provided the cash that supported the producers of luxury goods. Thus, as soon as this small sector of our population was hit by the stock market crash, they stopped buying luxuries and cut off the flow of funds on which business had depended greatly.

In 1929, few people were aware of how many holding companies existed in the United States, or the power which they wielded. A holding company is exactly what the name implies: it holds the ownership of other corporations and may provide over-all direction and management to its subsidiary companies whose stock it holds. . . .

During the nineteen-twenties, ingenious financiers, some honest and many otherwise, used the holding company device to put together vast empires, principally in the entertainment, railroad, and utility fields. One of the largest, and called "the world's safest investment," was the creation of English-born Samuel Insull. Once Thomas A. Edison's private secretary, he became a Chicago millionaire stock manipulator who dominated Chicago's political and social circles for many years. He built a reputation for being trustworthy. He also created an intricate pyramid of public utility holding companies that attracted money from thousands of widows, pensioners, aged people, and others who invested their life savings in this gigantic enterprise.

Insull's corporate manipulations and speculations with company funds brought about one of the greatest bank-ruptcies of all time. When the Insull system failed in 1932, it was worth almost three billion dollars and was produc-ing an eighth of all the electric power in the United States.

In effect what happened was this: Stock manipulators es-tablished a top holding company by selling bonds and stocks and used the money they received to buy up enough stock of existing companies to control them. Whenever the promoters wanted to raise more money, they created a sec-ond holding company, which in turn would buy up the first, and later they might organize a third, and so on, until a crazy hodgepodge of companies was created.

After the stock market crashed, there were no more cash customers to buy the securities. More important, as the de-pression deepened, operating companies made less and less money, so that the holding companies were not getting enough cash to meet the huge interest payments on the bonds they had sold, and this caused them to collapse like houses of cards.

The holding companies took all their subsidiaries' earn-ings which normally were used to expand operations and to buy expensive equipment and machinery. This meant fewer orders for the factories and less employment, which, because of the size of the power industry, had a depressing effect on the economy. Little wonder that Congress eventu-ally outlawed giant holding companies!

The Investment Trusts Collapse and Banks Close

Collapse of many investment trusts created additional hardship. Investment trusts had been invented many, many years before 1929, but never had they become so popular nor so easy to start. An investment trust is an organization that invests its money in securities—stocks or bonds—of other companies. For its income it depends on the divi-dends and interest received from the securities it owns.

One reason for the popularity of investment trusts—or mutual funds, as many are now called—is that an investor who does not trust his judgment of stocks and bonds can purchase shares of an investment trust which employs trained analysts and economists to manage its funds. Investment trusts were popular between 1926 and 1929 because they made money as stocks kept rising in value. Since the public did not bother to investigate before it bought, promoters of investment trusts had a field day—that is, until the market crashed.

Testifying before a committee of the United States Senate, Mr. Sachs, of Goldman Sachs & Company, stated in 1932 that his company had organized an investment trust, the Goldman Sachs Trading Corporation. Senator Couzens asked at what price the stock was sold.

MR. SACHS: At $104.

SENATOR COUZENS: And what is the price of the stock now?

MR. SACHS: Approximately $1.75.

Following the mid-Twenties, there was an increasing number of foreclosures on farms as mortgages became due and farmers were unable to pay. Banks found themselves loaded with unsalable property, which resulted in numerous failures. During the 1926–1928 years, 1,588 banks with deposits totaling $539,000,000 closed their doors.

Officers of stronger banks learned nothing from the numerous bank failures. They fell into the same trap by overextending credit, making loans on securities that were constantly rising in paper value only and on urban real estate which was enjoying a boom of its own.

Although bank closings during the Twenties did not bring on the depression, they were symptomatic of the precarious condition of the entire banking structure. It was inevitable, therefore, that, when the boom collapsed in 1929, many of the banks which had extended credit beyond reasonable limits were bound to suffer and contribute to the economic depression. Blame for the rash of bank closings should not be laid entirely on the bankers who were often overeager to lend other people's money. Much of the fault could be laid at the door of the Federal

Reserve Board, which was expected to set the banking tone for the nation.

Federal Reserve Policies

As Secretary of Commerce, Herbert Hoover repeatedly warned against the policies of the Federal Reserve Board, whose members (with one exception) Hoover described as "mediocrities."

"The Reserve policies . . . mean inflation with inevitable collapse which will bring calamities upon our farmers, our workers and legitimate business," Mr. Hoover said.

On the other hand, Roy Young, governor of the Federal Reserve Board, was said to have been laughing as he watched the rising prices on the ticker tape.

"What I am laughing at," he said, "is that I am sitting here trying to keep a hundred and twenty million people from doing what they want to do!"

In March, 1929, when President Coolidge left office, he dismissed the stock market with the happy comment that stocks were "cheap at current prices," and the country was "absolutely sound." It was not his responsibility to regulate the boom but up to the Federal Reserve Board, which Congress had created as a strong central bank. However, that group, many of whose members were profiting from the boom, was not about to do anything that would disturb the status quo. They felt that it could be as dangerous to curb the speculation and risk a bust as it was to let it march on unchecked. The latter seemed the more sensible course of action.

Holding the power to stop the headlong rush into disaster by increasing the rediscount rates, the governors hesitated, drew back, and stood by helplessly while one of their members—Charles Mitchell, chairman of the influential National City Bank of New York—announced that his bank was ready to lend money to all who cared to come and apply for it.

Meanwhile, the public was coming in such numbers to buy stocks on margin that the New York banks could not supply all of the money needed. They soon became agents for other banks that wanted to share in the money making. Not content with the usual interest rate of 5 per cent, they found that, as the frenzy in the stock market increased, interest rates went up, up, up, until 12 per cent was reached. The smartest banks of all were those which turned around, borrowed at 5 per cent from the Federal Reserve Bank, then loaned the same funds at 12 per cent.

As stocks continued their upward march during 1929 and as interest rates grew higher and higher, the Federal Reserve System still remained silent except for a few innocuous and meaningless statements. If anyone was thought to be responsible for regulating the New York Stock Exchange, it was Governor Franklin D. Roosevelt of New York, since the Exchange was located within his state and no Federal law had been created to regulate it.

With the Federal Reserve Board looking the other way, with no government agency to curb the speculative orgy, with corporations, banks, and individuals ready to loan money to speculators at unheard-of interest rates as high as 20 per cent, the stage was set for the biggest and most spectacular economic bust the world had ever seen!

Depression Farming: Drought, Dust, and Displacement

T.H. Watkins

Economic conditions during the depression were only one problem faced by American farmers. In the following excerpt from his book *The Great Depression: America in the 1930s*, noted historian and conservationist, T.H. Watkins explains how severe drought conditions and dust storms contributed to the displacement of many American farmers. Some moved to nearby states, Watkins writes, but others moved to the Pacific Northwest or California where they settled in cities or added to the population of migrant workers. The author discusses the problems these migrant workers encountered, including poor wages, disease, and intolerance. Watkins was an editorial consultant to the Sierra Club and has written many books and articles on history and conservation.

F or a quarter of a century, Caroline Boa Henderson and her husband Wilhelmine had raised a family and lived out the hardships and rewards of family farming on a homestead near Shelton, Oklahoma. "We have rooted deeply," she wrote in the summer of 1935. "Each little tree or shrub that we have planted, each effort to make our home more convenient or attractive has seemed to strengthen the hope that our first home might also be our last." But now: "[Our] daily physical torture, confusion of mind, gradual wearing down of courage, seem to make that long continued hope look like a vanishing dream."

A Disastrous Drought

In 1930, hail had destroyed their wheat crop. In 1931, terrible prices had undercut a reasonably successful crop. They could endure such drawbacks, as they had before. But then came drought, the worst drought in anyone's memory, day after day, week after week, month after month, year after year of little or no rain, until by 1935 they were facing ruin in a world ruled by the mocking oppression of dust. "There are days," she wrote,

> when for hours at a time we cannot see the windmill fifty feet from the kitchen door. There are days when for briefer periods one cannot distinguish the windows from the solid wall because of the solid blackness of the raging storm. Only in some Inferno-like dream could anyone visualize the terrifying lurid red light overspreading the sky when portions of Texas "are on the air."

The impact of this relentless siege of disaster cannot easily be exaggerated. Agriculture not only was the linchpin of the American economy in the monetary value of what it grew and nurtured—$9.5 billion even in the drought year of 1934—it produced the very stuff of life on which the rest of the nation's industry, society, and culture fed, physically and even psychologically. In 1934, nearly 30 percent of all Americans still lived on farms, and a good part of how the nation viewed itself was rooted in its agricultural traditions and experience. . . .

Now, both the image and the reality of the land were under assault. Natural cycles had combined with human miscalculation to produce the most devastating agricultural disaster in American history—and little the New Dealers [members of the government who hoped to alleviate the effects of the depression] could produce in the way of legislation or emergency measures would do more than provide intermittent and inadequate relief. Drought was nothing new, in this country or any other, but that of the 1930s, which continued through most of the decade—combining in some years with unprecedented heat waves—was "the worst in the climatological history of the country," according to a Weather Bureau scientist. It struck first in the eastern third of the country in 1930, where it crippled agriculture from Maine to Arkansas and where only Florida enjoyed anything that approached normal rainfall. It had been drought that had aggravated the terrible desperation of those farmers who had invaded the little town of England, Arkansas, in January of 1931, demanding food for their children, and drought that in 1930 had given the great Delta bluesman, Son House, the theme for "Dry Spell Blues": "Them dry spell blues are fallin', drivin' people/ from door to door,/Dry spell blues are fallin', drivin' people/ from door to door./Them dry spell blues has put everybody on/the kindlin' floor."

In 1932, the center of the drought started heading west, and by 1934 it had desiccated the Great Plains from North Dakota to Texas, from the Mississippi River Valley to the Rockies. In the northern Rockies in the winter of 1933–34, the snowpack was less than a third of normal, in the central Rockies less than half, and in areas of the southern Rockies barely a dusting of snow had been seen.

The Unprotected Soil Turned to Dust

Providence, fate, or some other cosmic force might be blamed for the drought itself, but not for the phenomenon that accompanied it over hundreds of millions of acres: most of that was inescapably man-made. The speculative dance of the war years and the twenties had abused millions of acres of farmland in the South and Midwest, as farmers plowed, planted, and harvested as much as they could as often as they could. Much of the topsoil was left so exhausted it could barely support the most undemanding ground cover, much less productive crops. Careless plowing had rutted the fields, leaving the land open to gullying from erosion. "Since the cover was first disturbed [in the nineteenth century]," a state commission of the National Resources Planning Board reported, "Iowa has lost approximately 550,000 tons of good surface soil per square mile, or a total of thirty billion tons." Iowa was not alone. "Approximately 35 million acres of formerly cultivated land have essentially been destroyed for crop production," the 1934 *Yearbook of Agriculture* reported, adding that "100 million acres now in crops have lost all or most of the topsoil; 125 million acres of land now in crops are rapidly losing topsoil. . . ." At the same time, decades of overgrazing by cattle and sheep ranchers in the western plains and valleys had left one former rich grassland

Drought and dust storms in the Great Plains contributed to farmers' problems during the Great Depression. In this photograph, soil drifts threaten to completely cover this farmhouse in Liberal, Kansas, in 1936.

after another stripped clean of ground cover, vulnerable to rampant wind and water erosion. Grass, a Texas sheepherder of the time commented, "is what counts. It's what saves us all—far as we get saved. Men and towns and such as that, don't amount to a particular damn anyhow. Grass does. Grass is what holds the earth together." Not everyone had understood that simple fact. Since the first great cattle and sheep herds had been turned out in the last third of the nineteenth century to feed on the rich grasslands of the plains and mountain pastures of the interior West, the grass had been steadily, ruthlessly overgrazed, until the earth over enormous stretches of land was no longer held together by anything but inertia. After the wartime and postwar booms of the teen years and the 1920s, more than half the grazing land in the western states was in a condition of soil depletion described by the Department of Agriculture as "extreme" or "severe."

The soil, loose and dry, lay unprotected from the winds, which repeatedly swept down on the ruined grasslands of the west, scooped them clean and carried the dust into the air, moving east to the exposed and waiting farmlands of the plains. Here, the winds deposited much of it, moved it around, added to it, filled the air now with the western grasslands dust and the plains farmland dust in a great choking geographic mix. Beadle County, South Dakota, November 11, 1933:

> By mid-morning, a gale was blowing, cold and black. By noon it was blacker than night, because one can see through night and this was an opaque black. It was a wall of dirt one's eyes could not penetrate, but it could penetrate the eyes and ears and nose. It could penetrate to the lungs until one coughed up black. If a person was outside, he tied his handkerchief around his face, but he still coughed up black. When the wind died and the sun shone forth again, it was on a different world. There were no fields, only sand drifting into mounds and eddies that swirled in what was now but an autumn breeze.

The dust did not always stay west of the Mississippi. When

conditions were right, the wind would carry it east on the jet stream in enormous clouds and drop it in the form of filthy unseasonal snow on Chicago, Indianapolis, Washington, New York, and even on the gently rolling decks of Atlantic liners. During just one storm between May 9 and May 11, 1934, an estimated 350 million tons of soil disappeared from the West and reappeared in the East. Chicago got four pounds of it for every person in the city, and Washington, New York, Boston, and other cities burned their streetlamps in the middle of the day.

Too Little, Too Late

The government did what it could. Interior Secretary Harold Ickes established the Soil Erosion Service under Hugh Hammond Bennett in August of 1933; the agency later moved over to the Agriculture Department as the Soil Conservation Service and Bennett and his people diligently organized farmers into soil conservation districts, but not all the reeducation, preventive measures, or reclamation work in the world could repair the damage of generations. In June of 1934, Franklin D. Roosevelt signed the Taylor Grazing Act, which authorized the president to withdraw up to 140 million acres of federally owned public land from application under any one of the three thousand or so public land laws on the books and to establish grazing districts whose use by the cattle and sheep industry was to be carefully monitored by a new Interior Department agency, the Grazing Service. The Service would be marginally successful in stabilizing the situation, but could do little to repair historical damage. Between 1933 and 1934, the Federal Emergency Relief Administration would spend $85 million to purchase and attempt to rehabilitate ruined farmland, but this program, too, was nearly helpless to reclaim land that nearly a century of abuse had left ruined.

Little helped. Human strength failed. Hope died. "[The] longing for rain has become almost an obsession," Caroline Henderson wrote in 1935. "We dream of the faint gurgling sound of dry soil sucking in the grateful moisture . . .

of the fresh green of sprouting wheat or barley, the reddish bronze of spring rye. But we wake to another day of wind and dust and hopes deferred. . . ." The Hendersons toughed it out and continued to work their land for more than two decades, but for thousands of other farm families the drought alone was more than they could endure.

The Dynamics of Dispossession

Many people simply pulled up stakes and abandoned their land, and even for many of those who might have stuck it out in spite of all that nature could do, financial circumstances would make it all but impossible. Resident and absentee owners alike lost their lands to foreclosure proceedings; according to Department of Agriculture reports, nearly two hundred out of every thousand farms in the states of the Midwest, the Central South, and the Plains succumbed to forced sales between 1930 and 1935. And when landlords failed, so did croppers and tenant farmers, and to the ranks of dispossessed owners were added thousands of men and women who were forced off land they had worked as if it were their own. . . .

No one knows precisely how many families were displaced in the early years of the New Deal—or just how many had left the land as the direct result of crop reductions or tractor use. However many, there was not much in the way of employment the affected states could offer these suddenly landless and workless thousands; in Arkansas, for example, the unemployment rate was 39 percent in 1933, and in Missouri, Oklahoma, and Texas it ranged from 29 to 32 percent. People began to leave their home states in growing numbers after the terrible summer of 1934. Oklahoma had a net loss of more than 440,000 people in the 1930s. Kansas lost 227,000. Throughout the Plains states, 2.5 million people ultimately would leave for other parts. Most of those parts were nearby; the greater portion of the internal population movement in the American middle in those years was from one state to a neighboring state. But some 460,000 people moved to the Pacific Northwest, where they found work on the building of Bonneville and Grand Coulee dams, found abandoned homesteads they could work in southern Idaho and the eastern valleys of Oregon and Washington, went into the ancient forests of the region as lumberjacks or joined the migrant workers in the hop fields and beet fields—or simply settled in the cities and collected relief checks where and when they could.

The Promise of California

Other thousands, particularly from the southwestern Plains states, headed for California. All logic dictated the move, so it seemed. After all, between 1910 and 1930 an estimated 310,000 southwesterners had already moved to the Golden State, lured by the promise of opportunity that had bathed California in the glow of hope ever since the Gold Rush of 1848–52. Residents of Oklahoma, Arkansas,

A Letter from the Dust Bowl

In the following letter, Caroline Henderson illustrates the desperation and determination of farm families during the dust storms of the 1930s.

Eva, Oklahoma
My dear Evelyn: June 30, 1935

In the dust-covered desolation of our No Man's Land here, wearing our shade hats, with handkerchiefs tied over our faces, and vaseline in our nostrils, we have been trying to rescue our home from the wind-blown dust which penetrates wherever air can go. It is almost a hopeless task, for there is rarely a day when at some time the dust clouds do not roll over. 'Visibility' approaches zero and everything is covered again with a silt-like deposit which may vary in depth from a film to actual ripples on the kitchen floor. I keep oiled cloths on the window sills and between the upper and lower sashes. Some seal the windows with

Texas, and other states who had fallen upon hard times now thought of all the cheerful letters they had been receiving from friends and relatives in California, took a look at the tormented land and overburdened cities of their own regions, and put together the wherewithal to get themselves and their families across the plains and deserts to the golden valleys of the West Coast. In one fifteen-month period alone, some 86,000 did precisely that, individually and as families, by car and by bus, most of them taking no more than three or four days to rattle down Route 66 to the border crossing at Yuma, Arizona. By the end of the decade another 220,000 or so would do the same.

If many of these people were hard-pressed by farm failure or urban unemployment, most were less than destitute or without family support. They had relatives waiting to house and feed them, if nothing else, and some even had

---

gummed-paper strips used in wrapping parcels, but no method is fully effective . . .

Naturally you will wonder why we stay here where conditions are so disheartening. Why not pick up and leave as so many others have done? Yet I cannot act or think as if the experiences of our 27 years of life had never been. To break all the closely knit ties of our continued and united efforts for the sake of a possibly greater comfort elsewhere seems like defaulting in our task. We may *have* to leave. We can't hold out indefinitely without some income, however small. But if we can keep the taxes paid, we can work and hope for a better day. We long for the garden and little chickens, the trees and birds and wild flowers of the years gone by. Perhaps if we do our part these good things may return some day, for others if not for ourselves.

A great reddish-brown dust cloud is rising now from the southeast, so we must get out and do our night work before it arrives. Our thoughts go with you.

Susan Winslow, *Brother Can You Spare a Dime?* New York: Paddington, 1976.

jobs waiting for them. That still left tens of thousands who legitimately could be described as rural refugees, and one thing they soon learned was that land monopoly and agriculture on an industrial scale was a California tradition and the opportunities to engage in family farming were limited to the point of nonexistence. More than 100,000 of the migrants consequently did not gravitate toward the state's farming regions, but to the city of Los Angeles, with some going down to San Diego or up to San Francisco. . . .

The Drifting Population of Migrant Workers

Most of California's new population would become irretrievably urban, whether it had started out that way or not, scattering through poor and middle-class white Los Angeles neighborhoods and out into the bungalow-and-apartment-building suburbs of Long Beach, Compton, Encino, Gardena, Covina, Southgate, Downey, and other towns. But some of those with rural roots would seek the work that was most familiar to them, joining California's drifting population of about 200,000 migrant farm laborers—the largest regional segment of the great army of migrant farm laborers in the United States, a constantly moving and nearly invisible population of as many as two million men, women, and children who cut cane in Florida and dug potatoes in Maine, picked peaches in Georgia and apples in Pennsylvania, plucked strawberries in Louisiana and dug sugar beets in Michigan, and harvested wheat from central Texas to northern Montana.

Some 110,000 people from the new migration would move to agricultural areas of California—more than seventy thousand of them to the San Joaquin Valley alone. Not all these new arrivals would become migrant laborers, of course, but most did, taking their place in the cheap labor pool that California's agricultural industry had come to expect as its due; for more than eighty years, it had capitalized upon successive waves of Chinese, white native Americans from earlier periods of economic stress, Japanese, Indian (from India), Filipino, and, most recently,

Mexican-American laborers. . . .

Before long, this latest resource of cheap labor would account for nearly half the total of all the state's migrant workers. Like their predecessors, most Anglo migrants confined themselves to journeys up and down the state, following the cycles of planting and harvest from the Imperial Valley to the Sacramento Valley and all the valleys in between, though some backtracked to the cotton fields and other irrigated crops of Arizona or continued straight up California to Oregon and Washington to work the hop fields and beet fields of the north. The average distance traveled from crop to crop every year, the State Relief Administration calculated, was 516 miles. The migrants frequently traveled and worked as families, living in the squalor of work camps either erected by themselves wherever they could with whatever they could or provided by the farmers. Whether self-built or furnished, these feculent little communities, often called "ditch camps" because they were located on the side of roads along which ran filthy water ditches, were disease-ridden and indisputably unfit for human beings. At one point, Carey McWilliams reported, fifty babies died of diarrhea and enteritis in one county during just one picking season; children in Tulare County were reported dying at the rate of two a day; and during an inspection tour of eighteen camps in the vicinity of Kingsburg in Kings County, one social worker found "dozens of children with horribly sore eyes; many cases of cramps, diarrhea, and dysentery; fever, colds, and sore throats." Hookworm, pellegra, and rickets were common.

Impoverished and Despised

Pay was better than it was in the depressed regions of the South and the Midwest, but whether by the day or by the amount of fruit picked or vegetables dug, wages were still far below what a family needed for decent upkeep. What was more, the seasonal character of the job made it impossible to accumulate a significant stake even when one or more members of the family made up to $3 a day, as many did. The recorded need for seasonal labor in the California fields over one two-year period, for example, ranged from a low of 48,173 workers in March to a high of 144,720 in September. Average annual farm labor income, as a consequence, never got much above $1,300 for each family—nearly $500 less than other Anglo California families (though $315 more than the average for *non-Anglo* Californians).

Huddling to wait out off-season unemployment in makeshift "shacktowns" and "Little Oklahomas" perched on the outskirts of agricultural service centers like Bakersfield, Fresno, and Modesto, collecting state relief, sending their children to local schools, the migrants soon earned the pious contempt of their neighbors in the traditional manner of humans rejecting outsiders who are unfamiliar and therefore vaguely threatening. Whatever their origin, they became known collectively as "Okies" and "Arkies," with a few "Texies" thrown in for good measure, and were subject to the kind of abuse and discrimination that the state's Mexican-American, Filipino, and African-American field workers had endured as a matter of course for decades. "These 'share croppers,'" one woman complained, "are not a noble people looking for a home and seeking an education for their children. They are unprincipled degenerates looking for something for nothing." Interviewing customers at several Sacramento Valley bars, a reporter collected a good run of comments: "Damned Okies." "No damned good. Don't do a damned thing for the town." "Damned shiftless nogoods." "Damned Okies. Damned bums clutter up the roadside."

They possessed a terrible patience, however, these despised migrants, as well as a burning determination and an anger to which someone would be forced to answer sooner or later. But it would be another season or two before the New Dealers would comprehend the full dimensions of what had fallen on these wanderers and begin, slowly and indecisively, to give them sanctuary.

The Migrant Youth of Depression America

Thomas Minehan

In 1932 and 1933, sociologist Thomas Minehan disguised himself as a hobo and interviewed teenaged freight travelers. Minehan believed that describing their life in statistical terms was inadequate, and he decided to paint a picture of the lives of these homeless boys and girls in his 1934 book *Boy and Girl Tramps of America,* from which the following account is taken. Minehan describes the often brutal environmental conditions the migrant youth faced and the ways they found to survive. The author also records the reasons they left home to ride the rails: many boys and girls left home because their families could no longer support them while others left because the stresses on depression families made life at home difficult.

Happy Joe and I sprawl on some wisps of straw in a box car, waiting for the hour when the eastern manifest freight pulls out. It is late afternoon and raining very hard, a cold autumn drizzle that chills through damp clothes and penetrates thin soles, and arouses a feeling of nostalgia for vanished summer and sadness for the memory of what life might have been. We have had our free bowl of soup and cup of stew at the mission, and an order to leave town before breakfast. The odor of wheat lingering in the wood of

Excerpted from *Boy and Girl Tramps of America,* by Thomas Minehan (New York: Farrar and Rinehart, 1934).

the box car revives our unappeased appetite and enhances the loneliness of the day and the misery of a box car in the rain. Why should anybody not a fool or a philosopher be taking the dreary road today?

"Did the old man kick you out?" I ask.

"Well, no." Loyal still to his family, Joe does not want to give the wrong impression. "He didn't exactly kick me out, but he gave me plenty of hints. He hasn't worked steady in the last three years," Joe explains. "There's seven of us kids at home, and I'm the oldest. I'm seventeen. I worked for about six months two years ago for a grocer who gave me no wages but, you know, food and stuff. Then he closed up. I couldn't get anything. The old man kept giving hints. Last fall they cut down on our relief. We had to go to bed because our house was so cold. I cut nine cords of wood for a man. He gave us two. That wasn't so bad, and I thought I'd stay until Christmas. I got the kids a duck, too, for Christmas, but I ain't saying how I got it. Then, before the old man could start giving any more hints, I scrams."

It is later in the fall now, almost snow time. The lumber shed, deserted and in decay, divides but does not stop the cold wind that charges full from the north. Fern and I listen for a train that is soon to come up the grade. She wears a boy's sailor blue mackinaw, a boy's cap, and with two pairs of overalls is not cold. But there was a thin scum of ice on our jungle water this morning, the last flight of ducks have gone south, and the wind is threatening snow. Fern limps a little from a sore ankle turned two nights ago when she stumbled over a switch, and with the day and a cold breakfast she is depressed.

"They were always picking on me," she replies in answer to my question. "At home or at school, it made no difference, everybody always blamed me for everything. Nothing I did ever satisfied anybody. I hated school worse than home even before the old man went on charity. I was always given the hard things to do in school, and at home if there was a dirty job I got it.

"I didn't have any clothes to wear to school. So one day

a guy says to me, 'Get wise, sister, get wise.' So I got wise. And the old man catches me taking my first two bits from a fellow and he goes kinda nertz. He calls me down on my knees in the kitchen and Ma comes in and takes my part. 'Why shouldn't she take two bits?' Ma says. 'Somebody in this house has to earn something.' And the old man slams the door and goes out to get drunk. 'Gimme that two bits,' Ma says. 'Gimme that two bits, you dirty slut, before I kill you.' So I says, 'Like hell you will.' And I scrams."

Why did they leave home?

The mission waiting room is a swarming ant hill of men who keep pushing in out of the cold and snow. Every available seat is taken. Men and boys crowd the aisles and cover the steps, leaving only a small lane for entrance and egress under the balcony and near the registration desk. Transients squat on knapsacks or stand in discouraged but talkative groups, waiting for the happy moment when stomachs can break their twelve-hour fast on bread and beans. New arrivals appear in the door in a cloud of steam, their snow-covered feet being the first portion of their body discernible as they clump down iron stairs. Outside a Minnesota blizzard howls a wolf-song through deserted snow-banked streets. Snow piles on window sills. Frost creeps over panes. The thermometer, dropping steadily, registers 27 degrees below zero.

Boo Peep and I rest our weary backs against the bricks of an unused fireplace. He sits on a pack; I on the floor, my heavy sheepskin serving not uncomfortably as a cushion and a shield against the blast of cold air that strikes us as the door opens. A small thin-framed lad, Boo Peep wears two cloth overcoats, the inner one cut off just below the waist. My larger bulk and bigger coat protect him somewhat from the draft. Fourteen hours he spent in a box car. He is still cold and hungry. A ring of bologna and a loaf of bread washed down with snow has kept him alive for two days, as he came up from the South and East. The sub-zero weather is not pleasant—particularly when, as in Boo Peep's case, you have no shoes. An old pair of four-buckle overshoes, miles too big and with several air holes, cover his feet. Two pairs of cotton socks, a pair of worn tennis shoes encased in a layer of newspaper have kept his feet from freezing—he thinks. Not until later will he know. Although he has been less than an hour in the mission, he seems to be thawing out. The blue cold is retreating from his face. He snuffles. At each snuffle, his whole body rises with the force of the inspiration. A deep cheek scar half an inch wide and twice that long, memento of a blow earlier in the fall from a railroad watchman, is suspiciously coloring and sore. Boo Peep is not quite fifteen.

"A guy's crazy to go out on a day like this if he doesn't have to. Why did you leave home?"

"I couldn't go back to high school in these pants. What the hell, I'd rather take to the road. The old man? I don't know where he is. I've had four of them. Every one worse than the other. Then, Ma died a year and a half ago. I stayed on with my stepfather for a while. He was a barber and he said he'd teach me the trade afternoons, and I could go to high school in the morning. But he took another woman. Naw, he didn't marry her. And she took a dislike to me as soon as she saw me. She gave me the dirt in all directions. They never bought me a pair of socks or gave me a nickel to spend. All I got was a dime from some of my friends for cutting their hair. So when I asked for a new pair of pants after working thirteen hours a day all summer and I didn't get them, I left."

Frank is almost eighteen. He raises his head across the collar of his coat.

"That's like the bastard I worked for," he contributes. "Milk fourteen cows a day, up before daylight and still working in the field when it's dark. And did I get any money after eight months' steady work? I got a pair of old boots with holes in them so big that I couldn't tell where the top was, and an overalls patched until it looked like a crazy quilt and when it got cold last fall they gave me a horse blanket smelling of liniment and manure to sleep under. And I thought, screw you, I'm hitting the road.

"Oh, sure, I got an old man, but he ain't worked in four years, and you know how it is. Four younger kids home. So I thought I'll work for a farmer and earn my board anyway. And did I work! And did I earn my board! So last fall I knew there was no use going home, and I just beat it."

Pete, a diminutive gnome with a slight limp, joins the discussion. His voice comes excited and asthmatic from a chest covered with fold upon fold of newspaper and clothing.

"Yes, and I'll bet you're glad you beat it. I know I am. Work! Work! 'Why don't you get work?' That's all I hear from the old man for a year. Cripes! What does he expect a kid to do?" The words come out of Pete's mouth bullet-like. "I try a job cleaning a shoe store every morning from four to six o'clock for a buck and a quarter a week. And one morning my mother forgets to wake me. And I'm canned. The old man goes nuts for a while. So finally I asks him, 'Why the hell don't you get work yourself for a change? You ain't done nothing now since the war!' Then he bangs me with a chair, and I lams it."

Pete's voice ends in a shriek. His small deep-set eyes flame indignantly at the memory of injustice. His voice forces itself more and more until it is wheezy and ineffectual as a locomotive losing ground on a grade.

Why did they leave home?

Still along the Mississippi River banks the sandstone caves are damp and chill. Three nights ago a hungry boy froze to death within a dozen yards of our cave, while above us a careless city celebrated. But hunger and cold and death ride the green light of every train the child tramp flips. Soon he knows them as old acquaintances. Below us, only a smudge of snow marks the end of winter. Already the Mississippi inches upward on the bridge piers with young freshets. And today a warm sun shines upon our doorway, drawing us out of our caverns as it draws the raccoon out of his hollow tree. It is a day when even the rheumatic old men venture out, the social leaders look up summer sailings, the penned-in worker begins to plan his vacation, and the child tramp starts to itch with a desire to travel which will not be denied. Well-thumbed time-tables are studied, routes compared, and experiences exchanged. By God, if nothing else happens this summer, we're going to see the country.

"Geez, it's two years ago since I left home, and I ain't never wanted to go back yet."

Jud, the hard-boiled, is talking. Elated with a new pair of work rubbers, a zipper-front jacket, and a barber school haircut, he looks upon the world as his oyster.

"No, sir, the old road looks good to me. Square meals don't come every day, but I eat better than I ate at home and no grief about the old man being out of work all the time and how he used to do so much when he was as old as I was, and then the snoopy old social worker coming around asking questions and the cops waiting for a chance to hang something on you. If they do give me a rap now nobody knows about it and if I haven't got a clean shirt there ain't nobody else showing off his new sport roadster."

"That's so for you perhaps, but I'd like to see my sister again." Flaxen-haired Fred is but sixteen.

On the road eight months, he has been living on his own for over two years. Mother dead, father dead, twelve-year-old sister in an orphan asylum in Milwaukee.

Fred's memories of home are pleasant. "Things were slick then. Nothing to do but go to school and play. And every evening after supper we used to gather around the piano while Mother played and we all sang songs in German. But then, I suppose—" His hands rise, his shoulders shrug, in an age-old gesture of resignation and impotence.

And while his voice does not break, in the corners of his blue eyes there gathers a suspicious mistiness. He blows his nose lustily between thumb and forefinger, snorting to distract attention.

I know Fred's story. So do all of us. Home might have been happy for Fred, playing with a younger sister, eating Mother's cookies, attending the circus with Father. But Father died and Mother followed six months later, and this morning as spring creeps over the frost-ribbed hills, Fred is a bum, welcome nowhere, pushed out of one city and into another, on the road because he has no home, no friends and no relatives. Still in his tired eyes shines something of the eternally unconquered Teuton, and the habits of cleanliness his mother taught him keep him neat and tidy on the road, the qualities of courage and honor his father inculcated keep him straight in the midst of a life of shame and dishonor.

"My old man was always mean," an Irish boy from Boston explains, "my stepfather, that is. My real father, I don't hardly remember him. He died a couple of years after coming back from the war. Gas. Everything was oke then. But my mother married about five years ago. My stepfather had two kids. A boy and a girl. The girl was all right, but I never liked the boy, nor the old man neither. I took a poke at the kid the first day he came to our house; I could lick him easy. The old man beat me. I hated him. And did I lick his kid before I left! Two black eyes, a broken ear and a bloody nose . . ."

Kay is fifteen. Her blue eyes, fair hair, and pale cheeks are girlish and delicate. Cinders, wind, and frost have irritated but not toughened that tender skin. Sickly and suffering from chronic undernourishment, she appears to subsist almost entirely upon her finger nails which she gnaws habitually.

"There wasn't"—she takes a finger away from her mouth long enough to join the discussion—"much else for me to do but go. There are eight younger kids at home and one older sister out of work. Dad hasn't worked steady for four years. Sis, for two. Mother got a job scrubbing—$7 a week, and that's all we had to live on except for some clothes we got from a lodge. We wouldn't take charity. So when a farmer offered me a chance to work all summer for potatoes and vegetables for the family last winter I took it. I could have stayed with his wife, but I thought maybe if I skipped around through the country I could earn some cash and send a few bucks home. But it don't look much like it now."

"You'd look fine sending anything home, kid" Helen, a

young box-car prostitute, sneers at Kay's threadbare boy's overcoat and holey overshoes. "If I ever get any money, I'll put it here." She pats her abdomen. "I lammed from home because I always wanted to see California. So when Frank says 'Let's go' I went. Wife or no wife could stop me although she did have Frank pinched."

Why did they leave home?

It is the middle of September and already a tinge of winter haunts the air in spite of the mellow sun of autumn and the warmth of early-changing, reddening leaves. Twelve boy tramps and three little girl companions sit in a natural clearing in a woods a hundred yards from a railroad grade fourteen miles south of Chicago. A spring bubbles from the ground in one corner, running away in a tiny stream to the woods. Here the child tramps wash their clothing. Bushes are hung with drying shirts, socks, underwear, and pants. Two boys try to bend a shoe nail with rocks as last and hammer. A Titian-haired girl of fifteen, extremely pretty and extremely thin, sews a patch on the seat of a boy's pants. The boy stands very still on a hummock. The girl sews very business-like, as she turns in the edges of the patch and reënforces the center. A second, blond girl boils coffee and potatoes and directs the barbecuing of a small hog. Except for the disproportionate ratio of boys to girls, the drying clothes and the deshabille of many, the gathering seems very much like a high school wiener roast, or a Sunday school barbecue. Nature has been kind to the farmers, and the farmers, with crops rotting in the fields, have been kind to the child tramps. There is food enough in the jungle to feed forty. Vegetables have been collected by the sack. Cantaloupes and apples stand in a pyramid on the ground. The hog, of course, was not a gift. But, then, he might have been hit by a truck.

Ragged, smiling Texas, merry as usual, is returning with a knapsack full of bread which he has begged uptown. He recounts his experiences and success gustily and with the pardonable braggadocio of one who has accomplished something.

". . . and one woman asked me why did I leave home, and I answers, 'Hard times, lady!' just like that. 'Hard times, lady, hard times!'"

His auditors laugh.

And hard times it seems to be, lady.

Three hundred and eighty-seven out of four hundred and sixty-six boys and girls stated definitely that hard times drove them away from home.

A New Deal for the American People

Alan Brinkley

In this overview, Alan Brinkley explains the the New Deal
from its roots in the politics of earlier decades to its role in
expanding the federal government's influence in American
life. Brinkley summarizes the achievements and setbacks of
the New Deal during its three periods of reform. Brinkley is
a professor of history at Columbia University in New York
and author of several books on the Great Depression and
the New Deal, including *The End of Reform: New Deal
Liberalism in Recession and War,* and *Voices of Protest:
Huey Long, Father Coughlin, and the Great Depression.*

Franklin Roosevelt broke with precedent within a few
hours of being nominated for president in 1932. He
flew to Chicago to deliver his acceptance speech in person,
becoming the first presidential candidate ever to fly in an
airplane and the first to appear before his party's convention as the nominee. In his speech to the Democratic delegates, broadcast to the nation by radio, he promised "a
new deal for the American people." The phrase became the
popular label for his administration (1933–1945) and its
many domestic achievements. The New Deal attempted
many things in its effort to end the Great Depression and
reform the American economy. It failed at many of them.

Excerpted from "The New Deal: An Overview," by Alan Brinkley, *Social Education,* vol. 60, pp. 255–58, September 1996. Copyright ©1996 by the National
Council for the Social Studies. Reprinted with permission.

But its successes were numerous and significant enough to establish it as the single most important twentieth century episode in the creation of the modern American state.

The Roots of the New Deal

Roosevelt entered office with no single ideology and no single, clear plan for dealing with the Depression. But the programs of the Roosevelt administration did have ancestors. The New Deal reflected progressive ideas that Roosevelt and most of his original associates had absorbed in their political youths early in the century: an impatience with economic disorder; an opposition to monopoly; a commitment to government regulation of the economy; and a belief that poverty was usually a product of social and economic forces, not personal moral failure.

The New Deal also drew heavily on the experience of its leaders in the economic mobilization for World War I and from the policy experiments of the 1920s, both of which involved efforts to harmonize the economy by creating cooperative relationships among its constituent elements. The New Deal was eclectic, pragmatic, and frankly experimental—a combination of several quite different ideologies and traditions.

The major domestic achievements of the New Deal took shape during three distinct periods of reform. During the first months of Roosevelt's presidency, the administration moved energetically to stop the economic panic that had engulfed the nation in 1932 (and had led to Roosevelt's decisive electoral victory). From early 1935 to mid-1936, as the president prepared for reelection, Roosevelt launched a second major series of reforms, which historians have often called the "second New Deal." A third, and less productive, period of activism began in mid-1937 and continued through 1938 as the administration searched for ways to increase its influence within the government and for a solution to a serious new recession.

In the first days after his inauguration in 1933, Roosevelt moved energetically both to deal with the most urgent crises facing the nation and to make his own personality the most important political force in America. On March 4, 1933, he delivered an important inaugural address that, while best remembered for the statement "The only thing we have to fear is fear itself," was more notable for the veiled but unmistakable warning that if normal political efforts were not enough to deal with the crises, he would seize broad emergency powers usually reserved for wartime. He began a series of "fireside chats" over the radio through which he explained the actions of the government to the public. He courted the press eagerly and effectively. And he made certain always to appear vigorous and optimistic. That was partly to distract attention from the fact that polio had robbed him of the use of his legs and that he spent most of his days confined to a wheelchair.

Most important, he won passage of a series of major pieces of legislation. The desperate economic situation, combined with the substantial Democratic victories in the 1932 elections, gave Roosevelt unusual influence over Congress in the first months of his administration. The celebrated first one hundred days of the new administration produced a federal program to protect American farmers from the uncertainties of the market through subsidies and production controls (the Agricultural Adjustment Administration). It created a new federal regulatory agency to oversee the stock market (the Securities and Exchange Commission); a reform of the banking system to include a system of insurance for deposits (the Federal Deposit Insurance Corporation); and a series of relief measures to aid some of the approximately fifteen million unemployed Americans (among them the Civilian Conservation Corps, the Civil Works Administration, and the Federal Emergency Relief Administration). The early New Deal also began a bold experiment in flood control, public power, and regional planning (the Tennessee Valley Authority).

The National Industrial Recovery Act (NIRA), the single most ambitious undertaking of the first one hundred days, contained a guarantee to workers of the right of collective bargaining and helped spur major union organizing drives in many industries. It created a substantial federal public works program (the Public Works Administration). Most importantly, and least successfully, it established the National Recovery Administration (NRA), which attempted to stabilize prices and wages through cooperative "code authorities" involving government, business, and labor. Among the inspirations for this great experiment was the American experience in mobilizing its economy for World War I. An experience that had left many Progressives with a dream of re-creating the supposedly harmonious war economy in peacetime.

These and other early initiatives created broad popular support for the Roosevelt administration and halted the rapid unraveling of the financial system. They did not, however, end, or even significantly soften, the Great Depression. The NRA not only failed to revive the industrial economy; it contributed to further restrictions on production and artificial increases in prices. In the end, it also became one of several crucial New Deal programs—the Agricultural Adjustment Administration was another—that the Supreme Court, dominated by conservatives, invalidated on the grounds that they exceeded Congress's constitutional authority.

The "Second New Deal"

In the spring of 1935, responding to the setbacks in the Court, restiveness in Congress, and a growing popular clamor for more dramatic action, the Roosevelt administration proposed (or endorsed) several important new initiatives. The National Labor Relations Act, also known as the Wagner Act, revived and strengthened the protections of collective bargaining contained in the original (and now invalidated) NIRA. It also created the National Labor Relations Board to help enforce the guarantees it promised workers. New relief programs, of which the most prominent was the Works Progress Administration, created hundreds of thousands of jobs for the unemployed. Highly publicized, if largely symbolic, measures—a tax on large fortunes and an assault on utilities-holding companies—and the president's increasingly harsh attacks on corporate selfishness gave at least the impression that the New Deal was fighting monopoly.

The most important achievement of 1935, and perhaps of the New Deal as a whole, was the Social Security Act, which established a system of old age pensions, unemployment insurance, and welfare benefits for groups that were thought to deserve special protections, among them dependent children and disabled persons. This act created the framework that shaped the American welfare system throughout the remainder of the century.

Roosevelt's landslide reelection in 1936 produced large Democratic majorities in both houses of Congress and pre-

The President Asks Americans to Do Their Part

During his administration, Franklin D. Roosevelt held "Fireside Chats" over the radio where he explained the government's actions to the American people. Roosevelt asked the American people for support of the National Recovery Act in the following excerpt from his "Fireside Chat" given on July 24, 1933. The badge of honor he refers to was a blue eagle with the words "NRA Member" above and "We Do Our Part" below.

If all employers in each competitive group agree to pay their workers the same wages—reasonable wages—and require the same hours—reasonable hours—then higher wages and shorter hours will hurt no employer. Moreover, such action is better for the employer than unemployment and low wages, because it makes more buyers for his product. That is the simple idea which is the very heart of the Industrial Recovery Act [NRA].

On the basis of this simple principle of everybody doing things together, we are starting out on this nation-wide attack on unemployment. It will succeed if our people understand it—in the big industries, in the little shops, in the great cities and in the

dictions—from the president's supporters—of great new achievements and from his opponents—of an executive dictatorship. Instead, the administration encountered a long string of frustrations. They were partly a result of the president's own political errors.

Emboldened by his political triumphs and angry at the stubbornness of his opponents—the Supreme Court among them—Roosevelt set out in 1937 to consolidate his own authority within the government in ways that provoked powerful opposition. Early in the year, he proposed a "reform" of the judiciary (known first to his opponents and then to almost everyone as the "court-packing plan") designed to stop the string of reverses his programs had been suffering in the Supreme Court. He asked Congress to ex-

---

small villages. There is nothing complicated about it and there is nothing particularly new in the principle. It goes back to the basic idea of society and of the nation itself that people acting in a group can accomplish things which no individual acting alone could even hope to bring about. . . .

There are, of course, men, a few of them who might thwart this great common purpose by seeking selfish advantage. There are adequate penalties in the law, but I am now asking the cooperation that comes from opinion and from conscience. These are the only instruments we shall use in this great summer offensive against unemployment. But we shall use them to the limit to protect the willing from the laggard and to make the plan succeed.

In war, in the gloom of night attack, soldiers wear a bright badge on their shoulders to be sure that comrades do not fire on comrades. On that principle, those who cooperate in this program must know each other at a glance. That is why we have provided a badge of honor for this purpose, a simple design with a legend, 'We do our part,' and I ask that all those who join with me shall display that badge prominently. It is essential to our purpose.

Susan Winslow, *Brother Can You Spare a Dime?* New York: Paddington, 1976.

pand the number of justices, which would allow him to appoint members sympathetic to his ideas and hence tip the ideological balance of the Court. In one sense the proposal succeeded; two of the existing justices, probably in response to the threat, began voting to uphold New Deal achievements, which created an effective liberal majority. But the "court-packing plan" did lasting political damage to Roosevelt and was finally defeated by Congress.

At about the same time, the administration proposed a plan to reorganize the executive branch in ways that would significantly increase the president's control over the bureaucracy. Like the court-packing plan, executive reorganization evoked strong opposition from those who feared a Roosevelt "dictatorship" and failed in Congress; a watered-down version of the bill finally won passage in 1939.

A New Response to Recession

The largest domestic event of Roosevelt's second term was the severe recession that began in the fall of 1937 and continued through most of 1938—a result at least in part of a premature effort by the administration to balance the budget by reducing federal spending. The New Deal responded in two ways. First, it launched a new rhetorical campaign against monopoly power; many liberals believed monopolies had deliberately caused the recession in an effort to discredit the New Deal. The centerpiece of this effort was a great public investigation of the issue by the Temporary National Economic Committee, a specially created body composed of members of both the executive branch and Congress. By the time the TNEC completed its work, however, the nation was at war and the antimonopoly fervor had cooled; it had little lasting impact. At about the same time, the president appointed an aggressive new director of the antitrust division of the Justice Department who launched prosecutions unprecedented in their number and range. The antitrust division, too, lost its effectiveness once World War II began, but not before achieving a permanent expansion of its bureaucratic capacities.

The administration's second response to the 1937 recession was ultimately more significant. Responding to the urgings of liberal economists and others in his administration, Roosevelt abandoned his efforts to balance the budget and launched a $5 billion spending program in the spring of 1938 to increase mass purchasing power as an antidote to the recession. Few Americans were yet much aware of the ideas of John Maynard Keynes, whose theories would soon transform economic thought throughout much of the world. But the spending program of 1938 was consistent with, and at least indirectly influenced by, what would later become known as Keynesian economics.

The last major domestic achievement of the Roosevelt administration was the passage in 1938 of the Fair Labor Standards Act, which established a national minimum wage and set limits on hours of work. By the end of the year, the New Deal had effectively come to an end. Roosevelt himself went on to win an unprecedented third term in 1940, and a fourth in 1944, and to lead the nation through a great world war. But his efforts to reform the American economy no longer generated broad congressional or popular support. By 1939, his efforts were turning increasingly to the great international crises that would dominate the last five years of his life. World War II, for all the horror it created, would do what Roosevelt's New Deal policies had never been able to do: end the Great Depression and usher in a period of vigorous economic growth.

Roosevelt's Lasting Impact

In retrospect, the New Deal has often seemed as significant for the things it did not do as for the things it achieved. It did not end the Depression and the massive unemployment that accompanied it. It did not—the complaints of conservative critics notwithstanding—transform American capitalism in any genuinely radical way. Except in the field of labor relations and a few other areas, corporate power remained nearly as free from government regulation or control in 1945 as it had been in 1933. The New Deal did not end poverty or effect any significant redistribution of wealth. Nor did it do much to address what became some of the principal domestic problems of the postwar era, among them the problems of racial and gender inequality.

Even so, the achievements of the Roosevelt administration rank among the most important of any presidency in American history, for at least three reasons.

First, the New Deal created a series of new government institutions that greatly, and permanently, expanded the role of the federal government in American life. The government was now committed to providing at least minimal assistance to the poor and unemployed, to protecting the rights of labor unions, to stabilizing the banking system, to building low-income housing, to regulating the financial markets, to subsidizing agricultural production, to using its fiscal policies to stimulate economic growth, and to doing many other things that had not previously been federal responsibilities.

As a result of the New Deal, American political and economic life became much more competitive than ever before, with workers, farmers, consumers, and others now able to press their demands upon the government in ways that had once been available only to the business interests.

This was the origin of the frequent description of the government created by the New Deal as a "broker state," that is, a state brokering the competing claims of numerous groups.

Second, the New Deal produced a new political coalition that sustained the Democrats as the majority party in national politics for more than a generation after its own end.

Finally, the Roosevelt administration generated a set of political ideas—known to later generations as New Deal liberalism—that remained a source of inspiration and controversy for decades, helping to shape the next great experiment in liberal reform, the Great Society of the 1960s.

The Emergence of Federal Public Assistance

John F. Bauman and Thomas H. Coode

Although social work developed as a profession in the 1920s, providing relief to those in need had been dominated by private, voluntary agencies, and social workers focused their efforts on rehabilitating their clients, hoping to end their dependence on relief. However, according to John F. Bauman and Thomas H. Coode, when faced with the vast numbers of jobless Americans during the depression, social workers appealed to the federal government to create a public welfare system. In response to this demand, the authors write, Franklin D. Roosevelt's administration created the Federal Emergency Relief Administration (FERA). Bauman and Coode explain that FERA's philosophy followed the social worker's view that cash was preferable to the humiliating food and clothing donations and that work was better than relief. Bauman is a professor of history and social science at California University of Pennsylvania, in California, Pennsylvania. Coode teaches at Volunteer State Community College in Gallatin, Tennessee.

I n the fall of 1933 the recently appointed director of the Federal Emergency Relief Administration (FERA), Harry Hopkins, launched a grass-roots inquiry into the condition and mood of depression-wracked America. From Washington, D.C., Hopkins dispatched a corps of sixteen reporters who were charged with investigating the enormity of the country's welfare problem and the effectiveness of the nation's local relief structure. His chief investigator was Lorena Hickok, a veteran journalist and confidante of Eleanor Roosevelt. Hopkins instructed Hickok "to go out around the country and look this thing over. I don't want statistics from you. I don't want the social-worker angle. I just want your own reactions, as an ordinary citizen. Go talk with preachers and teachers, businessmen, workers, farmers. Go talk with the unemployed, those who are on relief and those who aren't; and when you talk with them don't ever forget that but for the grace of God, you, I, and any of our friends might be in their shoes. Tell me what you see and hear. All of it. Don't ever pull your punches.". . .

The State of the Union

Hopkins's reporters witnessed the agony and despair of the Great Depression captured so poignantly in James T. Farrell's trilogy, *Studs Lonigan* (1932–1935), and in Jack Conroy's biting *The Disinherited* (1933). Behind the horror of the nation's faceless mass misery, loomed equally horrifying facts. During the year 1932, net income plummeted from $90 to $42 billion. Four months before the New Deal [a body of legislation created during Franklin D. Roosevelt's presidential administration] began, *Business Week* found over 15,000,000 unemployed, or about 31 percent of those normally occupied. The magazine revealed 17 percent jobless in agriculture, 45 percent unemployed in the extractive industries, 46 percent in manufacturing, 10 percent in public service, over 10 percent in the professions, and 35 percent out of work in the domestic and personal services.

Operations in America's key industries sputtered to near halt. Seventy percent of the nation's coal miners were idle, and the industry journal *Iron Age* reported in 1932 that steel plants were operating at only 12 percent of capacity.

U.S. Steel's 1929 payroll of 225,000 full-time workers fell to almost zero in early 1933. For the thousands who retained their jobs, starvation wages often prevailed. Garment workers toiled for abysmal pay. Employees in Baltimore clothing firms averaged eight dollars for a forty-hour week. *Scribner's* reported in March 1933 that throughout the East, females in the garment trades earned less than five dollars a week. Some women garment workers in Massa-

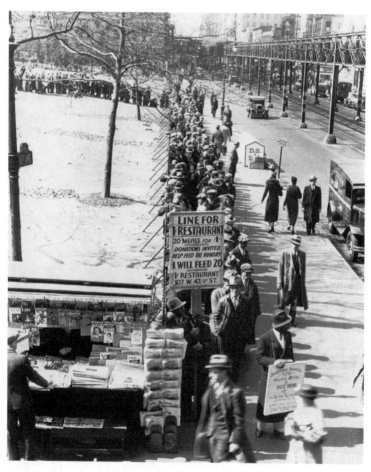

Soup kitchens and bread lines were often the only food sources for millions of unemployed Americans during the Great Depression.

chusetts labored for five or six cents an hour. The highest paid employees earned only seven dollars for a forty-eight-hour week. Half the women employed in Pennsylvania earned fewer than seven dollars a week; 20 percent earned under five.

The nation's farmers were virtually bankrupt. Farm prices declined 61 percent from 1929 to 1933, while total farm income plunged from $13 billion to $5.5 billion. One observer wrote that "it [was] almost impossible to describe the distress that [existed] among farmers." Wheat prices fell to the lowest level of the century, while the tax burden on wheat farmers had doubled since World War I.

In the Great Plains, bread lines snaked past grain elevators bulging with wheat. Wheat priced too low to move was piled high along railroad tracks. Montana wheat, which had been $100.00 a bushel in 1920, sold for only $19.23 in 1932. Thousands of farmers jammed the relief rolls in the Dakotas, Nebraska, and Oklahoma. Once rich agricultural states like Iowa groaned under the weight of mortgage debt. Sixty-five percent of the state's 214,000 farmers were precariously overmortgaged. In 1932, 60 percent of North Dakota's farms were dispossessed by mortgage and tax sales. On one April day in 1932, a fourth of rural Mississippi was auctioned on the block. Farm foreclosures in America were so numerous that Metropolitan Life Insurance Company organized a special farm department to handle them.

In urban America, city after city faced bankruptcy. The relief burden was overwhelming, the tax base too narrow, and both individual and corporate losses due to bank closings were ruinous. In New York City a future New Dealer, Rexford Tugwell, pondered whether modern times had ever witnessed so much distress just from sheer hunger and cold. City public health nurses found thousands of children famished. True, most of the apple vendors had disappeared from the city street corners by late 1932; hapless and dispirited, they crowded the bread lines and soup kitchens instead.

Problems in the South

In the South, where rural poverty had always been wide-spread, the Great Depression merely made matters worse. By Roosevelt's inauguration in 1933 the South had one-third of the nation's population, yet only one-fifth of its wealth, 20 percent of its wages; 27 percent of the country's property value, but only 14 percent of its bank deposits. With much of the nation's mineral wealth and hydroelectric potential untouched, the rural South had more farms than any other region, but the average acreage per farm was the smallest of any section.

Long mired in economic doldrums, southern farmers suffered further losses with the depression. In 1929, cotton returned $1.25 billion; three years later it was $374,000,000. In two years the drop was 62 percent. In 1932, forced farm sales throughout the country were 46 per thousand; North Carolina counted 68.2 per thousand; and in Mississippi, foreclosures hit an unbelievable 99.0 per thousand. By early 1933, sixty thousand farmers had lost their land. Farm cash income in Louisiana fell from $170,000,000 in 1929 to $59,000,000 in 1932, a decline of 65 percent.

With rural poverty so pervasive, thousands of southerners fled to nearby cities looking for work. However, for the South's unemployed, rural as well as urban, there were no alternative occupations, only inadequate relief. Even the old category known as "Negro jobs" virtually ceased to exist as southern whites now flocked to these positions. Nor did the depression in the South spare the fortunate who had jobs, for wages steadily declined. By 1932, industrial labor in the South earned sixteen cents an hour less than the national average. Per capita income in Louisiana in 1933 was only $222 a year, less than half of what it had been four years earlier.

Outside the South, in industrial states like Pennsylvania, the value of industrial products plummeted from over $8 million in 1929 to under $3 million in 1932. Wages dropped to less than half in the same years. The state's Department of Welfare estimated that one-third of the Commonwealth's people were entirely without income. At U.S. Steel's huge Homestead plant near Pittsburgh, only 424 workers were employed full-time in March 1932 as opposed to the average payroll of 5,235 three years earlier. Meanwhile, in the small mill town of Donora, only 277 people out of the town's 14,000 population had jobs in 1932.

A Whole Nation Suffers

It was no better in the Middle West where in 1933 some Ohio counties had over 70 percent of their population on the welfare rolls. In that year, almost 700,000 Ohioans were unemployed—about 37 percent of the state's normal working force.

Visitors to West Virginia and Kentucky coal counties described appalling conditions. One European visitor to Kentucky wrote: "Of all the desolate, god-forsaken spots I have ever known, American mining camps are certainly the worst. . . . Such abject poverty must be seen to be believed." Kentucky and West Virginia mining families burned furniture to keep warm, ate dandelions and blueberries, and, often evicted from their rented hovels, spent winters shivering in grimy tents.

Even the awesome splendor of the Rocky Mountains failed to disperse the pall of depression. In Colorado, per capita income by 1933 had fallen by one-third, and one-sixth of the state's working force was idle. Employment in Montana's mining and smelting industries declined by 60 percent from 1929 to 1933. Failures in New Mexico copper and coal mines drove down the assessed value of mineral production from a high of $37,000,000 in the mid-1920s to about $20,000,000 in 1932. Moreover, the value of New Mexico's agricultural crops stood at $9.5 million in 1932, down from $40 million several years earlier.

Elsewhere, California's once bountiful fruit harvests wasted on the vine while many of the state's city dwellers starved. Bank failures scarred the sunshine-drenched landscape of the Sacramento Valley; formerly powerful motion picture companies declared bankruptcy or fell into receivership. Some of San Francisco's fanciest restaurants closed, and in Los Angeles people whose gas and electricity had been turned off cooked over back-yard wood fires.

By March 4, 1933, the day Franklin Delano Roosevelt assumed the presidency, the nation's economy approached a standstill. Perhaps a third of the working force was unemployed, countless others worked for near starvation wages, and in many auto, rubber, steel, textile, and mining areas whole towns were virtually jobless. Corporate dividends were only a fraction of their 1929 values, and every day financial institutions foreclosed on hundreds of home mortgages; many other home owners desperately held onto their property, making 1929 payments in a 1933 economy. The suicide rate rose 25 percent in four years; more people left the United States than entered it, and at least a million migrants roamed the land, either on foot or stowed away on the undercarriages of freight trains. Thirty-eight states had closed their banks; nine million savings accounts had been lost; both the New York Stock Exchange and the Chicago Board of Trade locked their doors indefinitely.

Reexamining Social Welfare

Not since the Depression of 1892 had America confronted economic conditions dire enough to wrench the fabric of American culture and force the nation to reexamine cherished values and traditional institutions. In the 1890s, mass poverty and the fears of labor anarchism helped transform philanthropy into scientific casework and caused some welfare reformers to challenge laissez-faire capitalism by demanding social legislation regulating tenement housing, child labor, and factory conditions. However, despite the severity of the Depression of 1892 and of the depths of the subsequent recessions of 1907, 1914, and 1921, it was voluntary charity rather than government that provided the first line of defense against large-scale social insecurity.

Therefore, the Roosevelt administration's decision in 1933 to launch the Federal Emergency Relief Administration (FERA) stands as a landmark in American social welfare history. The decision, which climaxed a decade of intense modernization and professionalization in the area of social welfare, inaugurated the intervention of the federal government into the world of public assistance. Fearing that the fabric of American culture was threatened by mass joblessness and the other social structural dislocations caused by technological change, progressive-minded, middle-class New Dealers deemed federal action crucial to preserve the "American Way of Life."

Economic collapse on the grand scale of the Great Depression exposed weaknesses in the nation's moral fiber as well as the more serious abscesses vitiating the culture. Depression, for example, laid bare the gnawing poverty and rampant poor health indigenous to the nation's many mining camps, textile villages, and scattered tenant farms. Federal intervention, it was hoped, would impose scientific standards of relief and, through the accumulation of knowledge and federally sponsored social engineering, restructure society and abolish such cultural malformations as the mining camp.

Plainly, in Hopkins's eyes, bold, experimental federal relief programs required close monitoring to gauge their positive or negative effect on the jobless. Was federal relief destructive of American values, or would works programs better strengthen the American value structure? How did politics undermine the government's objective to reinforce American culture? These were a few of the many questions that troubled Hopkins and his aides as the Federal Emergency Relief Administration determined to use federal policy to shore up the nation's moral fiber.

The American welfare system that emerged by 1935 reflected the outcome of a clash of ideas about joblessness, poverty, and relief that swirled around private and state welfare agencies and through the corridors of the Washington bureaucracy during the dolorous months of 1933 and 1934. This ideological ferment over the role of welfare in America formed the essential backdrop for Hopkins's broad inquiry into the extent of poverty and the effect of joblessness and relief on American families.

Social Workers Faced New Challenges

During the 1920s, social workers had advanced into the foreground among those groups such as businessmen, urban planners, lawyers, and physicians seeking to fashion higher standards of efficiency in their professions. Throughout America, voluntary welfare organizations, family societies, children's aid societies, settlement houses, and other charity associations, organized at both the community and state level, championed the efficient coordination and delivery of services administered by professionals adhering to the tenets of scientific casework.

According to the private social agency, casework relieved the emotional stress or psychological trauma that impaired a client's ability to function effectively in modern society. Social workers, especially those trained at schools that integrated the psychology of Sigmund Freud with the friendly-visitor principles of Mary Richmond, eschewed material relief (charity) as abhorrent to sound casework practice. In this view, material relief, whether in the form of cash, clothing, or food, encouraged dependency and, therefore, impeded the necessary social and psychological rehabilitation of the client. . . .

Despite their disdain for the dole, social workers were cowed by the enormity of the Great Depression. Indeed, social workers implored the government to shoulder the massive burden of direct relief. By 1931, voluntary agencies across the nation tottered under the weight of rising caseloads. A study of thirty-two private family welfare agencies in Pennsylvania showed that between 1929 and 1932 professional staffs increased 23 percent while caseloads rose 131 percent. Alarmed by the trend, in 1930 President Herbert Hoover, buoyed by a deep-seated faith in the resiliency of voluntarism, created the President's Emergency Committee on Employment (PECE)—which became, after 1931, the President's Organization on Unemployment Relief (POUR). Other than urging business to rehire workers, PECE, and POUR essentially provided national direction, moral support, and boosterism for giant fund-raising activities to undergird voluntary relief. But it was all for nought. As the depression worsened, private benevolence among both the rich and not-so-rich declined; and, more seriously, voluntary-agency endowment income plummeted in concert with the national economy.

Exhausted and faced with depleted resources, social professionals who in the 1920s had prided themselves on having moved beyond amelioration to curing the cause of dependency, solemnly repressed their penchant for clinical approaches and discarded psychiatry for the grueling human salvage task. By 1932, agency after agency cut their budgets for "service" in order to extend coverage for material relief.

The Need for a New Welfare System

At the La Follette-Costigan Committee hearings on Federal Cooperation in Unemployment Relief in 1932, prominent social workers such as J. Prentice Murphy, Linton Swift, William Hodson, and Karl de Schweinitz conceded that voluntarism had collapsed. Emergency relief was too little and too late; relief workers described the poor scrounging for bits of decaying fruit and vegetables on city piers. Finally, the passionate and eloquent director of the Philadelphia Jewish Welfare Federation, Jacob Billikopf, reminded the committee of the prophet Isaiah's admonition that "when a man is hungry he is likely to fret himself, and in cursing his king and his God his heart is likely to be filled with revolt and rebellion."

Hours of horror-ridden testimony by social workers, mayors, and civic leaders, backed by intense lobbying efforts, produced on May 12, 1933, the Federal Emergency Relief Administration with $5 million in direct or matching grants to be channeled by FERA through states and localities. Although FERA dispensed relief through state emergency relief bureaus, it nevertheless exercised considerable central authority over local relief standards, demanded accurate data reporting on joblessness, reemployment, and relief expenditures, and oversaw numerous relief experiments, mostly in the area of self-help.

Social workers enthusiastically involved themselves in fashioning the new public welfare edifice. Professional altruists envisioned a "system under which men and women of sympathy and training could administer public welfare according to the best preaching of scientific social work." Relief should be coordinated centrally, directed by nonpolitical professionals, and permanently funded by government appropriations. As former chief of the New York Temporary Relief Administration, Federal Emergency Relief Administrator Harry Hopkins presented impeccable social work credentials; naturally Hopkins surrounded himself with fellow professionals such as Jacob Baker, Aubrey Williams, and Joanna Colcord.

FERA had the full support of charity organizations, settlement houses, and other urban reformers identified with professional altruism in the 1920s. Dazzled by FERA's potential as an instrument for achieving higher professional standards of social service, practitioners in the nation's 5,000 local emergency relief bureaus shaped relief after the professional image. In Philadelphia, professionals from the Family Society, Union Benevolent Association, and Jewish Welfare Society not only staffed the County Relief Board but also worked jointly or cooperatively on individual cases in order to shield "sensitive middle-class" clients from the stigma of public relief.

Accordingly, FERA's goals and standards reflected social work ideals. FERA field workers fought for adequate relief in cash rather than in humiliating food, clothing, and coal orders; FERA demanded thorough case investigations and relief tailored to the particular needs of individual families. Finally, for those capable of useful employment, FERA prescribed work instead of direct relief.

Under Hopkins and his core of professional social workers, FERA projected a psychosocial view of relief founded upon numerous studies of the human tragedy of unemployment. Social workers probed the mental state of jobless families whose savings vanished, whose homes were lost, and who dwelled on the precipice of despair. Students of the jobless counted the depression's toll in broken homes, evictions, overcrowded housing, impaired health, and the rising incidence of nervous disorders such as neurasthenia and psychoasthenia. How long, they asked, could the "respectable" or "deserving" poor maintain their moral and ethical principles; at what point does a man's faith in humanity and himself dissolve and "does he become downhearted and brooding and dangerous?"

Providing Work, Not Relief

Clearly, as William Bremer has observed, FERA looked beyond the manifest purposes of relief to its latent function of preserving the present and future social order. Rumors that the long-term jobless viewed flour as "manna from heaven" reinforced social workers' belief that cash was the most effective form of direct relief since it "conserved and restored the unemployed's normal activity of a producing and consuming citizen."

Although FERA opposed food orders and clothing doles, it supported experiments in self-help as psychologically rehabilitating. Thrift gardens, cooperative enterprises, and model farming communities received almost ecstatic support from FERA. However, work programs occupied the foreground in FERA's war on poverty. In advocating work programs, social workers carefully avoided linking work with relief. Relief work conjured up too vivid images of the nineteenth-century workhouse with its stone pile and wood yard. They campaigned, instead, for a "real-jobs" program, not "work for relief." Work should be suited to the skills and aptitude of the applicant and be rewarded by "prevailing wages."

The Civil Works Administration (CWA), Harry Hopkins's first large-scale emergency employment program, passed all the professional tests. Created in November 1933 to alleviate the rising tide of joblessness through the harsh winter of 1933–1934, by the time it was terminated on April 3, 1934, CWA had employed 4,260,000 people at prevailing wage rates. Moreover, CWA accepted all applicants; workers were not forced to pass a means test proving eligibility for relief. While social workers praised CWA, conservative businessmen vilified it as an extravaganza of "boondoggling." Locating jobs for over 4 million people necessarily involved employing a fair number of workers at leaf-raking tasks, park manicuring, or even research on the history of the safety pin. In the spring of 1934, Hopkins and Roosevelt called the emergency over and ended CWA. But for Hopkins and FERA social workers, the CWA experience confirmed that work and not direct relief was the "American Way." The American worker has "a right to a job," declared Homer Folks of the New York Charities Aid Society. Bemoaning "wasted manpower," Corrington Gill, later assistant administrator of the Works Progress Administration (WPA), joined Hopkins in extolling work as an "antidote for joblessness, which focused a person's productive energies and mental talents and self-respect." However, to Hopkins's chagrin, the objective of "real work" collided with the American reverence for private enterprise. Capitalism proscribed government competition in the marketplace no matter how noble the objective; nor would the private sector tolerate wage rates for public work competitive with rates paid by industry lest it lure the jobless into dependency. As a result, perceptive observers asked whether linking wages paid for works projects to a relief budget produced "real jobs" freed from the stigma of charity.

Although a social worker himself, Hopkins abjured what he believed to be the "nosy sentimentality" of social work and advocated in its place practical humanitarianism. Pledged to bureaucratic efficiency, he contended that government relief stood the ground between radical revolution and the preservation of the American Way of Life. A liberal and practical idealist, Hopkins neither trusted business's enlightened self-interest nor saw any limits to the politician's lust for power. Yet, despite his cynicism, Hopkins aspired to erect a politically chaste relief structure built around a works program, ironically the most politically volatile form of assistance.

Life in the Civilian Conservation Corps

Donald Dale Jackson

The Civilian Conservation Corps (CCC) was one of the first agencies created by the government to help needy young men and their families during the depression. After interviewing many former CCC enrollees, journalist Donald Dale Jackson chronicles their experiences, including the advantages and disadvantages of camp life. While working in the CCC, most of the former enrollees learned valuable lessons that changed their lives, Jackson writes. Moreover, the author points out, the many surviving buildings, roads, and other structures serve as lasting reminders of their work. Jackson is a frequent contributor to *Smithsonian* magazine and the author of several historical and biographical books.

"There were 30 boys from my county in Arkansas who went into the CCC the same day in 1936. We took a train west from Little Rock, and they called our names when we stopped at Clarksville. It was about midnight. They put us on a truck and hauled us to a camp in the woods at the end of a dead-end road, in rugged country. It just worried me. I was 17 and scared of most everything."

"The boys in camp came out in their skivvies hollerin' 'Fresh meat!' They meant us. We were all poor, hardly any-

Excerpted from "They Were Poor, Hungry, and They Built to Last," by Donald Dale Jackson, *Smithsonian*, December 1994. Reprinted with permission from the author.

body had been away from home before. Three of the 30 ran off that night and never came back. They issued us two dress uniforms and two work uniforms and two pairs of Army shoes, and that scared me too because it was more clothes than I'd seen before. And they said that if we lost any clothes our parents would have to pay, and I knew mine couldn't."

The Legacy of the CCC

Wayman Wells, a 75-year-old retired machinist, smiled as he recalled the skittish teenager he was on that long-ago summer midnight he became a member of the Civilian Conservation Corps (CCC). But like every other CCC veteran I met on a swing through four states in search of them, he remembered with pride his time in what was arguably the New Deal's most popular agency: "I believe I'd be there yet if they'd-a let me," he allowed.

Wells and the other men whose lives were changed for the better by the experience are one of the great legacies of the program that began at the dawn of Franklin D. Roosevelt's (FDR's) first term in 1933 and persisted until 1942. Another is the work they left behind, a splendid heritage of parks, dams, bridges, buildings, roads, and hundreds of conservation and restoration projects in every corner of the country. . . .

The original CCC got out of the blocks with what may be an all-time record for bureaucratic speed. Only 35 days elapsed between FDR's Inauguration and the enrollment of the first CCC boy—they were always called "boys"—on April 7, 1933. In that time, legislation was written, passed and signed, guidelines were set, campsite selection begun and, most remarkable of all, four Cabinet departments— Labor, Interior, Agriculture and War—were harnessed together to run the program. By July there were 274,375 boys in 1,300 camps.

To qualify, a boy had to be between 17 (18 at first) and 25 (28 later on), single, jobless, in good physical condition and needy. He signed up voluntarily at the local relief agency designated as the selection office. He enrolled for a six-month term, which he could extend for up to two years—longer if he was promoted to a leadership job. Five percent of the original 250,000 washed out in the first few months, most for refusing to work or going AWOL. Enrollees were paid $30 a month, $22 to $25 of which was sent home to their families. At its peak, in September 1935, the CCC mustered 502,000 members in 2,514 camps. Overall, 2.9 million served in nine years.

The Army built and ran the camps, which normally included four barracks with 40 to 50 men in each, along with a mess hall, recreation building, officers' quarters, a school for night classes, and a latrine and bathhouse separate from the barracks. The boys got up to a bugler's reveille, stood morning and evening formations, and showed up on time for meals or went hungry. When they trucked or trudged to work each morning, the Army bowed out and, most often, the U.S. Forest Service took over. Civilian foremen and "local experienced men," called LEMS, ran the work crews. Most of the work was manual labor; their tools were shovels and mattocks and sledgehammers, double-edged axes and crosscut saws. The bulk of the CCC's 200,000 black enrollees served in segregated companies. The rules were relaxed for Native Americans and for World War I veterans. The veterans were, of course, older men; and in the case of the Indians, the tribal council administered the projects, and enrollees were assigned to work in their own communities.

Helping Youth and Creating a National Treasure

The average CCC enrollee, according to a statistical portrait compiled by the agency, joined at 18½, stayed in for nine months, and gained from 12 to 30 pounds and a half-inch in height during his tour. He had finished the eighth grade, had held no regular job before the CCC, and had three to four family members dependent on his paycheck. Sixty percent were from small towns or farms. My interviews and research on CCC vets led me to add a few wrinkles to this portrait: I found that as a group they were obedient, patriotic (nearly all had served in World War II), resilient, grateful for the chance ("but I enjoy it more now than I did then," one said) and, to a man, convinced that the CCC is just as good an idea today as it was in 1933.

But if the CCC was a lifeline for the undernourished sons of the Depression, it was a boon of another kind for the country at large. CCC veterans have only slowly come to realize that the work they performed to help their families survive produced a national treasure of fine and lasting structures.

The masonry dam and bridge at Cumberland Mountain State Park near Crossville, Tennessee, built with hand-hewn sandstone, is a graceful yet solid edifice reminiscent of a Roman aqueduct. "I've met three old boys who claim they built that dam by themselves," Wayman Wells joked. The red pine log headquarters of the Chippewa National Forest in Cass Lake, Minnesota, one of the largest log buildings anywhere, is a masterpiece of precisely notched and grooved logs. The magnificent amphitheater at Mt. Tamalpais State Park in California, modeled after a Greco-Roman theater in Sicily, contains 5,000 stones weighing more than 600 pounds each. The limestone boathouse at Backbone State Park in Iowa, a delicate building with intricate and playful stonework, stands guard like a miniature castle over a CCC-made, 135-acre lake.

Robert Ritchie, a CCC vet from Hansell, Iowa, who worked at Backbone Park, expressed the late-blooming pride that many veterans share: "I thought of the C's as just a phase in my life, but as you go on, you feel that it, that you, were a part of the country and of history. We have this park; it was wilderness before, and now it's a nice place to go, and I had something to do with that. I was part of an important event."

A New Way of Life

Life in the CCC, with such niceties as three squares a day, indoor plumbing and electricity, was a step up for many boys from destitute rural families. "It was better than what I was used to," Clinton Boyer of St. Louis said. "At home we had no running water and used oil lamps." Lonnie Goddard of Bradley, West Virginia, recalled making a single egg do for two meals on his family's Appalachian farm. "I'd have the white for breakfast and put the yellow on corn bread for lunch at school."

Goddard's most vivid memory of the CCC is the careless waste of food. "I was on KP the first weekend I was in, and we had weenies in bread dough, but only about half the company was there and we threw a lot of it in the garbage. I was thinking about the people who could use it, like my family."

These were boys whose horizons were pinched by poverty. Doyle Jones of Jamestown, Tennessee, recalls every detail about his train ride to CCC camp because he'd never made a trip like that before. "They took us on the Southern Railway to Knoxville and then by the Louisville and Nashville to Chatsworth, Georgia. I recollect it even now because there wasn't much going on in my life at the time." At camp, Jones was startled to find such exotic foods as bananas and oranges on his tray. Jones' family used his $25 monthly allotment to pay off their grocery bill. "Kirby Johnson at the store, he'd just subtract $25 from what they owed."

They remember the food with a fondness born in deprivation. "Oh, they really fed us, especially breakfast," recalled Harry Marsanick of Florissant, Missouri, "ham and potatoes and sausage, all the eggs you wanted. The kitchen was enough to keep me happy." Slumgullion, [stew or hash], and the dish known to generations of servicemen as "SOS" were staples, along with fish on Friday and chicken on Sunday, and it was all fine with them. "Bread on the table, that's what it was about," said George Legg of Oak Hill, West Virginia. "Warm clothes and your own bed. It was three hots and a flop."

In 1942, when CCC funding stopped and most of the boys had changed to other uniforms, the agency issued a report summarizing its accomplishments. The numbers on the volume and variety of work were awesome: 46,854 bridges of various kinds built, 3,116 fire-lookout towers, more than 28 million rods of fencing, 318,076 "check dams" for erosion control, 33,087 miles of terracing. CCC lads fought forest fires and mosquitoes and soil erosion, they planted trees and grass, and excavated channels, canals and ditches; they laid pipe and improved wildlife habitat and built or maintained thousands of miles of hiking trails. They did every conservation job that any land manager could think of. And some died: there were accidental drownings and falls; 47 were killed in forest fires; nearly 300 perished when a hurricane flattened three camps of war veterans on the Florida Keys in 1935.

Their foremen used blueprints for major jobs like the Crossville Dam, but they often worked without plans because plans were paper and paper meant more military involvement. "A lot of times they didn't have plans," said Michael Pierce, director of the CCC's St. Louis-based alumni organization. "Plans would bring the Army in, which meant nitpicking, and they wanted to keep the Army out as much as they could." In extremely cold or stormy weather they stayed in camp. "We didn't go out if it was colder than 5 below," Robert Ritchie of Iowa recalled. "We had three weeks like that once. The guys sat around making cigarettes with their machines."

Hard Work and Discipline

They went to work at 7:15 and quit at 4, with a break for lunch served back at camp or trucked to the site. "They brought lunch in big old kettles, and we'd eat the beans and applesauce all slopped together in our mess kits," Lonnie Goddard remembered. The work was tough. "I filled holes in a road," said Burl Hutchison of Columbus Junction, Iowa. "My station was the business end of a wheelbarrow or shovel. We called the wheelbarrows 'silver streaks' or 'Irish buggies.'" Goddard quarried and set sandstone. "We'd blast it and then split the rock into smaller chunks with hand tools and load it on trucks with a hand crank." His proudest accomplishment was a stone wall in a state park. "We dug footings and filled them with stone to a depth of 17 feet. Seventeen feet! Do you believe it? And it was beautiful."

The lucky ones learned about craftsmanship. Arthur Jackson, who later owned a successful drilling company in Lebanon, Tennessee, cut blocks of sandstone for the Crossville Dam. "It was amazing what the engineers could do with a bunch of ignorant kids," he recalled. "They were patient. They said we were going to do it right, and if you rebelled you got another job. They only wanted boys who were willing to learn."

The CCC boys were civilians, but G.I. discipline governed their camps. "When I first reported, the officers asked me some question and I said 'Yeah,' and they shouted 'What did you mean, Yeah?'" Burl Hutchison of Iowa remembered. "They wanted a 'Yessir,' and I was thinking, 'Oh my, what did I get into?'" "They had a bugle or a whistle for everything," Lonnie Goddard said, "and I was used to roosters and not a bugle waking me up. You made your bunk with six inches of white below the pillow, and everything had to be just so in your foot locker. If you threw your cigarette on the ground you wore a butt can around your neck for a day."

They had to shave, bathe regularly and keep their hair short. Though the regimen varied with the camp commander, enrollees often had to salute officers, and bed checks were common. Toward the end of the CCC's existence, with war coming on, they learned close-order drill. But there were some who never quite fathomed the military mind. "The captain asked some of us one time if we wanted to work in the kitchen," Doyle Jones of Tennessee said, "and this one boy—he was always a puzzler, he thought about things—he said, 'Well, I haven't *fully* made up my mind.' I laugh whenever I remember that. The officer just looked at him and said, 'Well, I have, you're not a-workin' in the kitchen.'"

The Advantages and Disadvantages of Camp Life

Camp canteens sold candy, soap, cigarettes and sometimes beer in exchange for chits from canteen books the boys bought for a dollar. Every camp had a sports program, invariably including baseball and boxing and sometimes basketball; 20 CCC boys were signed by major league baseball scouts, and future Hall of Fame infielder Red Schoendienst served in a CCC camp in Illinois. There were libraries and night classes—though education was never considered to be the CCC's most successful undertaking, it became a more important goal as the program evolved. Everything from elementary school subjects to vocational training and even etiquette was taught in the camps. Nearly 8,500 CCC boys learned to read and write in fiscal year 1938–39.

Military doctors were assigned to each camp or group of camps. "Ours was a veterinarian, old Doc Briggle," Robert Ritchie of Iowa said. "He had one treatment, a fruit jar full of 'physic' pills about the size of a pea. If you broke your leg that's what you got." Arthur Jackson of Tennessee went on sick call with the flu, and the doctor gave him Epsom salts in a cup. "He said it's to discourage goldbricking. It liked to kill me. It ruined me for cups, I'll say that; I still won't drink water from a cup."

Practical jokes were a CCC tradition. New arrivals were dispatched to "water the flagpole." There were dozens of variations on the "snipe hunt": rookies raced off in quest of "striped paint," "bunk spacers," "sky hooks" and other imaginary objects. It was a simpler time: they gleefully short-sheeted one another's beds and tied neatly folded clothing in knots—"that would kind of disappoint you, especially if it was 15 minutes to reveille," said Burl Hutchison.

They concocted their own slang. A cigarette was a "stiffy," its makings, tobacco and paper, were "sawdust and blankets." The officers' orderly, who delivered meals to the brass, was known as "Dog Robber" because he got the choice leftovers the dog might otherwise have enjoyed. If you wanted something at the end of the mess table, Lonnie Goddard remembered, you called out "Butts on the beans!"

or whatever it was, and you finagled a drag off another's cigarette by crying "Butts on that cigarette!" In the evenings they played cards or Ping-Pong or music. Guitar picker Doyle Jones joined a band that played for local square dances, while Wayman Wells recollected Arkansas as "harmonica country—those boys could wear a harmonica out."

The rules prohibited the boys' owning a car, but many officers looked the other way as long as they parked the car elsewhere. "I kept my Model T a quarter-mile away on a farm," Robert Ritchie said. "For a dollar a month the farmer let me put it in a corn crib out of the weather." He and other car owners ferried their friends home weekends for a fee, one of several money-making hustles that flourished in the camps. Wayman Wells bought $1 canteen books at a discount from boys who needed money, then resold the books at face value. He also sold suits for a company that gave him one free for every four he sold. Arthur Jackson cut hair for a dime a head. Robert Ritchie made more as a loan shark than he collected from the government and spent it all on shirts, pants and underwear. When he got out he owned three foot lockers full of underwear.

Dealing with Conflict

CCC boys were by and large neither rebels nor troublemakers; they had chosen to be there, and most accepted the discipline and hard work. But from the beginning there were some who did not, and there were occasional uprisings if not full-scale mutinies. Desertion, always a concern, accounted for 11.6 percent of those leaving the corps in 1937, and the percentage increased in later years. A boy was counted a deserter if he was AWOL for eight days. Nobody pursued them, but Harry Dallas of Overland, Missouri, ran into an ex-enrollee 58 years later who was worried that they might still be looking for him. Most deserters left in the first few days, often out of homesickness.

They staged work stoppages and food strikes to protest curfews, cold-weather work and the quantity or quality of the food. In Wayman Wells' Arkansas camp the issue was neckties. "We wore wool uniforms and neckties for retreat review in summer when it was real hot, and they checked to make sure our ties were tight. Well, we called a food strike and nobody ate supper for three days. The doctor got into it, and they finally said we could unbutton the top button of our shirts and wear the tie loose."

The real conflict was not between CCC enrollees and the military but between the boys from the C's and townfolk in nearby communities. Some towns posted "No CCC Allowed" signs. "I think people in general looked down on us," Carl Denoff of Lansing, West Virginia, said. "It was like we were trash, we weren't recognized as equal. But when we'd pass farmhouses on our way to town the girls would holler and wave." On weekends they rode to town, where they sometimes scuffled with the local boys. "That's what bound us together," Lonnie Goddard said. "If the boys in town jumped you they'd have to whip all of us. We were like brothers."

If a CCC boy acquired a girlfriend he could escort her around town, but bringing her back to camp was a no-no, except at chaperoned functions. The boys in Robert Ritchie's Iowa company had nicknames for the girls. "A redhead from the town of Strawberry Point, we called 'the Strawberry Roan.' I was at a CCC reunion not long ago, and I mentioned that, and this woman sitting a few seats away heard me and piped up, 'That was me.' She'd married a CCC boy."

Hundreds of other marriages resulted, but relations between CCC lads and local girls also left a truckload of sour memories. Harry Dallas of Missouri was seeing a girl until "a car drove up to camp and her mother got out and gave me a lecture: 'I don't want my daughter associating with your type. We don't cotton to your kind.' I never saw that girl again." Wayman Wells and his friends found a novel way to fight back. "They had pie suppers in town. You bought a pie, and the girl who baked it sat with you, but the girls wouldn't sit with us. They always had a vote for the prettiest girl, you know, so we ran one of our guys,

Leon Ogden, and there was enough of us that we won. He got the prize as prettiest girl. We called him 'Sis Ogden' after that. But that broke the ice. Pretty soon we started dating town girls."

Lessons Learned in the CCC

Ask a CCC veteran what he got out of the experience and invariably his first response is that he learned to "get along with other people." But this doesn't mean an appreciation of ethnic or cultural diversity, it means something much simpler: this was often the first time they had been *anywhere;* the CCC was their first exposure to life beyond home, farm, village and schoolhouse. One camp's slogan was: "Join the CCC and see the world, a shovelful at a time"; the CCC was their first narrow glimpse of how many shovelfuls there are.

Most of them learned important lessons as well. "Discipline, that was the key," Harry Dallas told me. "You agreed to do something and you did it. I learned a work ethic, how to do things safely and right. Whenever I see that CCC postage stamp, you know, the one with the CCC boy carrying that pickax on his shoulder, it bothers me because that was unsafe—we learned not to carry them that way. You could turn and knock somebody in the head. There was pride in the work. We built something, and I knew I helped and I saw the result. It was something you could take pride in, and there wasn't a lot of pride available in those days."

Often enough, the CCC transformed shy, backward country boys who thought of themselves as losers into physically stronger, effective men. Self-esteem, we call it today. "I felt I was going downhill, like the CCC was the bottom of the barrel," said Robert Ritchie, "but I wasn't alone, and I came out positive, more positive as time passed." "I was scared to death of everything," Arthur Jackson of Tennessee recalled. "Just timid. I didn't think I could talk to people. I'd only gone to third grade. The C's gave me confidence that I was as good as anybody. It made me know I could do things, gave me some push. I'm proud that I worked on that Crossville dam. I wasn't afraid to tackle anything after that."

When CCC vets go in search of their old camps, as many of them have done, what they find is weeds, trees, an occasional cement foundation slab—nothing that looks familiar, nothing to mark their passage. The Army broke down the prefabricated buildings and hauled them away soon after the CCC expired in 1942. Most veterans react as Harry Marsanick did when he revisited the site of his camp in Missouri: "I was surprised. I was there 15 months, and it was like it never happened. I thought there would have been something there."

The men I interviewed were unanimous in their belief that the CCC was positive for them and the country, and they think it would work again—as indeed it has in CCC-like state programs and in small-scale federal models. "So many crafts don't have apprenticeships nowadays," Wayman Wells said. "A new CCC could restore them." "Think of all it might do," Harry Dallas added. "The roadside car junkyards, for example. They could clean all that up." Many veterans have doubts about whether today's young people are as hungry or as willing as they were, and most realize that this generation grew up in an America that survivors of the 1930s can barely recognize.

Still, they hanker for tribute, for recognition of the CCC's success. Veneration, appreciation, respect—they want what our fathers and grandfathers always want. Today there are a few scattered CCC museums, a restored camp in northern Minnesota, a statue in Los Angeles, and those glorious monuments in wood and stone. That and their memories.

Perhaps, in the end, that's enough. "I tried to find my camp at Crossville," Arthur Jackson said, "and I couldn't locate a trace of it. But that's all right. I can still picture it in my mind, and I know what we did was lasting, and that's what matters. It's not a sign or a marker or a camp, it's what we did that counts."

The Works Progress Administration: Criticism and Praise

Robert S. McElvaine

Finding work during the depression was difficult and, to help alleviate this problem, the government created the controversial Works Progress Administration (WPA). In this excerpt from his book *The Great Depression: America, 1929–1941*, Robert S. McElvaine, a noted authority on the depression, explores the conflicting goals and interests of the WPA. For example, in order to help the morale of the unemployed, the WPA tried to find people work; however, in order to encourage private employment and discourage dependence on federal programs, WPA wages were substantially lower, which was not good for morale. McElvaine also discusses the WPA's much praised Federal One project, which funded support for the arts and artists. McElvaine is a professor of history at Millsaps College in Jackson, Mississippi, writes for the *History News Service*, and is the author of several books on the depression.

T he most important aspect of the New Deal [a body of legislation created during Franklin D. Roosevelt's presidential administration] from a political perspective in 1936 was the Works Progress Administration (WPA). Created by executive order after the huge Emergency Relief Appropriation of 1935, the WPA was placed under the direction of Harry Hopkins. The President divided the nearly $5 billion made available by Congress in 1935 among several different agencies. Part went to the new National Youth Administration (NYA), which gave part-time employment to more than 2 million high school and college students, thus helping them stay in school. The NYA also assisted the 2.6 million young people who were not in school. Harold Ickes's Public Works Administration (PWA) and the Civilian Conservation Corps (CCC) received generous slices of the appropriation, too, but the largest share—$1.39 billion—went to the new WPA.

Although there were a sufficient number of make-work projects under the WPA to lend some credence to conservative complaints about one crew digging holes and another filling them up, the shovel-leaning and leaf-raking were only one side of a many-faceted organization. The WPA could not equal the PWA's accomplishments in public building, but it did construct or improve more than 20,000 playgrounds, schools, hospitals, and airfields.

Providing Jobs, but Inadequate Pay

There were, however, serious problems connected with the WPA. Although work relief was far more expensive than direct payments to the unemployed, almost everyone preferred government jobs to a dole. The brief Civil Works Administration (CWA) experience had been gratifying. "A workless man," Harry Hopkins observed, "has little status at home and less with his friends." "Give a man a dole," the WPA administrator said on another occasion, "and you save his body and destroy his spirit. Give him a job and you save both body and spirit." Many WPA workers agreed. "Please continue this W.P.A. program," a group of workers in Battle Creek, Michigan, wrote to the President in 1936. "It makes us feel like an American citizen to earn our own living. Being on the dole or relief roll makes us lazy and the funds are not enough to live decent on." A county relief administrator in West Virginia noted as early as 1934 that work relief people "consider themselves as government workers—badly paid, or rather, inadequately employed. The general attitude seems to be," she went on, "that by going on relief one is working for the government. . . . People frequently call me up and say: 'I've been working for you for so long. Can't you do this or that for me[?]'"

Some WPA projects met the goal of sustaining workers' morale; many, unfortunately, did not. Pay was miserable. The nationwide average was $55 a month, much better than FERA relief payments, but an annual income of $660 amounted to barely more than half of a minimum subsistence budget of $1200. Nor was much security provided even for this tiny income. Working hours were often short, thus preventing laborers from obtaining their full potential pay. And there were no guarantees that jobs would continue or that checks would arrive on time. Such problems were frequently subjects of complaint by workers. "[W]hy can't every one be paid regularly as agreed or is it inafficiancy[?]" a Texas WPA worker asked Hopkins in a 1935 letter. "Here in Ft. Worth the mens' pay is from 4 to 6 days behind; + some of them have to go home because they are too week to work." A group of Wisconsin workers who said they were "not red, but red-white-and blue" criticized the President for saying American workers should be paid decent wages and then not doing it.

There were two fundamental reasons for the low wages. The first was obvious: there was not enough money to go around. The second concern was in some respects more significant. Committed as they were (hysterical charges by the Liberty League to the contrary notwithstanding) to maintaining the free enterprise system, Roosevelt and Hopkins wanted to be sure that work relief was not attractive in comparison with private employment. Hence they had to be sure that WPA earnings were kept at a sufficiently low level that the government would not be competing for workers with private enterprise. This was, of course, a rather silly concern while the unemployment rate was in the double digits, but the New Dealers remained convinced that strong incentives must be provided for those on work relief to return to the private sector as soon as *any* opportunity arose.

The Conflicting Goals of Work Relief

Yet this policy was in direct conflict with the stated objectives of using work relief to build morale and distinguishing WPA work from charity. Harry Hopkins correctly pointed out that "those who are forced to accept charity, no matter how unwillingly, are first pitied, then disdained" by others. People on direct relief were unable to avoid the stigma attached to charity and the resulting assumption that they were responsible for their own plight. People on the dole had to go through a humiliating "means test." The original hope—fulfilled briefly under the CWA—was that a work relief program could dispense with this demeaning procedure. The goal was summed up by New York social worker William Matthews when he said, "The sooner work relief can be given as nearly as possible the same status as that of work under regular conditions . . . the sooner it will command the respect . . . of the worker. . . ."

The trouble, simply, was that New Dealers wanted on the one hand to make work relief like a "real" job, but on the other to make it *un*like such employment. They sought to make WPA jobs attractive, so as to boost worker morale, at the same time they strove to make them *un*attractive, so as to encourage people to return to private employment. The result, inevitably, was a highly contradictory program. This was embodied in a policy that attempted to provide hourly wages similar to those paid by private businesses for the same sort of work, but limited the total monthly income of a WPA worker to far less than he might hope to make in the private sector. Hence those with the highest-paying jobs were allowed to work the fewest hours per month.

This was no way to provide a sense of security or build morale. WPA planners also failed to understand that manual labor was not a seamless web. Little attempt was made on most projects to match the strength, experience, and ability of a blue-collar worker with the job assigned to him. This was an indication of unconscious discrimination against lower-class people. When it came to the middle-class unemployed—or even to artists and writers—Hopkins and his associates tried to create jobs appropriate to their careers. (Hopkins was partial to artists. His family summered in Woodstock, New York, the noted artists' colony.) Manual laborers, though, were thought of simply as manual laborers.

There were other problems. President Roosevelt had promised when the organization was launched that the work would be "useful . . . in the sense that it affords permanent improvements in living conditions or that it creates future new wealth for the nation." Yet critics soon complained that much of what the WPA did was not "useful." In some cases they were right, but one of the principal reasons was that Roosevelt had pledged that the WPA would not compete with private enterprise. One wonders what such critics would have said if the organization *had* started to do useful things and thus had begun to compete with private business.

Criticism of Relief Agencies

Behind the other conservative misgivings lay the fear that bureaucrats like Hopkins—intellectuals who had never "met a payroll" or "faced an electorate"—were using the relief agencies to secure positions of power for themselves. There was also some concern that Hopkins and his assistants wanted to keep large numbers of people on relief so that they would be politically subservient to the WPA. Particularly disturbing to Vice President Garner was the practice of referring to WPA workers as "clients."

Other WPA rules were as constraining as the prohibition on competition with private industry. Concentrating on helping the unemployed get through a "temporary" crisis, New Dealers used all available funds for payrolls and provided scarcely any training to help workers obtain permanent employment. Similarly, the requirement that 90 percent of those hired must come from the relief rolls—well intentioned though it clearly was—served both to discriminate against those who had held out longest against going on the dole and to prevent the employment of skilled workers needed to undertake many "useful" projects. Finally, a WPA rule allowing only one member of a family to be employed discriminated against women (who never represented even one-fifth of WPA workers) and large families. Some of the latter actually found themselves with lower incomes under the WPA than they had received on the dole.

The greatest failing of the WPA, however, was that it never provided work for most of the unemployed (the figure hovered around 30 percent of the jobless on WPA rolls between 1935 and 1940). This left upward of 5 million jobless Americans on the tender mercies and empty treasuries of state and local governments. When he chose the work relief option, President Roosevelt had decided to end federal relief, which he characterized in words worthy of Herbert Hoover (but none the less accurate for that) as "a narcotic, a subtle destroyer of the human spirit." That the states were not up to the task they had amply demonstrated in the early thirties, but Roosevelt dumped back in the laps of the governors and legislatures the "unemployables." The results were similar to those that might be expected if Ronald Reagan had obtained enactment of his New Federalism plan in the 1980s. They are best symbolized by New Jersey's decision to issue licenses to beg to those who could not be helped by exhausted state funds. Also like the New Federalism plan, Roosevelt's 1935 decision that Washington "must and shall quit this business of relief" meant that the states with the greatest needs would have the smallest resources with which to meet them. By the end of the decade, ten poor southern states were paying less than $10 per month per family, considerably less than half the national average.

Despite all of the drawbacks, the WPA was far better than what had gone before it (which is almost to say that it was far better than nothing). For those who got jobs on its projects, the pitiful wages were usually, if not always, better than relief. For all the obstacles to the goal of morale-building, an unemployed person was more likely to maintain a bit of self-respect working on a WPA project than he was receiving direct relief. And the agency did add substantially to the common wealth—material and artistic—of the American people. The WPA was much less than it could have been and it was less innovative than might have been expected in the Depression era. It was, for that matter, a good deal less daring than its precursor, the CWA, had been. Yet it was innovative and daring in some ways, most notably in its attempt to provide public patronage for the arts.

Bringing Art to the People

A combination of factors—economic need, resurgent democratic values, Rooseveltian paternalism, and the quest for a distinctly American culture—came together in the mid 1930s to create the most notable experiment of the work relief program, Federal One. This was the use of a small but highly significant portion of WPA funds for an experiment in providing federal support for the arts in America. Although he had no special appreciation for "high culture" himself, as a gentleman Franklin Roosevelt believed fine music, art, and theater were essential to the good life. As part of his general attempt to democratize American life, Roosevelt wanted to make such culture available to the masses.

The 1935 relief appropriation included money designated for use in helping unemployed professionals. The WPA proceeded to set up four programs under Federal One: the Federal Art Project, the Federal Music Project, the Federal Theatre Project, and the Federal Writers' Project. (A fifth, the Historical Records Survey, was made a separate unit in 1936.) Harry Hopkins was among those who thought it was foolish and wasteful to put a concert violinist or a Shakespearean actor to work laying bricks. But Hopkins and a number of those who became involved with the WPA arts projects saw them as far more than a way to provide "suitable" relief work for artistic or educated Depression victims. They saw Federal One as a grand opportunity to fuse "high culture" with American democracy. The relationship between culture and democracy had long been a troubling question in the minds of some Americans. As democrats, some in the American arts community were concerned with bringing the arts to the people at large. At the same time, however, they feared that emphasis on numbers would inevitably lessen quality. Moreover, the dependence of artistic people on wealthy patrons often distanced the arts from "ordinary" folks.

A possible solution to some of these difficulties seemed to be federal patronage of the arts. In any case, private financial support practically dried up during the early Depression. As with so many other areas of American life, the Depression left many artistic people with nowhere else to turn for help but Washington. Dependence on federal financial assistance was not an unmixed blessing, however. Two principal, if vastly different, problems arose. The first was winning public support for the idea. Many people had a hard time accepting singing and acting as work. (We seem to have no trouble accepting the right of performers to make huge sums of money while working privately, but we balk at paying them much smaller amounts from our taxes.) Public support for federal arts projects was never strong. In the end, this proved fatal.

The other problem was the possibility that as Washington began paying the pianist it would want to call the tune. Even if there were no conscious interference—and who could be sure there would not be?—the possibility that bureaucracy would stifle creativity was omnipresent. Yet this possibility never seriously materialized. Instead, the WPA arts projects gave several million Americans their first opportunity to experience "high culture" and many people were enabled to participate in WPA-sponsored community symphonies, amateur theaters, and the like.

Writing America

The least controversial of the Federal One projects was the Historical Records Survey, which inventoried local government records across the country. It performed a useful service and did so efficiently and without stepping on many conservative toes. The same could nearly be said about the Federal Writers' Project. Writers had originally been left out of the plans for arts projects, but after some of them complained the FWP was created. Although the Historical Records Survey succeeded in using previously untrained personnel, good writing was not so easily obtained. Many self-described "writers" who joined the project might not have been so classified by literary critics. In fact, many people—teachers, librarians, and others from white-collar occupations—who were not writers but did need relief were assigned to the Writers' Project. Trying to make a virtue of necessity—as well as to emphasize the democratic nature of the project—FWP Director Henry Alsberg said, "We must get over the idea that every writer must be an artist of the first class, and that an artist of the second or third class has no function."

Be that as it may, the FWP suffered no shortage of first-class writers. Among those who were employed by the Writers' Project were Richard Wright, Saul Bellow, Ralph Ellison, John Cheever, Jack Conroy, Conrad Aiken, Arna Bontemps, and Margaret Walker. Several of these great talents would likely have gone undeveloped had it not been for the FWP. The project did not allow much creative writing on WPA time, but working hours usually amounted to only thirty per week. "The simple act of providing writers and would-be writers with jobs that gave them a livelihood without unduly taxing their energies," FWP executive Jerre Mangione later contended, "turned out to be the most effective measure that could have been taken to nurture the future of American letters." Richard Wright was perhaps the best example of what the project could do for a young writer. He used his spare time to write *Native Son,* which won him acclaim while he was still an FWP employee. Ralph Ellison summed up the effect of working on the project: "Actually to be *paid* for writing . . . why that was a wonderful thing!"

What they were paid to write was a variety of what has been called "American stuff." Included was a series of inspired state guides. This was part of the mid-thirties revival of interest in all things American. It extended in the work of the FWP to the collection of folklore, studies of ethnic groups, "life histories" of individuals from many backgrounds, and the reminiscences of some 2000 former slaves. The last item, in particular, was a priceless historical treasure that would have been lost if not for the work of the Writers' Project. These efforts, under the guidance of Benjamin Botkin, emphasized the belief that "history must study the inarticulate many as well as the articulate few."

An Eclectic Music Project

Federal Music Project Director Nikolai Sokoloff was also concerned about the inarticulate many, but he sought to raise them to an appreciation of fine music. An elitist where culture was concerned, Sokoloff of necessity had to reach for a mass audience if he was to find employment for some 15,000 out-of-work musicians. And the wide variation in their talent and skills obliged him to be more eclectic than he desired. Since instrumental music was unlikely to be perceived as carrying leftist messages, the FMP remained less controversial than some of the other WPA arts projects. The Music Project organized orchestras across the nation in cities that had not known them before, but it was prevented by political opposition from taking classical music to many areas its leaders had originally intended to reach. Concerts and music lessons were provided free or for nominal charges.

The accomplishments of the Federal Music Project were significant, but came to far less than some hoped for. Charles Seeger of the Music Project, along with Alan Lomax of the FWP, undertook a remarkable effort to collect and preserve America's folk music. Their accomplishment was magnificent, but Seeger's grand hope to integrate "popular, folk, and academic music into a distinctively American idiom" was never approached. Nor did the advances made by the FMP generally survive. Orchestras formed after World War II appear to have had their roots in WPA symphonies in fewer than ten cities.

The Controversial Murals

More controversial than the historical, writing, or music projects was Holger Cahill's Federal Art Project. Project Director Cahill and his associates were firm believers in the ideal of cultural democracy; they expressed their goal as "art for the millions." Cahill insisted that the audience for plastic arts under the FAP be broadened greatly from those who had frequented galleries and museums in the past. Franklin Roosevelt agreed with the objectives, if not always with the content of the art that was aimed at the millions. The President guessed—optimistically—that only 10 percent of the American people had ever had an opportunity to view a "fine picture." For a brief time the FAP changed that. By 1938 works done by Art Project painters and sculptors were on view in many parts of the country. An FAP exhibit at the New York World's Fair in 1940 was seen by more than 2 million people. The most lasting—and perhaps the most impressive—of the Art Project's achievements were the murals its artists painted in public buildings across the nation. The decisive influence came from Mexican painters of propaganda murals, particularly Diego Rivera and Clemente Orozco, who spent the early years of the Depression being paid large fees by the likes of the Ford and Rockefeller families to paint anticapitalist murals in such incongruous places as the San Francisco Stock Exchange Club, the Ford-supported Detroit Institute of Arts, the RCA Building in Rockefeller Center, and the Dartmouth College Library. Like the products of other WPA arts projects, the FAP murals represented part of the renewed interest in American life. Victor Arnautoff's "City Life" in San Francisco's Coit Tower is one of the best examples. The subjects of many, however, were too labor-oriented to suit conservatives in Congress. Charges of "Communism" grew louder as the Depression decade neared its end.

The quality of the work done by FAP employees varied widely, of course. So did the opinions of critics on its overall merit. As with the Writers' Project, the Art Project provided a livelihood for some artists who would go on to great careers, among them Jackson Pollock, Willem De Kooning, Anton Refregier, and Yasuo Kuniyoshi. Critical controversy, like that over social content, centered on the murals. Post office murals (most of which were done outside the FAP jurisdiction) tended to celebrate the "masses" and the oppressed laboring class. While Ford Madox Ford, the English art critic, said the quality of FAP work was "astonishingly high," American photographer Alfred Stieglitz said he had nothing against putting unemployed artists on the federal payroll, but they should not be allowed to get near paint. Stieglitz characterized some of the project's work as "the rape of the walls." President Roosevelt, as was his wont, took a middle ground on the murals: "Some of it good," he said, "some of it not so good, but all of it native, human, eager and alive—all of it painted by their own kind in their own country, and painted about things that they know and look at often and have touched and loved." Roosevelt's knack for understanding the public mood was once again evident in this assessment.

If the social content of a mural could raise the eyebrows of members of the House Committee on Un-American Activities, a theatrical production could appear to be outright subversion. The Federal Theatre Project, directed by the former head of the Vassar College Experimental Theatre, Hallie Flanagan, was the most important, the most controversial, and hence, the shortest-lived of the Federal One projects. Flanagan had been a classmate of Harry Hopkins at Grinnell College. One actress who worked with her described her as having "the spirit, the soul, and the dedication, and the drive" of Eleanor Roosevelt. The FTP director was dedicated to building a truly national theater, one that would provide food for thought as well as for actors' stomachs. One of her ideals was to use drama to create public awareness of social problems. Hopkins promised a theater that was "free, adult, uncensored." That was a tall order, but in its brief history the FTP often approached the ideal.

The FTP played a role similar to those of the other arts projects in stimulating and encouraging talents that would remain important for decades after the program's demise. A very abbreviated list of its directors, playwrights, actors, producers, composers, and technicians gives an idea of the FTP's contribution: Orson Welles, Arthur Miller, Dale Wasserman, John Huston, Joseph Cotten, Jack Carter, E.G. Marshall, Will Geer, Arlene Francis, Canada Lee, Howard Da Silva, Burt Lancaster (who began as an aerialist in an FTP circus), John Houseman, Lehman Engel, George Izenour.

An Open and Uninhibited Theatre

Even more important than the individual careers that were spurred on by the FTP was the stimulus the project provided for the American stage through its openness to new ideas. Far more than other government agencies of the Depression era, the Theatre Project treated black Americans as highly capable, basically equal human beings. The FTP established sixteen "Negro Units" around the country. Casts almost always remained segregated (the notable exception being a Newark production of *The Trial of Dr. Beck*), but the roles were not. That is to say that black actors were no longer confined to "Negro" roles. The great departure was initiated by John Houseman, who codirected the Harlem FTP unit with black actress Rose McClendon. When the Federal Theatre began, the Harlem riots of 1935 were only a few months in the past and the usual offensive roles for black performers were wholly unacceptable. Houseman decided to put on a black production of a Shakespearean classic. If the idea was to be accepted it would have to be a first-rate production, and Houseman needed the best possible director. His friend Orson Welles, not yet twenty years old, quickly agreed to take the job. Welles's wife, Virginia, had the inspiration to make the first production *Macbeth,* set in Haiti with Voodoo priestesses as the witches. A troupe of African drummers (including a genuine witch doctor) was hired. At their request WPA requisition forms were filled out for five live black goats, which they proceeded to sacrifice in the theater's basement, so that the skins could be stretched for drums. With such authenticity, the *Voodoo Macbeth* was a smashing success.

Despite a few cases of attempted censorship, the Federal Theatre was remarkably uninhibited in its offerings. Most notable among its innovations were the "living newspapers." These were plays in the new form of documentaries that took a stand on issues of the day, provided information about them, and advocated a course of action. The New York group first put on *Triple-A Plowed Under*, a play that called for farmers and consumers to work together against greedy middlemen. Despite its agrarian subject matter, *Triple-A Plowed Under* was a stunning success, both critically and at the box office. So were such other living newspapers as *Power*, which demanded public ownership of utilities; *Injunction Granted,* a play that dramatized the anti-union actions of the courts; and *Created Equal,* which dealt with conflicts between property owners and citizens throughout American history. Right-wing critics charged that such productions were propaganda for the New Deal—or for something worse. Garrett Garet wrote in *The Saturday Evening Post* in June 1936 that *Triple-A Plowed Under* employed such "logotypes of Communist propaganda" as "hunger" and "starvation." Two months later another piece in the same periodical claimed that the Federal Theatre's "hair [was] full of Communists" and Flanagan was trying to "Russianize" the American stage.

Although the conservative critics finally had their way, the accomplishments of the Federal Theatre Project in its brief history are most impressive. In addition to its remarkable efforts in the legitimate theater, the FTP put on radio drama, children's plays, puppet shows, and circuses. In less than four years, approximately 30 million people attended productions of the FTP. Here, albeit all too briefly, was art for the millions.

CHAPTER 3

The "Golden Age" of Radio

Radio in the 1930s: An Overview

Tom Lewis

In the following overview, Tom Lewis discusses radio's impact on American life during the 1930s. Despite their often desperate economic troubles, Lewis writes, Americans were reluctant to part with the radios that kept them connected with the world. Controversial talk radio hosts voiced people's fears, Lewis observes, and to calm those fears, President Franklin D. Roosevelt explained his administration's policies and gained citizen support during his radio "Fireside Chats." Moreover, unlike the serious programming of the 1920s, Lewis explains, popular comedies like *Amos 'n' Andy* offered relief from the stresses of the depression. Lewis is an English professor at Skidmore College in Saratoga Springs, New York, and the author of *Empire of the Air: The Men Who Created Radio*.

I live in a strictly rural community, and people here speak of "The Radio" in the large sense, with an over-meaning. When they say "The Radio" they don't mean a cabinet, an electrical phenomenon, or a man in a studio, they refer to a pervading and somewhat godlike presence which has come into their lives and homes.

—E.B. White, 1933

Excerpted from "A Godlike Presence: The Impact of Radio on the 1920s and 1930s," by Tom Lewis, *OAH Magazine of History,* Spring 1992. Reprinted with permission from the author.

The Impact of Radio

As we look forward to high definition television bringing satellite-transmitted pictures from around the globe, we sometimes dismiss radio as merely a quaint prologue to the present. Radio was and is more than that. It defined the twentieth century as much as the automobile. The *first* modern mass medium, radio made America into a land of listeners, entertaining and educating, angering and delighting, and joining every age and class into a common culture. The various entertainers in the thirties and forties—the "golden age" of broadcasting—captured the imagination of millions. People talked then as much about the schemes of Amos and the Kingfish, [characters from the radio comedy *Amos 'n' Andy*], or the visitors to Fibber McGee and Molly [characters from the radio comedy of the same name], as they talk today about Murphy Brown's new baby, [a controversial episode of the situation comedy, *Murphy Brown*, that stimulated discussion in the 1990s on family values], or the latest video footage on the TV news. Radio created national crazes across America, taught Americans new ways to talk and think, and sold them products they never knew they needed. Radio brought them the world.

The new medium of radio was to the printing press what the telephone had been to the letter: it allowed immediacy. It enabled listeners to experience an event as it happened. Rather than read about Charles Lindbergh meeting President Calvin Coolidge after his flight to Paris, people witnessed it with their ears and imaginations; rather than learn of President Franklin D. Roosevelt's thoughts on banking from a newspaper story the next day, people listened to their president speak to them from the White House. The radio, which knew no geographic boundaries, drew people together as never before. Soon, people wanted more of everything—music, talk, advice, drama. They wanted bigger and more powerful sets, and they wanted greater sound fidelity. Radio became a "godlike presence," as the essayist E.B. White described it, that overtook American lives and homes.

Radio meant that for the first time in history one person with a microphone could speak to many, influence them, and perhaps change their lives. The concept borrowed the metaphor from a farmer scattering seeds across a field. Now a single speaker could sow seeds of information, propaganda, entertainment, political and religious fervor, culture, and even hatred across the land. The farmer's phrase, the word that changed the nation, was *broadcasting*. . . .

Entertaining Depression America

Through the economic turmoil of the Depression, radio was one of the most important forces keeping the nation together. By the thirties, radio had pervaded the consciousness of every American, subtly changing the way they thought and lived. There were 19,250,000 radio sets in America, and it was not unusual for a person to regard the radio as the most prized of possessions. Even though a quarter of the nation was unemployed, radio continued to grow in popularity. It enabled people to leave the economic trials and wretched conditions besetting the country. Social workers found that Americans would sooner sell their refrigerators, bath tubs, telephones, and beds to make rent payments, than part with the box that connected them with the world.

The nature of broadcasting was changing, too. While there still were inspirational and educational talks, and classical music programs, serious dramas, infrequent analyses of current events, and even the occasional protest talks, broadcasters offered a decidedly lighter fare of comedy, variety, and popular music. Vaudeville theaters, were now only a memory, and performers like Eddie Cantor, the Marx Brothers, George Burns and Gracie Allen, Jack Benny, and Ed Wynn successfully made the transition to the new medium. Listeners came to regard radio less as a medium for the transmission of culture and education and more as an easy way to escape their condition. As a most astute advertising agency head once said, America should laugh and dance its way out of the Depression.

The most popular program that brought the most laughs was of course "Amos 'n' Andy," which NBC broadcast at 7:00 each weekday evening. A publicity picture of the pair suggests what the show was about. One man sits on a barrel. He is wearing a shirt open at the throat, an unbuttoned vest, rumpled work pants, and shabby shoes. Another, dressed in dark wrinkled pants, a mismatched worn dress coat, white dress shirt and a wide tie, stands authoritatively beside him. Chewing on a stogie, he places his right hand on the other's shoulder, while his left grips the lapel of his jacket. Atop his head at a rakish angle, rests a derby hat. Thick lips, and the vacant look in their eyes are the most prominent features of their dark faces. They are Charles J. Correll and Freeman Fisher Gosden, not black men, but a black face comedy duo. In 1933 they earned $100,000 from NBC; more than Babe Ruth; more than the president of the network that employed them; more than the president of RCA; indeed, more than the President of the United States.

The Role of Advertising

"Amos 'n' Andy" and almost all the other popular radio shows had commercial sponsors that brought the networks and stations money. The list of broadcasts, punctuated by commercial announcements written by clever advertising agencies, grew as the decade advanced. By the early thirties commercials had become the standard way of financing broadcasts. Convenience goods, consumed by millions, became the most popular products to sell, accounting for 86 percent of the network and 70 percent of the non-network advertisements in 1934. Cigarettes (Lucky Strikes and Chesterfields), cigars ("There's no spit in Cremo Cigars!"), toothpastes (Ipana and Pepsodent) coffees (Maxwell House and Chase and Sanborn) and laxatives (Haley's M-O) proved especially popular.

More and more, advertisers—and the enormous revenues they offered to networks and small stations—controlled the content of broadcasts. Advertising agencies in

New York, rather than stations and networks created programs to meet a specific need of the client, and they hired audience rating companies to measure the response. Clever copy writers dramatized commercials and sometimes wove them into variety and comedy material. The singing commercial began to take form, too:

When you're feeling kinda blue
And you wonder what to do,
Ch-e-ew Chiclets, and
Chee-ee-eer up!

Gone was the ten minute sales talk for "Hawthorne Court," a suburban apartment development in Queens, New York, the radio advertisement in 1922 that had started it all. Now commercials were short, snappy, and often full of humor. To one wag of the time, radio was simply "a new and noisy method of letting peddlers into your home."

News and Commentary

News and commentary were not popular with advertisers or broadcasters. On 12 and 13 March 1933, two typical days, listeners in New York had the following choices: WEAF carried only Lowell Thomas, who devoted his fifteen minutes as much to commentary as to news, and a fifteen minute talk direct from Berlin by the chief European correspondent for the *New York Times*, who assured listeners that Adolf Hitler's rise to power was "no cause for general alarm" even though Jews were fleeing into Poland by the thousands. WJZ offered a fifteen minute news broadcast at 2:00 PM and fifteen minutes of Walter Winchell's Broadway gossip at 9:30. To lend more drama and immediacy to his stories and to suggest they were fresh off the wire, he introduced them with meaningless tapping on a telegraph key and then shouted "Flash."

That stations were uninterested in the news seems all the more extraordinary when one considers the events at the beginning of March, 1933. In Los Angeles the coroner had counted 110 deaths caused by an earthquake that struck the area. In Montgomery, Alabama, the second trial of nine black youths from Scottsboro who had been charged with the rape of two white girls was getting under way, and was already clouded by charges of the blacks' mistreatment in jail. In Berlin, roving bands of Nazi youths were attacking Americans. Chancellor Adolf Hitler's National Socialists had won resounding victories in municipal elections throughout Prussia. Showing at the Palace in New York was *Mussolini Speaks*, a biography of the Italian dictator with a running commentary by Lowell Thomas. Undergraduates at the universities of Glasgow and Manchester, following the lead of the students at Oxford, passed a resolution refusing to bear arms "for King or country." In St. Petersburg, Florida, Colonel Jacob Ruppert, owner of the New York Yankees was trying to get Babe Ruth to sign a new contract for $50,000. Before the Newaygo County courthouse in White Cloud, Michigan, the sheriff and his deputies used tear gas to disperse 400 men gathered to protest a mortgage foreclosure sale of land belonging to a fellow farmer. And Helen Keller revealed that one day while she was having tea in Lady Astor's London drawing room, her companion, Mrs. Macy, haltingly and with a quiver signed in her hand the pronouncement of her fellow guest George Bernard Shaw: "All Americans are deaf and blind—and dumb."

Dark messages did come through the air, however. From Detroit Father Coughlin excoriated the rich for having been "dulled by the opiate of their own contentedness" and organized his listeners into the "National Union for Social Justice" and the "Radio League of the Little Flower." Often implying anti-semitism, he denounced international bankers, blaming them for the Depression and suggesting that "Democracy is over." A startling number of listeners agreed. When a Philadelphia station asked its listeners if they would like to hear Coughlin or the New York Philharmonic on Sunday afternoons, the vote ran Coughlin 187,000; Philharmonic 12,000.

From Baton Rouge Huey Long raged against "lyin'

newspapers" promised "Every Man a King," and complained that though the Lord had invited the world to a feast "Morgan and Rockefeller and Mellon and Baruch have walked up and took 85 percent of the vittles off the table." He had an engaging conspiratorial way of bringing his audience into league with him:

> Hello friends, this is Huey Long speaking. And I have some important things to tell you. Before I begin I want you to do me a favor. I am going to talk along for four or five minutes, just to keep things going. While I'm doing it I want you to go to the telephone and call up five of your friends, and tell them Huey is on the air.

Listeners did. Across the land they organized "Share the Wealth" clubs. Until his assassination in September, 1935, many thought the Kingfish offered them the way to economic salvation.

A President Speaks to the People

The few news events that did make the radio were those orchestrated by Franklin Delano Roosevelt. After his inauguration on March 4th, the new president had declared a banking holiday as "the first step in the government's reconstruction of our financial and economic fabric." Farm leaders urged the President to take on sweeping new powers as a "Farm Dictator." And Congress rushed to approve an administration bill to sell beer and wine with 3.2 percent alcohol.

Roosevelt used radio to unite a fearful nation and to expand his popular appeal. When four out of every five newspapers declared their opposition to his policies, he spoke directly with the American people through his "Fireside Chats." And the people believed him. At 10:00 PM, Sunday, 12 March 1933, the end of his first week in office, the President delivered his first talk to explain the banking crisis. To prepare for it Roosevelt lay on a couch and visualized those whom he was trying to reach, ordinary people trying to get on with their affairs, who had little under-

During the Great Depression President Roosevelt's radio broadcasts, or "Fireside Chats," were often a source of comfort and hope for millions of Americans.

standing of the reasons why they couldn't cash a check or withdraw their money. "My friends, I want to talk for a few minutes with the people of the United States about banking," Roosevelt began,

> First of all let me state the simple fact that when you deposit money in a bank, the bank does not put the money into a safe deposit vault. It invests your money in many different forms of credit. . . . In other words, the bank puts your money to work to keep the wheels of industry and of agriculture turning around.

After explaining how "undermined confidence" caused a run on the banks' deposits, the consequent need for a "bank holiday," and the plans for their reopening, he reassured his listeners, "I hope you can see, my friends, from this elemental recital of what your government is doing that there is nothing complex, nothing radical in the process." And he concluded:

Confidence and courage are the essentials of success in carrying out our plan. You people must have faith; you must not be stampeded by rumors and guesses. Let us unite in banishing fear. We have provided this machinery to restore our financial system; and it is up to you to make it work. It is your problem, my friends, your problem no less than it is mine. Together we cannot fail.

Listeners heard his basic lesson in banking and they understood; they heard his fundamental sincerity and they believed. From Santa Monica, California, Will Rogers made the ultimate pronouncement. Roosevelt "stepped to the microphone last night and knocked another home run," Rogers wrote in the *New York Times*. "Our President took such a dry subject as banking . . . he made everybody understand it, even the bankers."

Other talks by Roosevelt followed, three more in 1933, and sixteen in the following years. The flow of letters to the White House, from many of those Americans whom the President had envisioned, became a torrent. Some people placed Roosevelt's picture beside their radios, so they might see him as he spoke.

Efforts at Reform

By 1933, a minority who still dreamed that broadcasting might become a medium of culture, education and information, were pressing hard for reform. Through the National Committee on Education by Radio they encouraged sympathetic congressmen to propose legislation that would force the Federal Radio Commission to license stations with more power and more favorable places on the broadcasting spectrum, and they were hopeful of success when they learned President Roosevelt wished to create a communications commission. But the result of their efforts, the Communications Act of 1934 that created a Federal Communications Commission, only maintained the status quo. When a committee of the FCC held hearings on the role of education in broadcasting, the networks contended they already were devoting ample time to cultural enrichment, including shows like NBC's "Amos 'n' Andy." Nevertheless, the threat of legislation induced networks to create programs like "The University of Chicago Round Table" and "American School of the Air" to satisfy the FCC's stipulation that broadcasting be in "the public interest, convenience, or necessity."

It was not simply the threat of legislation that moved broadcasters to develop better programs. David Sarnoff, the president of RCA who had first proposed the "radio music box" in 1916 so that listeners might enjoy "concerts, lectures, music, recitals," felt that the medium was failing to do this. By 1937, RCA had recovered enough from the effects of the Depression for it to make a dramatic commitment to cultural programming. With the most liberal terms Sarnoff hired Arturo Toscanini to create an entire orchestra and conduct it. On Christmas night, 1937, the NBC orchestra gave its first performance—Vivaldi's Concerto Grosso in D Minor—in an entirely refurbished studio in the RCA Building. "The National Broadcasting Company is an American business organization. It has employees and stockholders. It serves their interests best when it serves the public best." That Christmas night, and whenever the NBC orchestra played over the next seventeen years, he was right.

RCA's rival, the Columbia Broadcasting System, hired writers like Archibald MacLeish, Stephen Vincent Benet, James Thurber, Dorothy Parker, and Norman Corwin, among others, to write first-rate radio dramas. The most prolific and some would consider the most successful was Corwin, who often interwove political and social themes into plays like "They Fly through the Air with the Greatest of Ease." Broadcast in February 1939, the drama served as Corwin's aesthetic response to the cold-blooded, fascist bombing of Guernica, Spain:

> A symmetry of unborn generations,
> Of canceled seed.
> The dead below, spread fanlike in their blood,
> Will bear nor more.

Toward the end of the decade events in Europe began to overtake radio. In March, 1938, Edward R. Murrow broadcast reports of Hitler's invasion of Austria for CBS. In the Munich crisis later that year, Murrow made thirty-five broadcasts. When German planes bombed London, listeners across the United States heard the reserved Murrow intone "This . . . is London." Politics had forced radio to enter the world of reality.

The End of an Era

On 20 April 1939, before the RCA pavilion at the New York World's Fair, David Sarnoff strode up to a podium and declared: "Now we add radio sight to sound"

> It is with a feeling of humbleness that I come to this moment of announcing the birth of a new art so important in its implications that it is bound to affect all society . . . an art which shines like a torch in a troubled world . . . a creative force we must learn to utilize for the benefit of all mankind.

An RCA camera at the "Avenue of Patriots," focussed on the trylon and perisphere. To the few hundred watching sets about the city the scenes were wondrous. Television had entered the modern world.

Political events would halt the true introduction of television until the end of World War II. By 1953, when there were more than 17 million television sets in the United States, many proclaimed that radio would soon die. Events would prove otherwise, of course. Only rarely does a new technology entirely eliminate an older one. While television changed the function of radio in society, it did not eliminate it. Through popular music, especially rock and roll, radio continued to shape American culture. The development of FM broadcasting (an invention of 1933 which did not become successful for more than three decades), the creation of National Public Radio in 1970, and radio talk programs of recent years, demonstrate the power of the medium. Radio still captures the imagination, too. As a child once said, he preferred radio over television because "the pictures are better."

Listening in the 1930s: Americans Remember the Radio

Ray Barfield

Those who grew up in the 1930s have vivid memories of the family radio. Ray Barfield, a radio historian, records many of these recollections in the following essay. Barfield includes, for example, descriptions of the varied styles and sizes of radios, accounts of difficulties with reception, and humorous tales of those who did not quite understand how the new technology worked. These stories reveal the tremendous impact radio had on the lives of both rural and urban Americans during the "Golden Age" of radio. Barfield is an English professor at Clemson University in Clemson, South Carolina.

"**B**ringing home the radio set" and looking for "the little man who lived in the [radio] box and made the music" are recurrent motifs in listener accounts from the Depression decade. When the creation of the Rural Electrification Administration and the building of giant dams made electric power available to farms and communities in the Appalachians, in the Midwest, and in the Western states, the first family purchase was often a radio. Many families outside the cities could not wait for the power lines to be strung, however, they chose to improvise with troublesome batteries. Whether in the city or the country, the household's first radio was typically borne home like a proud trophy, a symbol of victory in the family budget wars. And not only youngsters but their grandparents too wondered how the music and the voices got into and out of "that thing." Copies of the weekly *Radio Guide* were kept near receiving instruments, which were available in an increasing variety of packagings: cathedral radios for the pious and traditional, Deco radios for the fashionable, pipe-rack radios for lounging types, and consoles and square wood veneer table sets for everyone. Near the end of the decade, a few optimistic manufacturers added a "Television" function to the row of push buttons supplementing the tuning dials of some models.

Memories of the First Radio

The yowler was indeed being tamed. Less and less a novelty item, the family radio seemed more and more a household necessity. Often it was the single investment in family entertainment. Calling herself "a child of the Depression," Jeanette Caler declares, "Radio was our lifeline to the world." "It was our prized possession for a long time," Juanita Capell says of the round-topped table model that her parents purchased in the early 1930s: "My Mother and Dad had nine living children, and we had trouble all of us trying to hear what we wanted to. But we managed to work it out somehow. The day we got a Radio was a great event in our lives. We enjoyed it for many years. It was all the entertainment we had." Like many other contemporary grandparents, Joe Jones still treasures a receiver which came into the family in the early Depression years: "My Dad bought us a 1933 Philco console which I believe was one of the first radio sets to have amazing 'push buttons' to tune the station. That old Philco set is today down in my basement playroom, and it still works and plays. My grandchildren have a great time with the push buttons and love to listen to the 'old' radio. It still has the big old glass tubes which came in it, but when they wear out or break, that will be the end, as I understand none of the old tubes are made any more."

When they first encountered radio in the early 1930s, some listeners had difficulty understanding its precise nature. Evelyn B. Thomason reports that her grandfather was far too early in attempting interactive communications: "Vividly I remember when my father surprised us with our first radio. It was the most beautiful and wonderful thing I had ever seen, a thing of mystery and delight. One night we took our prized possession to my grandfather's room so he could listen to the returns being broadcast from a local election—probably county; I don't remember. Anyway,

Radio Innovation in the Thirties

Alan Voorhees, editor of the California Historical Radio Society Journal *and collector of Kadette radios, talks about one of the first companies to make radios that were accessible to all Americans.*

In the 1920s, when radio manufacturing was in its infancy, a young man in Ann Arbor, Michigan started making radios. Charles Verschoor didn't make his mark on the radio world, however, until 1931 when he started the International Radio Corporation. One of his first products was a diminutive little radio with a plastic case, the Kadette. The compact size of the radio was accomplished by using an innovative new circuit, one which strung all the tubes in series like Christmas tree lights. This set, which would operate on either AC or DC current no longer required a power transformer, and that made it lighter, smaller, and cheaper than the other sets on the market.

Its plastic case was noteworthy as well. Manufactured for International Radio by the Chicago Molded Products Co., it marked the beginning of a new era in cabinet design by being the first set housed in plastic. Its design was rather traditional, having a strong Gothic look with arches on the front of the case. The radio was a hit with the American public, and its popularity led everyone was intently listening when all of a sudden my grandfather held his hand up high and said in a loud, pleading voice, 'Repeat that, please!' We had a good laugh later, after explaining the situation to him, and we laugh about it to this day."

V.T. Chastain recalls,

> My father, W.H. Chastain, had the first radio in the Holly Springs community ten miles north of Pickens, South Carolina. It had been a gift from friends in Michigan, and, since electricity had not yet come to our area, the radio had to be run off of a six-volt battery borrowed from the car for

to the almost immediate profitability of International Radio. Within two years, International Radio was the only Ann Arbor corporation that was still paying dividends to its shareholders.

Other innovative sets followed in rapid order. The following year the Kadette Jr. appeared. It had two dual-purpose tubes and was the world's first pocket sized set—albeit a coat pocket sized one. By this time the first Kadette model had been refined into the handsome Kadette Jewel, which appeared in five standard color combinations. Like with some other Kadette models, Chicago Molded Products made a few cases in other, often unusual, color combinations.

In 1936, just as Sears was jumping on the bandwagon with its first Bakelite set, the "Streamliner" (model 4500) in basic black plastic, International was releasing the Kadette Classic—a set with a cabinet molded in three different plastics. It was ultimately available in seven color combinations, among them an ivory case with contrasting grill and green, yellow, rose, or blue top and a jet-black case with an ivory grill and a bright vermilion red top. The set resembled a colorful room heater, and the front and the back looked basically the same allowing the radio to be placed away from the wall and still be attractive from behind.

Alan Voorhees, "International Radio Corp." *Antique Radios Online.*

that purpose. At first WSM, Nashville, Tennessee, was the only station, but later we also got WFBC from Greenville. Reception was pretty good if the weather was good, but bad weather brought static. Programs consisted of country music and boxing. . . . Neighbors from all around congregated at our house to see and hear the amazing radio! One man I remember in particular really enjoyed a certain musical rendition, and he told Dad, "Make 'em play that one again, Wade." Nothing Dad could say would convince him that the musicians were in Greenville and not somewhere, somehow, inside that box!

The Man Who Lived in the Box

At the age of about four, some sixty years ago, Rachel P. McKaughan was engaged in the natural childhood process of discovering the dimensions of the world, often understanding new things by analogy: "I saw [just] about the first airplane in the sky that I'd ever seen. I asked my dad how it flew, and he said there was a man in it who flew it! (A child at that age has no concept of distance and size perspective.) Later we got a radio in the home, our first. When he turned it on, I asked if that was the tiny little man who could fly an airplane! I thought someone had to be in 'the box' doing all that talking."

Trina Nochisaki was born in 1927 and dates her earliest radio recollections from about 1930. Her account pictures a family strongly committed to the medium:

We had two radios in our house. One was a magnificent Stromberg Carlson model the size of a modern day hutch with curving legs and beautiful retractable doors covering the radio part of this piece of furniture. We really didn't get to listen to it much because it was in the "parlor" and my hard-working parents had little time for sitting in this room.

The other was a Philco table model radio which was in our multi-purpose room (dining room, den). I remember my parents listening to Father Coughlin, Amos and Andy, and

Fibber McGee. . . . And I can't recall how many times I tried to sneak up on the real little people I just *knew* lived in the radio—if only I could catch them unawares.

By about 1934, B.A. "Gus" Wentz was gathering the first remembrances of his life in the part of the house which his family had designated "the radio room." He says, "I remember looking into the back of the radio to try to see the 'little people' in there. The radio—an Air Castle, I think—stood on a table in the corner next to the stairs. We kids would vie for choice seats on the stairs as the family hovered around to hear the Sunday evening lineup (after church, of course). Some folks in the church would actually miss evening services to catch Fred Allen, Jack Benny, George Burns and Gracie Allen, the first time I was ever aware of a conflict between radio and 'duty to God'."

A Variety of Styles and Sizes

For many who were young children in the early 1930s, the receiving instruments seemed to loom very large. Paul F. Snow first encountered radio through a neighbor's Atwater Kent "powered by a wet storage battery with a monster horn speaker." "The first one that I remember," Ellen Edmonds says, "was a large cabinet that sat in the living room or 'parlor'. . . . It had a small dial that was orange when it was on. Later on, after my father passed away, we moved to the mountains of western North Carolina, near Marshall. We lived on a small farm and we owned a small 'table model' radio with a large battery. Our listening pleasure was measured by the life of the battery (we did not have electricity or inside plumbing)." For Dottie Zungoli, whose family owned the first receiver in a newly electrified Philadelphia neighborhood, the programs were delightful, but they emerged from an early combination radio-phonograph that seemed an aesthetic compromise: "It was a great big ugly thing, and on the other side of it was a Victrola."

For Mary Lee McCrackan, the listening experience was defined not by the size of the radio but by the dimensions of the house. Having known very early broadcasting in Chicago, Illinois, and in the Deep South, she moved to Richmond, Virginia, to live with her father, who

> had remarried after being an eligible widower for fourteen years, and I came along in the deal. We lived on the third floor of the Antebellum Matthew Fontaine Maury House. It was a perfect setting for listening to such scary radio broadcasts as Sherlock Holmes and "The Hound of the Baskervilles." The description of the hounds on the radio and the associated sound effects were scary in the extreme. It was late on a cold Sunday afternoon, and the backyard shadows from the fig tree coupled with the howling wind were more than I could take. My father and mother had gone to the university to prepare for the next day's classes, but I telephoned and asked that they return home at once.

Problems with Reception

During the 1930s Bill Buri spent most of his childhood in an aunt's home in the coal-mining regions of Pennsylvania, and there he encountered the uncertainties of reception. "We would get really weird stations because it was up there in the mountains. We used to get WJZ and WOR from New York, KDKA from Pittsburgh, WBZ from Boston, and WBZA, Springfield. Sometimes if the weather was right, we'd get Canadian Broadcasting at night. We had two identical radios—I think they were Emersons—and they looked like cathedrals. In the spring when the weather got warmer, I had a little hut in the attic; they had a bed up there and a German helmet that my uncle had brought home from World War I. You could get better stations up in the top of the house." In Ardmore, Pennsylvania, George A. Walker, Jr. knew similar difficulties: "There were always frustrating periods, early on, with trying to pick up special stations or broadcasts that were beyond the capability of our radio. It got better as time went on. The stations themselves added more power, and the radios got better and better."

In those days of variable reception, a change of residence

could prompt the buying of a radio. "It was a long time before we had a radio of our own," Lois Robinson says. The purchase came after her family moved in 1930 from Greenville, Mississippi, to Chicago, Illinois. That new console "had a curved dial with numbers on it, and when it was turned on, the dial glowed a light orange color. Radio wasn't 'instant on' at first. It had to warm up a little before you could hear a program." The move to the city also underscored a startling contrast in listening matter: "We used to listen to the police calls late at night. In Greenville, as our funny friend Boola Woods used to say, we heard, 'Calling both cars! Calling both cars!' Greenville wasn't a very big place. But listening to police calls after we moved to Chicago was scary."

Helen J. Tidwell's memory of her family's investment in radio blends elements of humor and sacrifice:

> My father traded one of his best "milk" cows for a console type radio. A beautiful piece of furniture, up on four legs, speakers covered with a fabric, dial, and four knobs, it was placed in our "parlor." The first morning after obtaining the "Squawk Box" (as [it was] sometimes referred to), my mother tuned in to a program called "Don McNeill's Breakfast Club." On that particular morning they had a cow moo-o-o-o-ing on the program. (Don't know if we had Elsie the Borden cow back then or not.) My mother called to my father in another room and said, "Daddy, your cow is on the radio." Being only four or five years old, I wondered how Daddy's cow got in that radio and when it would come out. It never did!

Adapting to the Radio

Historian Robert A. Waller tells of growing up in the mid-1930s on a farm in central Illinois: "In the days before FDR's New Deal REA brought electricity to rural America, the first radio I can remember was battery operated from a wind charger on the top of our tenant farmer's home. On becalmed days, there were sometimes limited or no evening programs when the battery had not retained or received enough of a charge to operate the system." Jim Harmon, author of *The Great Radio Heroes*, *Radio Mystery and Adventure and Its Appearances in Film, Television, and Other Media*, and other studies of the popular arts, says, "Our family first got electricity in the house and radio the same Christmas, when I was three. I do remember, somehow, I do. We lived in the rather rural town of Mt. Carmel, Illinois. The year was 1936. On Sundays, we all listened together to Jack Benny, Fred Allen, and the rest. I would lie on my stomach, hypnotized by the yellow eye of the dial. I've heard others say the same thing, but I know this is no false memory."

Sometimes the receiver had to be placed inconveniently because of the antenna's location. Absalom W. Snell's family experienced that problem when he was a teenager in the late 1930s: "We spent most of our time in the evenings in a bedroom with fireplace heat. The radio was located in the living room, which was not heated and seldom used, so that an antenna could be connected. One end of a multi-strand wire was connected to a high chimney and the other to a cypress pole installed for that purpose. The antenna suffered a lightning stroke, and the multi-strand wire was completely destroyed. The attached solid wire conducted the lightning to the window sill, then to the electric wire in the wall, causing damage to the wall."

Living in a city in the mid-1930s did not guarantee immediate access to a radio, as Dr. Jeanne Kenmore well knew: "In 1935 I was twelve years old. We did not have a radio! Depression days. We children saw one movie a year, but somehow—I suppose from conversations at school—we learned what we were missing. My mother, my two younger brothers and I lived in an 'upper' duplex in Minneapolis. In that city a duplex has two floors which are identical. Downstairs there was a woman with her two children about my age. So, I crouched down under a window on the front porch to try to hear the downstairs radio. When the weather was decent and a window was open, I had a perfect seat, months on end."

In Ann Chase's family, as she remarks with an unblinking directness learned from Depression-era spareness, the family radio purchase became a test of financial stability: "My father was never fired from a job—he was famous for giving them up, usually right before some big expenditure. [One day] I was playing with my friends when a large truck stopped outside our house. The driver, with his helper, dismounted and, with great authority, opened the back doors. There, surrounded by emptiness, sat an impressive floor model radio. This radio was placed in the hall below the stair, not too far away from the living room or the kitchen, so that the sound that emerged could reach the ears of either the resting or the busy."

The radio became a popular form of entertainment during the 1930s. For many who grew up in depression-era America, listening to the radio is one of their fondest memories.

Growing Up with Radio

Joan Waller grew up in the Chicago suburb of River Forest, populated by doctors', industrialists', and other professionals' families. In her home, she remembers, radio was
very much a part of the children's play:

> The radio occupied a prominent place at the end of the liv-
> ing room. Couch cushions on the floor provided seating as
> well as something soft to lie on while engrossed in daily
> radio episodes.
>
> My father's return home from work occasioned the only
> brief interruption. When Dad opened the door and called,
> "Is anyone at home?" my two brothers, two sisters, and I
> would run and give him a hug, check to see if he'd brought
> us any presents, and then rush back to our programs.
>
> I remember the day when a new remote control radio ar-
> rived at our house. What magic. Not only could we change
> programs by rotating the dial from across the room, but
> now we could even change the stations in our house from
> the house next door. While one of us took the magic box and
> rotated the dials from next door, the rest of us listened to the
> stations changing inside our house and signaled through the
> window to let the dial changer know it was working. We
> continued to change places until each of us had had our
> turn. Though this proved to be great fun, we soon tired of
> our new "toy" and returned to serious radio listening.

Even if they were born into very different settings, children of the 1930s could view the arrival of the radio in similar ways. Max Salathiel was born on a farm in Central
Oklahoma in 1935, and in his youth he heard members of
his extended family appear on national broadcasts. "I grew
up with radio," he declares. "My earliest memories are of
my dad bringing in a box in late 1938 with a brand new
Zenith table model receiver. It was battery operated as we
didn't have electricity. We had a windcharger mounted on
a windmill to charge the battery. The glass dial on the radio

had a sailing ship etched on it. When you pushed a knob on the front of the radio at night, the dial would light up, displaying the frequencies and the ship." Bill Anthony recalls his early days in the city: "It all started for me in 1937, when my father came home from work with a new Zenith radio under his arm. Funny, I was only seven at the time, but I can still picture that quite clearly as though it just happened. I then started to try to tune in distant stations and even drew a picture of the dial on paper and clearly marked the numbers from the dial when I got those wonderful stations that we were not supposed to get in Pittsburgh. Every Sunday at seven, my mother would clean up after dinner, and we would all sit down to listen to Jack Benny. I remember how delighted I was that the show made my father laugh because times were tough, and he worked hard to buy that radio and [meet] all of our other needs." He adds, "The love affair with radio continues to this day, as I am an avid Old Time Radio collector (and have been for twenty five years)."

Malcolm Usrey, a children's literature scholar, weighs the value of radio in his Texas childhood:

In the 1930s and 1940s, the Texas Panhandle was not a cultural desert, but neither was it a cultural oasis. Live musical and dramatic performances were rare, with only Amarillo large enough to support serious cultural events, and for the most part, they were suspended during World War II. There was no "little" theater, though most high schools offered one dramatic performance, the annual "senior play." County fat stock shows and county fairs and the Texas Panhandle State Fair in Amarillo drew larger crowds than concerts and plays. Rural churches had their all-day Sunday singings, which lasted for two to four hours after a "dinner on the ground," leaving only those with the strongest lungs to sing the hours away into the late afternoon, time to return home and take care of farm chores—milking, feeding animals, gathering eggs. Every county seat had at least one film theater, and Amarillo may have had two or more, but the small towns and villages did not have theaters.

County seats also had small libraries, usually a small room in the court house or in a store building on the main street. Many rural people never saw the inside of a library, never read a newspaper, never read a magazine. But nearly everyone had a radio.

My family acquired its first radio in the mid-1930s, when I was about five or six years old. It was an elegant piece of furniture and an astounding piece of equipment, a large, three-feet tall Zenith with a dark mahogany finish. It had a worldwide band and was powerful enough to bring in KGNC in Amarillo about seventy five miles away, KRLD in Dallas about 300 miles away, and sometimes stations in San Antonio and New Orleans.

The author of a survey of Sherlock Holmes's appearances in several media, Gordon Kelley also feels that he was born at the right time to appreciate radio's value:

I was born in 1934, a time when the family radio was the center of most people's lives. We could only afford one radio because the Depression was still evident in the small farm town where I lived, but we really didn't need more than one because listening was a family affair.

My family lived about twenty miles south of Indianapolis, and we were fortunate in being able to get four local stations and one from Cincinnati (WLW). The reception on our large and heavy table top cathedral radio was quite good. We only had AM radio during the times I was growing up, and it was subject to all of the atmospheric disturbances that most of us today do not notice on the more prevalent FM band. There would be lots of static during the summer months when electrical storms were common, and our radio squeaked and squawked each time we changed stations. I still have this radio in working condition, and it hasn't changed at all. All the noises are still there, but there isn't much of anything to listen to.

Creating Consumers: The Radio Soap Opera

Marilyn Lavin

In the following article, Marilyn Lavin, a professor of marketing at the University of Wisconsin in Whitewater, Wisconsin, examines the emergence of the radio soap opera. During the 1930s, Lavin writes, most women spent their daytime hours at home with only the radio to keep them company. She points out that when radio stations discovered that housewives enjoyed serial dramas about women like themselves, advertising agencies began to see these stories as a way to sell products. She notes, for example, that script writers would incorporate dialogue about products into the stories, and radio stations would encourage listeners to send in for family photographs of the soap opera characters that included product endorsements. According to Lavin, these strategies were some of the first attempts to encourage mass consumption.

The 1930s have emerged as an important moment in consumer history, even though the decade presents somewhat of an anomaly. The thirties witnessed the widespread want and deprivation associated with the Great Depression, and, at the same time, those years were the occasion of rapid advances in mass consumption. In seeking

---

Excerpted from "Creating Consumers in the 1930s: Irna Phillips and the Radio Soap Opera," by Marilyn Lavin, *Journal of Consumer Research*, vol. 22, no. 1, June 1995. Copyright ©1995 by Journal of Consumer Research, Inc. Reprinted with permission from The University of Chicago Press and the author.

to explain how the majority of people in the United States dealt with economic hardship and simultaneously desired a growing assortment of consumer goods, historians have given special attention to the role of the media—particularly radio—in creating a national consumer culture. They have noted that it was in the 1930s that phrases such as the "American Way of Life" and the "American Dream" that are associated with material as well as social and political well-being came into common usage, and they have shown that during the decade such diverse groups as middle-class whites, blacks, and working-class ethnics for the first time shared a devotion to a set of nationally broadcast radio programs and advertisements.

Soap opera, one of the radio formats originated in the 1930s, was well suited to play an important role in encouraging mass consumption. First, serial programming turned individual housewives across the nation into a mass audience that faithfully tuned into each daily episode. Second, soap operas provided role models of "real life" families who overcame adversity and successfully attained the American Dream of middle-class well-being and happiness. And finally, serial programming permitted the development of characters with whom the audience could identify and who could serve as trusted friends and experts. . . .

The Origin of Radio Soap Operas

Soap operas developed as a result of the convergence of four factors during the early 1930s. First, radio became an established communication medium in the United States. Second, advertising agencies became increasingly involved in the development of programs that would suit the needs of their clients. Third, Americans generally agreed that the most socially acceptable roles for married women were those of housewife and mother. And finally, advertisers recognized women to be the purchasers of the majority of household consumer goods.

Exclusively a local medium in the early 1920s, radio had become national in scope by 1930. The National Broadcasting Company (NBC), organized in 1926, had 61 affiliated stations, while the Columbia Broadcasting System (CBS), established in 1927, had 79. As the networks formed, the American people enthusiastically accepted the new means of communication. Sales of radios increased 1,400 percent between 1922 and 1929 and, even in the Depression years of 1930 to 1932, 4.6 million sets were sold. By 1934, CBS reported that more than 90 percent of all nonfarm households owned radios.

By the late 1920s, concern that advertising had saturated the print media caused advertising agencies to overcome their initial fears that listeners would reject direct sales messages broadcast over the radio, and they began to pursue the use of radio as an advertising medium. As an initial step, agencies such as J. Walter Thompson began to interweave casual references to the sponsor's product into program dialogue. To be successful, the approach required close ties between the program and the product, and a number of agencies enlarged their radio departments to begin production of radio programs tailored to their clients' needs. The multiple demands of the new broadcasting format led the secretary of one agency to question "Shall we entertain, and in entertaining hope to sell; or shall we continue to sell as in the past, and make use of entertainment as one the several techniques of selling?" Despite such ambivalence, by 1931 the agencies wrested control of radio program production from the networks. In exchange for a 15 percent commission on gross costs, the agencies hired writers, announcers, actors, and directors; supervised scripts; wrote commercials; booked air time; devised premium offers; and oversaw broadcasts.

Discovering a New Audience

By 1928, the viability of commercially sponsored radio programming during evening hours had become apparent. When the agencies and the networks next looked toward the daytime hours, the most obvious potential audience was the 23 million housewives in the population of 37 million women between the ages of 16 and 64 counted in the United States census for 1930. Although economic necessity forced many wives to seek employment in low-paying jobs during the Depression, work outside the home was inconsistent with the social ideal for married women at that time. Indeed, 82 percent of male and female respondents to a 1930s survey held the opinion that a married woman with a husband capable of supporting her should not work to earn money. Charged with responsibilities for home maintenance and child rearing, housewives spent the majority of their daytime hours at home, where, isolated from social contact with other adults, they were likely to look to the radio for stimulation.

Housewives were not only an available audience, but, for program sponsors, they were also a desirable one. By the late 1920s, writer, Carl Naether, who provided instructions on advertising to women, claimed that "Shopping is as much a woman's business as making money is a man's." In a similar vein, Mrs. Christine Frederick, who dubbed the American housewife "Mrs. Consumer," advised that "The American male . . . seems to enjoy himself most at earning, while content to leave the pleasure of spending to his women." She also estimated that women controlled 90 percent of the expenditures of most households.

With the advent of the Depression, housewives' purchasing roles assumed even greater importance. During the 1930s, most families did not face catastrophic hardship, but according to Susan Ware, they often needed to "Use it up, wear it out, make it do, or do without." Housewives spent their household dollars cautiously. In a period when weekly food budgets averaged $5 for a family of six, one woman reported she and a friend bought two pounds of hamburger for a quarter each week, and that they took turns paying the extra penny.

As late as 1930, radio limited its daytime hours to cooking and household-advice broadcasts. Although women in those early days of the Depression sought money-saving recipes and household tips, those offerings were not alone sufficient to sustain listener interest. For daytime radio to serve sponsors' needs, a new entertainment format that would encourage housewives to listen during morning and afternoon hours had to be developed.

Attracting the Housewife Audience

Chicago was the scene of two efforts to develop the daytime serial in 1930. As a member of the Blackett-Sample-Hummert [advertising] agency, Frank Hummert was making his initial, albeit unsuccessful, attempts to adapt the serial to the needs of sponsors. At the same time, Henry Selinger, the station manager of WGN, was working to devise programming that would stimulate the sale of morning and afternoon radio time. . . .

Inspired by the success of the nighttime program, *Amos 'n' Andy*, Selinger believed the serial format might be transferred to earlier listening hours. In the spring of 1930, the station manager commissioned a staff writer to develop a daytime serial that featured an Irish-American mother and her daughter, Irene. The initial reactions of potential sponsors were not promising. The Super-Suds Company first declined to be involved with *The Sudds;* likewise, a margarine maker rejected a retitled version, *Good Luck Margie.* Several months later, Selinger gave the serial assignment to Irna Phillips, who had joined the station only a few months earlier. A 1923 graduate of the University of Illinois and a drama teacher in the public schools of Missouri and Ohio, Phillips had no experience in script writing, advertising, or any other aspect of broadcasting. Following Selinger's instructions, however, she added a third character, Sue Morton, a young woman who lived with the mother and daughter, and prepared 10 scripts that established a general story line of intergenerational misunderstanding and conflict between "Mother Moynahan" and the younger women. Broadcasts of *Painted Dreams,* which is considered to be the first soap opera, began on October 20, 1930, but sponsors continued to reject the unproven program format.

For almost a year, WGN aired *Painted Dreams* as a sustaining program; that is, the station underwrote the costs of production in the hope of attracting an audience large enough to gain commercial sponsorship for the program. During the same period, Phillips worked to develop an entertainment vehicle that appealed specifically to housewives. Surviving scripts and plot outlines indicate that *Painted Dreams* relied on an ongoing story that pitted the "modern" Irene against her more traditional mother. The first soap opera, however, also included poetry, music, and philosophy. The inclusion of those materials was not accidental. Phillips was aware that Swift, Montgomery Ward, and other advertisers had used such features "to appeal to women listeners, not only sectionally but throughout the country." Phillips's correspondence also contained a reference to the program preference test conducted by Montgomery Ward. Montgomery Ward had sponsored a contest in which entrants were offered an opportunity to win $10,000 in prizes in exchange for their evaluation of four different formats the retailer was presenting during its 8:30 A.M. program. The 70,000 respondents overwhelmingly chose *Beautiful Thoughts—Bits of Song and Sentiment to Brighten the Day*.

Satisfying Advertisers

In the era before media rating services, programmers used "mail hooks" (offers of small premiums to listeners who sent a stamped, self-addressed envelope) to generate fan mail. That mail in turn provided a means of assessing the magnitude of the listening audience for potential sponsors. The mail hook that Phillips chose to demonstrate the popularity of *Painted Dreams* revealed her willingness to use the proven appeal of "homey" poetry and philosophy to facilitate the audience's acceptance of her more innovative daytime serial effort. In April 1931, after *Painted Dreams* had been on the air for about six months, Phillips used a twofold appeal to her listeners: in keeping with the established taste of her daytime audience, she offered listeners who sent in a stamped, self-addressed envelope an autographed copy of a poem that had been presented on the broadcast; at the same time, she attempted to stimulate her listeners' involvement with the story by urging them to write and indicate whether their favorite character was the "charming blue-eyed Irene . . . the practical mysterious and loyal Sue . . . or . . . the ever-understanding lovable Mother Moynahan."

In the fall of 1931, Mickelberry Products Company, a Chicago meat packer, took on sponsorship of *Painted Dreams*. At the same time, Phillips's salary rose from $50 to $100 per week. Those two events, occurring in the depth of the Depression, suggest that Phillips had developed a commercial daytime format capable of attracting and sustaining the interest of the daytime housewife audience.

While Phillips worked to attract listeners, she recognized that the program format she was developing had to meet the needs of advertisers. Early in 1932, she wrote "any radio presentation which is sponsored in order to be of utility to its sponsor, must actually sell merchandise; otherwise the object of radio advertising has failed." Consequently, she followed the lead that advertising agencies had established for nighttime programming and closely tied the plots of her early serials to the sponsors' products.

For Marshall Field and Company, the manufacturer and wholesaler of Zion Curtains, Phillips proposed the program *Looking through Your Curtains,* which centered around the theme "life is a curtain through which we look." For Brown Beauty Baked Beans she created *Life's Patchquilt*, in which Betty Brown visited Aunt Martha in each episode and heard a different uplifting tale related to a piece of the quilt. Regarding Betty, Phillips wrote: "there is definite merit in the fact that Betty Brown, who will do the commercials is always a part of the script." Phillips's most blatant efforts to tie together advertising and programming occurred, however, with her first soap opera, *Painted Dreams,* and its successor, *Today's Children. . . .*

Selling Goods

When *Today's Children* began national broadcast in September 1933, it joined Frank and Anne Hummert's serial,

Betty and Bob, which had been sponsored by General Mills on the NBC network since October 1932. In December 1933, the Hummerts' *Ma Perkins,* underwritten by Procter and Gamble, became the third soap opera on NBC. The presence of those three programs in the radio network's daytime schedule indicates that, as early as 1933, major consumer product companies considered the soap opera format a viable means of reaching the housewife. Moreover, soap opera sponsorship served not only to build product awareness, but it also became an important means of directly stimulating product sales.

Only weeks after *Today's Children* began network broadcast, Phillips offered her listeners a family picture that had been taken by Mother Moran at the engagement party for boarder Kay Norton and her fiancé Bob Crane. To increase requests for the photo, Phillips wrote a special plea that was delivered by daughter Frances at the end of one episode.

> Friends, I dont [*sic*] know just how to begin. Perhaps I should say to all you good people who have sent for a picture of *Today's Children,* thank you. You cant [*sic*] know how much we appreciate the wonderful response of friendship and cooperation you have given us. I couldnt [*sic*] begin to tell you what it has meant to all of us, and most of all to Mom. Perhaps you dont [*sic*] know that it was Mom's idea to offer you a picture of *Today's Children,* and she asked the Pillsbury people to send them out for her. All you had to do to get your picture was to send in the word "balanced" from any size sack of Pillsbury Flour, or the label from a package of SnoSheen Cake Flour to show your interest . . . I'm asking you to send for your picture not for myself . . . but only for my mother, for I want her to able to show the Pillsbury Flour Mills Company each and every one of you—her friends—are with her.

For Phillips, the engagement picture photograph had a dual purpose. Like the mail hooks she had used previously, the family picture offer was a means of measuring the size of her audience. In addition, it served to strengthen the bond between her listeners and the program characters. Frances used the term "friends," not "listeners," to encourage the audience to write for the picture. The mail hook was a photo of the Moran family, a premium that allowed the radio audience to see the characters they could previously only imagine. Finally, because serial fans wanted their favorite programs to continue "forever," Frances clearly explained that sending for the picture was a sign of goodwill to Mother Moran that would be used "to show the Pillsbury Flour Company each and every one of you— her friends—are with her."

For Pillsbury, the engagement picture offer also had multiple purposes: it provided assurance that *Today's Children* attracted a large audience, and it served as a direct advertising vehicle. . . .

Using Premiums

In the spring of 1934, Phillips and Pillsbury devised another mail offer. This time they offered their audience, in return for a flour label, a book detailing the history to date of the Moran family. The book also included poetry selections recited on the program, but the highlight of the volume was a sketch that daughter Frances had drawn of Mother Moran. This sketch was purportedly necessary because "Mom would never have her picture taken"; in reality, a photo was impossible because Phillips was the voice of Mother Moran as well as of Kay Norton. The book offer elicited enthusiastic response, and Pillsbury received more than 250,000 requests for the premium. Such results suggest the strong ties radio listeners had established with the serial's characters. The president of Pillsbury's advertising agency believed that "the amazing allegiance of hundreds of thousands of women" extended to the sponsor's products, and he praised the daytime serial as a means by which "the flour-buying audience can be reached—and sold."

In 1934, a survey directed by Daniel Starch for CBS revealed that 78 percent of all radios were in use during daytime hours. Those findings made the use of mail hooks to verify the existence of the daytime listening audience unnecessary; at the same time, however, sponsors recognized that premium offers could play an important role not only in gauging the sizes of audiences for specific shows but also in the actual sale of goods. As noted in the preceding paragraph, listeners bought more than 250,000 bags of Pillsbury flour in order to send for the *Today's Children* history. At about the same time, Procter and Gamble also increased its detergent sales when 1,000,000 members of its *Ma Perkins* audience responded to an offer of a package of flower seeds in return for an Oxydol box top and 10 cents. At least one actress reportedly complained, "For heaven's sake, do I have to read this glop?" when rehearsing the following copy for a costume jewelry premium: "Why it [the broach] gleams like virgin gold, and just look at those gorgeous colors—exactly like a rainbow and sunset coming together in a resplendent display of almost unimaginable beauty." Nonetheless, premium offers tied to soap opera plots and requiring the purchase of the sponsor's product flourished in the 1930s. Pillsbury, in fact, considered such selling efforts so important that the company reported its mail offer results to its salesmen, who, in turn, shared the information with retailers. . . .

The premium offers that Pillsbury and other consumer product sponsors of the soap operas made during the 1930s clearly indicated the relationship between the purchase of advertised goods and the continuation of a serial. For their part, the sponsors were specific about their purpose; on the 1,000th broadcast of *Today's Children,* the president of Hutchinson Advertising stated: "The Pillsbury Flour Folks . . . offer no apologies for the fact that it is a commercially sponsored program; that it is put on the air to increase the use of Pillsbury's products." He also reported that many listeners wrote to Pillsbury to compliment the company on "the restrained manner, inoffensiveness, and brevity of the advertising announcements."

Hutchinson's latter statement reflects the advertiser's ongoing concern about audience reaction to broadcast selling messages. By the 1,000th episode of *Today's Children,* manufacturers had, for almost a decade, used radio to promote a wide assortment of consumer products. Nonetheless, sponsors and their advertising agencies remained sensitive to the possibility of offending listeners. In 1935, the Women's National Radio Committee, representing 27 women's organizations, including the American Association of University Women and the American Legion Auxiliary, had put forth a standard for assessing advertising. That body recognized that "radio offers an opportunity to the manufacturer to visit every potential buyer's home." The committee argued that, consequently, the "manner of bringing the product to the attention of the buyer [should be] exactly the same as the manufacturer's crack salesman would employ if he were magically given entrée to every consumer's home." Hutchinson may have been aware of the committee; indeed, he appeared to paraphrase its statement when, on the 1,000th-anniversary program, he voiced his hope that "*Today's Children* and Pillsbury's products long continue as welcome visitors" in listeners' homes.

The Press-Radio War

Gwenyth Jackaway

Whenever technological innovation creates a new media, conflict with the old media is inevitable, writes Gwenyth Jackaway, a professor of communications at Fordham University, in New York City. At first, print journalists were unsure how to handle radio, but when newspapers were getting scooped, they put political, economic, and legal pressure on radio to prevent radio broadcasts of the news. Eventually, Jackaway writes, the newspapers lost the press-radio war as well as their monopoly over the flow of news.

S ome 60 years ago, after holding a monopoly over the news gathering and distribution process in America for more than a century, the newspaper industry found itself facing new competition. Radio had arrived, and with it came a new channel for the dissemination of information. Not surprisingly, print journalists were livid. They spent nearly a decade trying to block the emergence of broadcast journalism. This inter-media conflict is known as the press-radio war. And it is just one of a number of such media wars—battles that have been waged between old and new media. Media wars are conflicts between existing and emerging media industries which take place at the time of technological innovation in communication. They have occurred with the introduction of almost every new medium in this century. Both the newspapers and the film industry

Excerpted from "America's Press-Radio War of the 1930s: A Case Study in Battles Between Old and New Media," by Gwenyth Jackaway, *Historical Journal of Film, Radio, and Television*, Spring 1994. Reprinted with permission from the author and Taylor & Francis, Ltd., 11 New Fetter Lane, London, England EC4P 4EE.

fought the introduction of radio. Hollywood also balked at the introduction of television. Broadcast television struggled against the introduction of cable. In recent years both the newspapers and cable have been fighting with the phone companies. Why are these battles continually waged? What are they really about? . . .

Building Alliances

A key issue at stake in the debate over providing radio with wire service bulletins was the role of the newspaper in the institutional structure of the journalism industry. The entry of radio as a new 'player' was menacing to the established news distribution structure that defined the journalism industry in America by the 1920s: the newspaper-wire service alliance. Prior to the advent of broadcasting, news moved from the wire services, through the newspapers, to the people. It was a network-like arrangement, with newspapers across the country linked to the wire services, upon whom they depended for the majority of their news. If the press associations provided radio with the news they needed, news could now bypass the newspapers, thus shifting the flow of news in society. Information would now move from the press associations through the radio to the public. Ultimately then, the anti-radio newspapers, which constituted the majority of the nation's papers, were fighting to retain their long-established role in the process of news distribution. It was a fight for self preservation. It was a fight that could only be won if all journalists banded together.

What was needed was alliance-building. The anti-radio journalists had to convince their pro-broadcasting colleagues of the dangers of radio. They argued that providing broadcasters with news posed a fundamental threat to the existence of all newspapers. This view was expressed, for example, in an *Editor and Publisher* article, "Giving News to Radio Viewed as Menace to Newspapers by Many Editors." In it, one editor stated that he did not think that the wire services, "which are created and operated for the main purpose of disseminating news to newspapers, should distribute news through radio" before newspapers have a chance to publish such news. Speaking of the press associations, he said that "their main customers, their original customers and the customers they are created to serve are the newspapers, and their first duty is to the newspapers." In the same article, Joseph Pulitzer took the position that "the news associations exist for the purpose of disseminating news to the public through the newspapers," and that therefore "only on rare occasions such as Presidential elections should the news be released for dissemination by radio prior to publication." We hear in both of these comments the clear assertion of a 'natural order' to the flow of news in the culture. According to this point of view, wire services provided the newspapers with news. If they changed this role, they were deviating from their 'true' identity.

Not everyone agreed. In 1928 the AP joined the other wire services in providing radio with election returns. This was in accordance with the AP rules that had been adopted 4 years earlier. But in the wake of the elections a number of journalists complained that this practice rendered their own papers obsolete. "It is not fair," one member complained, "for several hundred publishers to gather news and then have it given to the public before they are able to publish it themselves." Richard Jones, publisher of the Tulsa Tribune asked, "has the Associated Press decided to kill the newspaper business in the United States?" Charles Whaite, President of the Southern California Newspapers Association, said that it was beyond his comprehension "why the publishers of newspaper should be expected to pay the expense of gathering news and then turn it over free to a competitor."

An editorial in *Editor and Publisher* observed with anger that the newspaper industry "apparently, is only a queer kind of business which gives its product away to a competitor, and stands idly by to see a natural and rightful function supplanted." An expression of frustration came from Walter Humphreys of the Temple Telegram in Texas. "We fight the growing encroachment on our field by the radio," he complained, "only to have the news organization to which we belong turn around and help the radio thumb its nose at our honest efforts. Every bulletin we printed in our extra was second hand. The radio with the assistance of the Associated Press scooped us miserably." Humphrey's words convey the sense of betrayal many papers seem to have felt when the news for which they had paid was being turned over to the broadcasters, to be aired before the papers even had a chance to print it. . . .

Tipping the Scales

There were other factors as well. The fall of 1932 had brought yet another presidential election, and with it, once again, the matter of providing radio with election returns. The elections that year were characterized by a comical series of events in which the various wire services offered their services to the networks for a fee, then retracted their offers, and then ended up providing the returns for free. The nation's newspapers were quite upset, and the wire services received many letters of protest. Letters from small newspapers complained that by providing news of the election to the broadcasters, the Associated Press "had entered its service into direct competition with member newspapers." Richard Lloyd Jones, publisher of the Tulsa Tribune predicted that should the AP continue the policy it put into effect on election night, "it will become the best agency in the country to destroy the newspapers." Another letter, from Walter Humphreys of the Temple Telegram, a small newspaper in Texas, complained that the AP had "rendered all of our election activities . . . futile and helpless."

In response to the widespread protests to the provision of the networks with election returns both the AP and ANPA both polled of their membership. These surveys revealed strong opposition throughout the journalistic community to the practice of supplying radio with news of any kind. About 70 per cent of the AP members responding to the survey opposed giving news to the broadcasters. The minority in favor either owned or were affiliated with radio stations. Since all papers, large and small, held equal power when it came to voting on AP policy matters, the results of this survey suggested what the outcome would be when the membership brought this issue to a vote at its annual meeting in the following spring.

Meanwhile, a media event raised the saliency of the issue. In the first week of March 1932, Charles Lindbergh's infant son was kidnapped, and radio was there to cover the story live. According to the *New York Times*, nearly 700 bulletins were broadcast within the first 72 hours after the boy was reported missing. It was a big story, one that captured the nation's attention, and many journalists were upset once again to be scooped by the broadcasters. Print journalists also complained about the quality of the radio coverage itself, accusing the broadcasters of being inaccurate and sensationalist. One article in *Editor and Publisher* noted that the "problem of spot news broadcasting and the amount of harm caused by the frequent radio bulletins on the Lindbergh story" were the focus of "increasing debate among newspaper executives." Another article, just prior to the annual gathering of the AP and ANPA in April, predicted that the subject of competition with radio was likely to be a topic of heated discussion, "particularly since the situation has been aggravated by the recent spot broadcasting of news of the Lindbergh kidnapping by radio corporations with announcers at the scene of the activity."

Attacking the Enemy

By the time the various wire services and press associations came together for their annual conventions in Washington that year, they were ready to take action. In April of 1933 all three wire services agreed to cease providing radio with news bulletins. For the AP this meant that election returns and other items of "transcendent importance" would no longer be supplied. For the UP and the INS this meant a complete cessation of their long practice of giving news to radio for free. It seems that dissatisfaction among print journalists had reached a state of 'critical mass'. The anti-radio forces finally had their wish. Enough journalists had come to see radio as a threat to newspaper-wire service relations. The nation's journalists had agreed at last to put aside their differences and unite forces against radio, in order to protect the institutional structure of their industry. This meant the broadcasters were forced to find new ways of obtaining bulletins for their newscasts. By the fall of 1933, CBS established a full-fledged news division. NBC followed suit, on a much smaller scale. The networks were free at last, or so it seemed, from their dependence upon the print journalists for their news bulletins.

Print journalists could finally direct their energies toward a battle with the 'enemy'. United at last in the name of protecting their industry, the press now had to defend the boundaries of its territory. If they were to retain their control over the process of news gathering and dissemination, they had to find ways to prevent, or at least limit the development of broadcast journalism.

Successful military campaigns are conducted by attacking the enemy from several directions simultaneously. It seems the exertion of pressure from multiple points overcomes the opponent. So it was with this phase of the press-radio war. The 'attack' of the press on radio took three forms: political lobbying, economic boycott and legal action. For a time, it worked. So effective were the attacks of the print journalists that only a few months after the networks began broadcasting their own news, they appealed to the press to meet with them and negotiate a 'peace agreement'.

Using Political Pressure

What kind of pressure did the journalists use to get the broadcasters to the bargaining table? The answer to this question explains the Biltmore Agreement. Newspaper and broadcasting industry representatives met at the Hotel Biltmore in New York City. The meeting took place in early December of 1933, and was called in response to a telegram from William Paley, president of CBS, to the

ANPA. He had requested a meeting between the two industries for the purpose of ending "the long standing dispute as to news broadcasting," and suggested that perhaps it would be possible to work out a plan "whereby the broadcasters may have access to news without gathering it themselves, and under arrangements that would be mutually satisfactory." The very one-sided terms of the Biltmore Agreement suggested total surrender. The plan called for the networks to cease their news-gathering operations. In exchange they would be supplied, twice a day, with five-minute news bulletins. The material for these bulletins would be provided by the three wire services to a new Press Radio Bureau (PRB). The PRB would function as a 'clearinghouse' for the news bulletins. Its job would be to rewrite the wire service copy into radio news announcements. Restrictions were placed on the scheduling of these newscasts, to insure that the bulletins were aired several hours after the morning and evening papers reached the news stands. The bulletins were to be aired without commercial sponsorship. All costs of running the Press Radio Bureau were to be covered by the broadcasters. In other words, the networks agreed to give up gathering their own news, and acquiesced to full press control over the content and scheduling of their newscasts. They also agreed to foot the bill for the expenses of having the press control their news. Independent broadcasters, who were also represented at the Biltmore Conference, did not agree to the terms of this plan.

What compelled the networks to agree to such a restrictive arrangement? Apparently, a combination of political and economic pressure. In 1933, print journalists had the serendipity of timing on their side. The Roosevelt Administration was in the midst of plans to revise the 1927 Radio Act. The "window of opportunity" was open, so to speak, for major changes in the area of broadcast legislation. Bills such as the Wagner-Hatfield Act were on the Hill proposing changes in the spectrum allocation process that would give more frequencies to non-commercial stations. In fact, the very economic structure of commercial broadcast was under fire from various lobbying groups, such as the National Committee on Education by Radio, the ACLU and the AFL, who were working to have commercials eliminated from the airwaves altogether. Some of these same groups were starting to challenge the growing power of the networks and were beginning to ask questions about monopoly. Commercial radio, and network radio in particular, was under attack. If ever the publishers had an opportune moment to frighten the networks into cooperating with them, this was it. They threatened to join the fight against commercial broadcasting. . . .

Using Economic Pressure

In addition to the threat of political lobbying, the print journalists had another weapon: economic pressure. Newspapers threatened to cease publication of the networks' programme listings. The issue of whether or not the newspapers should publish these listings free of charge had, in fact, been a matter of debate for quite some time. Most were opposed to the practice on the grounds that it gave free publicity to the sponsors whose company names often appeared in the titles of radio programmes (like the A&P Gypsies, for example). Yet papers continued the practice because every time they tried to stop publishing the listings the public complained. Obviously, the publication of these programme logs was important to the networks, for it told listeners what was on the air. It was also important to the advertisers, who preferred backing programmes that got mentioned in the newspapers.

The publishers came to the Biltmore conference with an advantage that the broadcasters lacked: a united front. NBC had no real news gathering division to speak of, and thus had very little to lose by agreeing to the plan. Indeed, given the political climate of the time, NBC's vulnerability on the subject of monopoly meant that they had a great deal to lose if they refused the publishers' demands. CBS was willing to fight, but it could not do so alone. Journalists were ready to threaten CBS with a boycott of its program listings. If only NBC's shows were listed, there might be an exodus of advertisers from one network to another. CBS felt it had to cooperate.

In exchange for acquiescing to the terms of the Biltmore plan, the networks were assured that newspapers would continue to publish all programme listings in full. As NBC president Merlin Aylesworth explained, "there was a general feeling on the part of the radio broadcasters that this cooperative experiment would result in all of the newspapers of the country rendering a program service . . . to the vast number of readers who listen to radio." Similarly, an article in *Broadcasting* reported that the networks were "virtually forced" into an agreement with the publishers in order to avoid seeing the majority of the nation's papers "eliminate all program listings and wage a bitter war on radio generally."

It was this combined threat of losing the programme listings and being faced with a "bitter war" from the newspapers that brought broadcasters to the negotiating table. Indeed, according to one article, several weeks before the Biltmore meeting the National Radio Committee of the ANPA, representing "the majority of the 1,800 daily papers in the United States," had approached the networks saying that they were ready to "ban together not only to eliminate radio program listings but to carry on a fight in Congress and in their columns against radio."

It may appear ironic that the journalists would have pressured the broadcasters into accepting an arrangement that involved wire service provision of news to radio. After all, the press spent nearly a decade of internal debate over whether to supply the broadcasters with bulletins. But now the process was under their control. Indeed, the Biltmore Agreement gave the journalists the best of both worlds. The terms of the arrangement stopped the development of network news. Once they formed an internal alliance, print journalists convinced broadcasters to yield control.

At the Biltmore Conference the press had achieved an important victory. Winning a battle, however, does not necessarily mean winning a war. Independent broadcasters had left the meeting without signing the agreement. This left the press with a serious problem, for only about 150 of the nation's 600 radio stations were network owned or affiliated. They lacked financial clout, but had the strength of numbers.

Independent stations needed a new source for their news. Before long, several news gathering agencies emerged to fill it. These were essentially wire services for radio reporters who gathered their own news and provided bulletins to the broadcasters by telegraph and teletype. Unlike the PRB however, these services placed no limitations on the time of day the newscasts could be aired, nor did they prohibit the stations from airing the news with commercials. The most successful was the Transradio Press Service, which had over 150 subscribers after only nine months of operation. Staffed largely by former employees of the CBS news division, Transradio had reporters in cities nationwide and soon posed serious competition for the PRB.

Protecting Intellectual Property

There was nothing that the press could do. There was no legal justification for taking action against Transradio simply for providing radio with news. What the journalists could do however, was to closely monitor the broadcasters for any violations of rules governing the flow of news. The press feared that the independent broadcasters might 'steal' news from the wire services or the newspapers. This would have constituted a violation of intellectual property rights laws governing news, and was grounds for legal action. The press shifted its attack strategy from a political and economic approach to a legal one. On the lookout for violations, they placed the broadcasters under close surveillance and took legal action when they found what they felt were infractions of the laws governing information use. . . .

When Yankee News Service, one of the first independent radio news associations, began operations, Editor and Publisher reported that several Boston newspapers were "keeping close check on the radio news service to determine the character of its bulletins and also if there is any duplication of their own contents." So great were the fears of news theft that some newspapers and wire services even made recordings of broadcasts to determine whether any news items had been taken from the press. As Abe Schechter, news writer for Lowell Thomas at NBC explained, they "were making a practice of keeping a stenographic record of our news broadcasts; in some cases they even recorded our newscasts on discs so they could check back and see whether we had swiped anything."

The broadcasters claimed that they were being falsely accused of wrongdoing. It seems, however, that their pleas of innocence were received with skepticism. This is evident from the fact that numerous articles appeared in the press trade journals at this time characterizing radio as a thief. In *Editor and Publisher*, for instance, broadcasters were accused of "filching" and "lifting" the news from newspapers. Similarly, the American Press wrote of the attempts of a radio station to "chisel" news from local papers for broadcasting purposes. At a meeting of the Inland Daily Press Association in 1933, a discussion was held about how to prevent broadcasters from getting news from newspapers and "bootlegging" it over the radio. The ANPA complained that broadcasters were "appropriating" the news without the consent of the publishers, and the Southern Newspaper Publishers Association portrayed the radio news commentators as being engaged in "news pilfering." This phrase also appeared in another report from the ANPA, which stated emphatically that publishers "should not tolerate a situation in which there is a general pilfering of our news."

Taking Legal Action

A number of lawsuits were filed by newspapers and press associations accusing radio of violating their property rights. Some of these cases included: *AP v. KSOO* (1933), a joint suit by four New Orleans newspapers against WDSU (1933), and *AP v. KVOS* (1935). In both cases the press charged that in making use of news taken from either the papers or wire services, the broadcasters were appropriating news that did not belong to them. In both cases the courts ruled in favor of the press.

After a number of cases in the lower courts, one of these radio news piracy suits reached the Supreme Court. In 1935, issuing a ruling in favour of the AP in *AP v. KVOS*, the Supreme Court established, as it had in the INS case, that those who gathered the news were entitled to protection from use of that news by competing news agencies. Federal policy had been reaffirmed regarding the control over the flow of news. Through the enforcement of established rules governing the use of news, the journalism industry was able to retain control over the information that flowed through its channels. Thus the use of legal action proved to be an effective means of protecting institutional territory.

In the end, of course, the press lost their war against radio. After the PRB had been in operation for just over a year, the success of Transradio Press attracted the attention of UP and INS. They wanted to compete for revenue available from the sale of news to radio. Both pulled out of their coalition with the AP in the spring of 1935, making their news available to the broadcasters once again. Once the united front collapsed, the nation's newspapers lost their power to hinder the development of broadcast journalism. In addition, an increasing number of newspapers bought radio stations, drawn by the economic promise of broadcasting. In the period between 1934 and 1938, for example, the number of newspaper owned or affiliated stations more than doubled, from 100 to 211. With the collapse of the wire service coalition, the broadcasters were free to develop their own news divisions. Although the PRB continued for another 3 years before dying quietly in 1938, the battle between the old and new institutions of news dissemination was over at last.

With the advent of radio news, the institution governing the gathering and dissemination of news in this country was changed forever. The arrival of this new medium posed a serious challenge to the established institutional structure of journalism. While neither newspapers nor wire services went out of business, they lost their monopolistic control over the flow of news to the American public. Radio, with its capacity to transmit news instantaneously to a mass audience, fundamentally changed the information ecology of the nation. Change triumphed over resistance. The broadcasters won the press-radio war. But for a time, the print journalists fought hard to block the development of a new medium of information transmission. And their fight offers important insights into the nature of inter-industry conflict in the communications industry at the time of technological innovation.

Martians Invade the Airwaves in 1938

Edward Oxford

In the following article, historical writer Edward Oxford tells the story of the most famous radio show ever broadcast: Orson Welles's adaptation of H.G. Wells's *The War of the Worlds*. Oxford explains that in an attempt to achieve authenticity, Welles and his associates prepared a radio adaptation of the science-fiction novel that many listeners believed was an actual Martian invasion. Providing excerpts from the actual broadcast, Oxford demonstrates how the show could deceive so many listeners. He also relates often humorous stories of audience reactions. Once the broadcast was over, Oxford explains, controversy followed, and commentators debate to this day what the audience reaction means about the impact of the media.

A little after eight P.M. on Halloween eve 1938, thirteen-year-old Dick Stives, his sister, and two brothers huddled around their family's radio. They were in the dining room of their grandfather's farmhouse near the hamlet of Grovers Mill, four miles east of Princeton, New Jersey. Their mother and father had dropped them off there and gone to the movies.

Tuning In on Sunday Night

Dick worked the radio dial, hunting for the station that carried the *Chase and Sanborn Hour,* his—and the nation's—favorite Sunday evening program. As he scanned the airwaves, Dick tuned in the local affiliate of the Columbia Broadcasting System (CBS). A commanding voice—that of Orson Welles—riveted his attention.

". . . across an immense ethereal gulf, minds that are to our minds as ours are to the beasts of the jungle, intellects vast, cool, and unsympathetic, regarded this earth with envious eyes and slowly and surely drew their plans against us. . . ."

Dick Stives turned the dial no further. Instead, during the next hour he and millions of other listeners sat glued by their radios, convinced by an alarming series of "news bulletins" that monster aliens from Mars were invading America. Dick's village of Grovers Mill—the supposed landing site for these invaders—became the focal point of a panic wave that rapidly swept across the nation.

The program—the *Mercury Theatre on the Air* adaptation of H.G. Wells's *The War of the Worlds*—would later be remembered as the most extraordinary radio show ever broadcast. And Orson Welles, its brilliant young producer, director, and star, would be catapulted to nationwide fame overnight. . . .

For the next unforgettable hour, Dick Stives at Grovers Mill, along with several million other Americans, sat transfixed as the airwaves brought word of weird and almost incomprehensible events that seemed to unfold with terrifying reality even as they listened.

It was not as though listeners hadn't been warned. Most simply didn't pay close attention to the program's opening signature (or tuned in a few seconds late and missed it altogether): "The Columbia Broadcasting System and its affiliated stations present Orson Welles and the Mercury Theatre on the Air in *The War of the Worlds* by H.G. Wells. . . ."

Many in the radio audience failed to associate what they heard with prior newspaper listings of the drama. And, by the time a single station break came late in the hour with reminders that listeners were hearing a fictional story, many others were too agitated to comprehend that they had been deceived.

"Orchestrating" the Illusion

Skillfully choreographed by Orson Welles and John Houseman, the program—a play simulating a montage of real-life dance band "remotes" and news bulletins—began with deliberate calm. Millions of listeners, conditioned by recent news reports of worldwide political turmoil—and by their inherent trust in the medium of radio—believed what they heard.

Just two minutes into the show, audience perception between fantasy and reality began to blur when, following Welles's dramatic opening monologue, the microphone shifted to a "network announcer" reading an apparently routine report from the "Government Weather Bureau."

Programming then shifted to "Ramon Raquello and his orchestra" in the "Meridian Room" at the "Hotel Park Plaza" in downtown New York City.

During rehearsals for the show, Welles had insisted—over the objections of his associates—on increasing the broadcast time devoted to the fictional orchestra's soothing renditions of "La Cumparsita" and "the everpopular 'Stardust.'" As he had anticipated, the resulting "band remote" had a disarming air of reality—and provided emotional contrast to the intensity of later news bulletins.

Just when Welles had calculated that listeners might start tuning out the music in search of something more lively, an announcer broke in with a bulletin from the "Intercontinental Radio News": "Professor Farrell of the Mount Jennings Observatory" near Chicago had reported observing "several explosions of incandescent gas occurring at regular intervals on the planet Mars. . . . The spectroscope indicates the gas to be hydrogen and moving towards the earth with tremendous velocity."

The dance music resumed, only to be interrupted repeatedly during the next several minutes by other bulletins. The tempo of events—and listeners' interest—began to intensify.

From a "remote pickup" at the "Princeton Observatory," reporter "Carl Phillips" interviewed famous astronomer "Richard Pierson" (played by Welles). As the clockwork mechanism of his telescope ticked in the background, Professor Pierson described Mars as a red disk swimming in a blue sea. He said he could not explain the gas eruptions on that planet. But skeptical of anything that could not be explained by logic, the astronomer counted the chances against living intelligence on Mars as being "a thousand to one."

Then Phillips read a wire that had just been handed to Pierson: a seismograph at the "Natural History Museum" in New York had registered a "shock of almost earthquake intensity occurring within a radius of twenty miles of Princeton." Pierson played down any possible connection with the disturbances on Mars: "This is probably a meteorite of unusual size and its arrival at this particular time is merely a coincidence."

Again the program returned to music, followed by yet another bulletin: an astronomer in Canada had observed three explosions on Mars, confirming "earlier reports from American observatories."

"Now, nearer home," continued the announcer, "comes a special announcement from Trenton, New Jersey. It is reported that at 8:50 P.M. a huge, flaming object, believed to be a meteorite, fell on a farm in the neighborhood of Grovers Mill, New Jersey, twenty-two miles from Trenton. The flash in the sky was visible within a radius of several hundred miles and the noise of impact was heard as far north as Elizabeth."

Listeners leaned closer to their sets. In Grovers Mill, Dick Stives stared at the radio and gulped.

Gathering Listeners

Again the broadcast returned to dance music—this time to "Bobby Millette and his orchestra" at the "Hotel Martinet" in Brooklyn. And again the music was interrupted by a news flash. Having just arrived at the scene of "impact" on the "Wilmuth farm" near Grovers Mill, reporter Carl Phillips, accompanied by Professor Pierson, beheld police, state troopers, and onlookers crowding around what appeared to be a huge metallic cylinder, partially buried in the earth.

About this time, some twelve minutes into the broadcast, many listeners to the *Chase and Sanborn Hour*, momentarily bored by a guest musical spot, turned their dials. A lot of them stopped in sudden shock as they came upon the CBS wavelength. The events being described seemed real to listeners—quite as real to them as reports, not many months before, that Adolf Hitler's troops had marched into Austria.

"I wish I could convey the atmosphere . . . the background of this . . . fantastic scene," reported Phillips. "Hundreds of cars are parked in a field back of us. . . . Their headlights throw an enormous spot on the pit where the object is half-buried. Some of the more daring souls are venturing near the edge. Their silhouettes stand out against the metal sheen. . . ."

Professor Pierson described the object as "definitely extraterrestrial . . . not found on this earth. . . . This thing is smooth and, as you can see, of cylindrical shape." Then Phillips suddenly interrupted him:

"Just a minute! Something's happening! Ladies and gentlemen, this is terrific! This end of the thing is beginning to flake off! The top is beginning to rotate like a screw! The thing must be hollow! [shouts of alarm] Ladies and gentlemen, this is the most terrifying thing I have ever witnessed. . . . Wait a minute! Someone's crawling out of the hollow top. Someone or . . . something. I can see peering out of that black hole two luminous disks—are they eyes? Good heavens, something's wriggling out of the shadow like a gray snake. . . . I can see the thing's body. It's large as a bear and it glistens like wet leather. But that face. It . . . it's indescribable. I can hardly force myself to keep looking at it. The eyes are black and gleam like a serpent. The mouth is V-shaped with saliva dripping from its rimless lips that seem to quiver and pulsate. . . ."

Thirty state troopers, according to the reporter, now formed a cordon around the pit where the object rested. Three policemen carrying a white handkerchief of truce walked toward the cylinder. Phillips continued:

"Wait a minute . . . something's happening. [high-pitched, intermittent whine of machinery] A humped shape is rising out of the pit. I can make out a small beam of light against a mirror. . . . What's that? There's a jet of flame springing from the mirror, and it leaps right at the advanc-

The Golden Age of Sound Effects

In this excerpt taken from The Nostalgia Digest, *Todd Nebel reflects on the hard work and imagination of radio sound effects operators.*

During the golden age of radio, listener's imagination depended upon the sound effects which were presented in such a way that visual images in the mind was the final result. Much of this imagery depended upon the power of suggestion by actors in the radio program to achieve the desired effect. . . .

The sound effects operator had to have a good sense of rhythm, a working knowledge of music, appreciate dramatic values, know radio engineering and technique, be eager to experiment with new sounds, and be coordinated with good sense of timing.

From his position on the radio program stage he had to work closely with his director, all the while keeping an eye on the script which he was following. Many made a habit with their scripts of circling their cues in red pencil with additional markings of where the sound was to peak and where it was to be faded out. Many usually made the effort of practicing for hours on end with new sound effect ideas and getting the presentation of sounds just right for their performance. He also had to be a quick study with absolute dependability and have the ability to memorize cues in order that no time would be lost during the broadcast. It

ing men! It strikes them head on! Good Lord, they're turning into flame! [screams and shrieks] Now the whole field
by the woods has caught fire! [sound effects intensify] The
gas tanks, tanks of automobiles . . . it's spreading everywhere! It's coming this way now! About twenty yards to
my right [abrupt silence]."

Now terror was afoot. A series of voices—fictional "announcers," "militia commanders," "network vice presidents," and "radio operators"—took up the narrative. At
least forty people, according to the radio bulletins, lay dead

---

was none too easy to have 50 to 60 cues per program and be prepared with effect in hand for each one! Before the broadcast
many sound effects operators would arrange each effect or apparatus in the order in which it was to be used. Everything was
therefore at hand so that no time was wasted in getting it to the
microphone. The microphone was usually positioned on stage
with the actors and actresses in order that the sound effects could
be heard by them and they could thereby recognize and react to
the effect. All the while during the progress of the show the
sound engineer took his cues from the producer in the control
room who was hearing the entire show as one package. As a matter of record (although I have used the masculine pronoun to describe them), many sound effects operators during the golden age
of radio were women.

Every time the sound operator had created and proven satis-
factorily a new sound which was suitable as an effect for broadcast, he usually catalogued it and recorded it—no matter how
unimportant it may have seemed at the time. This way the studio's library of sound would have a sound effect on hand the next
time it might be needed for broadcast. Many of the more prominent "manual" sound effects used during the golden age of radio
were used on up till the demise of network radio and the advent
of television.

Todd Nebel, "The Golden Age of Sound Effects," *The Nostalgia Digest.*

at Grovers Mill, "their bodies burned and distorted beyond all possible recognition." And in a Trenton hospital, "the charred body of Carl Phillips" had been identified.

Spreading Fear

A current of fear flowed outward across the nation. Real-life police switchboards, first in New Jersey, then, steadily, throughout the whole Northeast, began to light up: "What's happening?" "Who's attacking America?" "When will they be here?" "What can we do?" "Who are they—these Martians?"

By now, according to the broadcast, "eight battalions of infantry" had surrounded the cylinder, determined to destroy it. A "Captain Lansing" of the "Signal Corps"—calm and confident at first, but with obviously increasing alarm—described what happened next:

"Well, we ought to see some action soon. One of the companies is deploying on the left flank. A quick thrust and it'll all be over. Wait a minute, I see something on top of the cylinder. No, it's nothing but a shadow. . . . Seven thousand armed men closing in on an old metal tube. Tub, rather. Wait, that wasn't a shadow. It's something moving . . . solid metal. Kind of a shield-like affair rising up out of the cylinder! It's going higher and higher! Why, it's . . . it's standing on legs! Actually rearing up on a sort of metal framework! Now it's reaching above the trees and searchlights are on it! Hold on [abrupt silence]."

In a matter of moments, a studio "announcer" gave America the incredible news:

". . . Those strange beings who landed in the Jersey farmlands tonight are the vanguard of an invading army from the planet Mars. The battle which took place tonight at Grovers Mill has ended in one of the most startling defeats ever suffered by an army in modern times; seven thousand men armed with rifles and machine guns pitted against a single fighting machine of the invaders from Mars. One hundred and twenty known survivors. The rest strewn over the battle area from Grovers Mill to Plains-boro crushed and trampled to death under the metal feet of the monster, or burned to cinders by its heat ray. . . ."

Grovers Mill's couple of hundred real-life residents hardly knew what to make of it all. Young Dick Stives was stunned. He and his sister and brothers pulled down the shades in the farmhouse. Their grandfather shoved chairs against the doors.

Teen-aged Lolly Dey, who heard about the "invasion" while attending a church meeting, consoled herself by saying: "I am in the Lord's House." Another resident, seeing what he thought to be a Martian war machine among the trees (actually a water tower on a neighbor's property), peppered it with shotgun blasts. One man packed his family into the car, bound for parts unknown. He backed right through his garage door. "We're never gonna be needing that again anyway," he muttered to his wife.

"The monster is now in control of the middle section of New Jersey," proclaimed the voice on the radio. "Communication lines are down from Pennsylvania to the Atlantic Ocean. Railroad tracks are torn and service from New York to Philadelphia discontinued. . . . Highways to the north, south, and west are clogged with frantic human traffic. Police and army reserves are unable to control the mad flight. . . ."

Life was soon to imitate art. A wave of terror, unprecedented in its scope and rapidity, swept across New Jersey. A New Brunswick man, bound for open country, had driven ten miles when he remembered that his dog was tied up in the backyard of his home. Daring the Martians, he drove back to retrieve the dog.

A West Orange bar owner pushed customers out into the street, locked his tavern door, and rushed home to rescue his wife and children.

Twenty families began to move their belongings out of a Newark apartment house, their faces covered by wet towels to repel Martian rays. Doctors and nurses volunteered to come to hospitals to help handle the "war casualties."

At Princeton University, the chairman of the geology department packed his field equipment and headed into the night to look for whatever it was that was out there. The governor of Pennsylvania offered to send troops to help New Jersey. A Jersey City man called a bus dispatcher to warn him of the fast-spreading "disaster." He cut their conversation short with: "The world is coming to an end and I have a lot to do!"

Meanwhile, on the radio, the "Secretary of the Interior," speaking in a voice much like that of President Franklin D. Roosevelt, announced that he had faith in the ability of the American military to vanquish the Martians. He solemnly intoned:

". . . placing our trust in God we must continue the performance of our duties each and every one of us, so that we may confront this destructive adversary with a nation united, courageous, and consecrated to the preservation of human supremacy on this earth."

A Trenton store owner ran out screaming, "The world is ending! The world is ending!" Another man dashed into a motion-picture theater in Orange, crying out that "the state is being invaded! This place is going to be blown up!" The audience hurriedly ran out to the street.

A woman in a Newark tenement just sat and cried. "I thought it was all up with us," she said. A man driving westward called out to a patrolman: "All creation's busted loose! I'm getting out!"

More grim reports issued from the radio. Scouting planes, according to the broadcast, had sighted three Martian machines marching through New Jersey. They were uprooting power lines, bridges, and railroad tracks, with the apparent objectives of crushing resistance and paralyzing communications. In swamps twenty miles south of Morristown, coon hunters had stumbled upon a second Martian cylinder.

In the Watchung mountains, the "22nd Field Artillery" set down a barrage against six tripod monsters—to no avail. The machines soon let loose a heavy black poisonous gas, annihilating the artillerymen. Then eight army bombers from "Langham Field, Virginia," attacked the tripod machines, only to be downed by heat rays.

Thousands of telephone calls cascaded into radio stations, newspaper offices, power companies, fire houses, and military posts throughout the country. People wanted to know what to do . . . where to go . . . whether they were safer in the cellar or the attic.

Word spread in Atlanta that a "planet" had struck New Jersey. In Philadelphia, all the guests in one hotel checked out. Students at a college in North Carolina lined up at telephones to call their parents for the last time. When a caller reached the CBS switchboard, the puzzled operator, asked about the end of the world, said: "I'm sorry, we don't have that information.". . .

The Grand Finale

Forty minutes into the broadcast, Welles gave his distraught audience a breather—a pause for station and program identification.

In the control room, CBS staffer Richard Goggin was startled as telephones there began to ring. That would only happen in an emergency. "Tension was becoming enormous in Studio One," he later recalled. "They had a tiger by the tail and couldn't let go."

For those brave enough to stay tuned, Welles was able to match the program's stunning first portion with an equally remarkable concluding sequence. In what amounted to a twenty-minute soliloquy, he, in the role of Professor Pierson, chronicled the events that followed the Martians' destruction of New York City. Welles's spellbinding voice—magnetic, doom-filled, stirring—held listeners mesmerized.

In the script, a stoic Pierson, still alive in the rubble, made his solitary way toward the ruins of New York, hiding from the invaders as he went. . . .

The joke was on the listeners. More than one hundred and fifty stations affiliated with CBS had carried the broadcast. About twelve million people had heard the program. Newspapers estimated that at least a million listeners, perhaps many more, had thought the invasion real.

Back in Grovers Mill, disenchantment began to take hold. Twenty-year-old Sam Goldman and three pals had been playing cards when they heard that the Martians were on the move down by the mill. They had thrown down their cards and jumped into a car, ready to face the invaders. "We got there and looked around," Sam said, "and nothing was going on."

A squad of New Jersey state troopers equipped with riot guns had deployed near the crossroads. They found little more than the dilapidated old mill itself.

Nearby, in their grandfather's farmhouse, Dick Stives, his sister, and brothers talked excitedly about the "men from Mars." Then their mother and father came home from the movies and told the children about the "make believe" on radio that everyone was talking about. Dick, more confused than ever, went upstairs to go to sleep, still half-sure that what he heard was "really real."

A Surprise for the Cast

For the players who had inadvertently just made radio history, the next hours turned into a nightmare. As soon as Welles left the twenty-second-floor studio, he was called to a telephone. He picked it up, to hear the irate mayor of Flint, Michigan, roar that his city was in chaos because of the program and that he, the mayor, would soon be on his way to New York to punch one Orson Welles in the nose.

"By nine o'clock several high-ranking CBS executives had arrived or were in full flight toward 485 Madison. We were in trouble," recalled Larry Harding, a CBS production supervisor for the *Mercury Theatre* show.

Policemen hurried into the CBS building. Welles, Houseman, and the cast were held under informal house arrest. Staffers hastily stashed scripts, memoranda, and the sixteen-inch acetate disks upon which the show had been recorded.

Welles was taken to a room on the seventeenth floor, where reporters battered him with questions about whether he knew of the deaths and suicides his broadcast had caused (none have ever been documented), whether he knew ahead of time how devastating an effect his show would have (he said he didn't), and whether he had planned it all as a publicity stunt (he said he hadn't).

Finally, at about one o'clock Monday morning, Welles and the cast were "released," free to go out into the streets of New York where not a Martian was stirring. Welles walked a half-dozen blocks to the Mercury Theatre, where, even at that hour, members of the stage company were still rehearsing their new play.

Welles went up on stage, where news photographers were lurking. They caught him with his eyes raised, his arms outstretched. The next day his photograph appeared in newspapers throughout the country, over a caption that blurted: "I Didn't Know What I Was Doing!", or words to that effect.

The next morning headlines in major city newspapers reported the hoax: "Radio Listeners in Panic, Taking War Drama as Fact" (*New York Times*); "U.S. Terrorized By Radio's 'Men From Mars'" (*San Francisco Chronicle*); "Radio Drama Causes Panic" (*Philadelphia Inquirer*); "Listeners Weep and Pray, Prepare for End of World" (*New Orleans Times-Picayune*).

Many of the listeners who had been deluded laughed good-naturedly at one another—and at themselves. Some professed not to have been taken in by what one woman called "that Buck Rogers stuff." But others turned their wrath on Welles, on the network, and on the medium that had turned their Sunday evening into a time of unsolicited terror.

CBS apologized to the public, but also pointed out that during the program no fewer than four announcements had been made stating that it was a dramatic presentation, not a news broadcast.

A subdued Welles, believing his career was ruined, dutifully followed suit. "I don't think we will try anything like this again," he stated.

For two or three days, the press would not let Welles, nor radio, off the front page. Media rivalry played its part;

newspaper publishers seemed anxious to portray radio—and Welles—as villains. The clipping bureau that served CBS delivered condemnatory editorials by the pound.

While newsmen "tsk-tsked," government officials fumed. Senator Clyde Herring of Iowa, reflecting the anger of many citizens, stated his support for legislation to curb such "Halloween bogymen." The Federal Communications Commission (FCC), flooded with complaint letters, tried to find a philosophical stance somewhere between imposing severe censorship and permitting unbridled expression.

Novelist H.G. Wells cabled his disregards from London. Although he had given CBS permission to air his novel, he complained that "it was not explained to me that this dramatization would be made with a liberty that amounts to a complete reworking of *The War of the Worlds*."

Realizing the Implications

But some columnists and editorialists began to perceive significant merit in the program. Essayist Heywood Broun interpreted the broadcast as a cautionary tale: "Jitters have come home to roost. The peace of Munich hangs heavy over our heads like a thundercloud." *Variety*, under a headline stating "Radio Does U.S. A Favor," described the program as a warning to Americans of the danger of unpreparedness.

In a column that turned the tide of public opinion in favor of Welles and company, Dorothy Thompson called the broadcast "the news story of the century—an event which made a greater contribution to an understanding of Hitlerism, Mussolinism, Stalinism, anti-Semitism, and all the other terrorism of our time than all the words about them that have been written by reasonable men."

Welles, to his relief, soon learned that he would not be consigned to durance vile [imprisonment]. "Bill Paley, the head of CBS, brought Orson and me up on the carpet and gave us a reprimand," Houseman later recalled. "But there was ambivalence to it. The working stiffs thought we were heroes. The executives thought of us as some sort of anarchists. But reason—and revenues—prevailed. A few days after the broadcast, when it was announced that Campbell's Soup had become a sponsor, the boys at the top began to think of us as heroes, or at least as employable persons, as well."

Some critics continued to decry the credulity of the American people. They spoke of the compelling power of the human voice emanating from the upper air. Radio, ominously, seemed able to reduce an entire country to the size of one room; it exerted unexpected power over susceptible millions.

For a book-length study titled *The Invasion from Mars,* Princeton University psychology professor Hadley Cantril interviewed scores of persons who had listened to the program. Speaking with them shortly after "that night," he received responses ranging from insecure to phobic to fatalistic.

"The coming of the Martians did not present a situation where the individual could preserve one value if he sacrifices another," Professor Cantril concluded from his research. "In this situation the individual stood to lose all his values at once. Nothing could be done to save any of them. Panic was inevitable."

Did Welles intend the panic? Had he hoped, by means of his magnificent dramatic powers, to gain all those headlines?

Houseman dismisses such conjecture as "rubbish." He declares: "Orson and I had no clear pre-sense of the mood of the audience. *The War of the Worlds* wasn't selected as a parable of invasion and war in the 1930s, but just as an interesting story unto itself. Only after the fact did we perceive how ready and resonant the world was for the tale. Our intent was theatre, not terror."

Welles and his players could not know that they had portrayed the shape of things to come. The program was, in a way, quite prophetic. Barely two weeks later, German foreign minister Joachim von Ribbentrop chillingly commented: "I would not be surprised if in the United States eye-witness reports are under consideration in which the

'Giants from Mars' marched up in brown shirts waving swastika flags."

Sooner than the peoples of the world could guess, a true nightmare—that of World War II—would be upon them.

Welles, of course, went on to memorable successes in motion pictures and theater. And his *War of the Worlds* broadcast became the most famous radio program of all time.

Talk Radio in the 1930s

Stephen Goode

Talk radio is nothing new. In fact, writes Stephen Goode, some of the most popular programming of the thirties was the political and social commentary of Father Charles W. Coughlin and Will Rogers. Goode describes the very different personalities and politics of these two radio personalities from Father Coughlin's serious conservatism to Rogers's casual and conversational liberalism. Goode is a staff writer for *Insight on the News*, an investigative weekly news magazine.

If you arrived at the home of almost any average American family in the evening during the 1930s, it's likely they'd be gathered around their radios. It probably would have been a console model—an Atwater Kent, for example, or a Philco—and it would have been the most prominent piece of furniture in the living room.

America's Relationship with the Radio

Family values were in. One of the era's most popular shows, *One Man's Family,* reached an estimated 28 million listeners (out of a total population of about 125 million) every Wednesday at 8 P.M. on the NBC network. At the beginning of the widely heard program, an announcer's voice said the show was "dedicated to the mothers and fathers of the younger generation and to their bewildering offspring.

In the 1930s, "radio was a companion. It was something very much like a friend, and people had a warm place in their hearts for it in ways we'd find schmaltzy and a bit simple," says Philip J. Harwood, an associate professor of communications at the University of Dayton in Ohio who specializes in the history of broadcasting.

Amos 'n' Andy, a comedy show about two black characters—performed, incidentally, by two white guys—also was wildly popular. Almost every American knew radio singer Kate Smith's great songs, "When the Moon Comes Over the Mountain" and "God Bless America." The telephone number most likely to be readily recognized by the average American was Murray Hill 8-9933, which is the number anyone could use to call the *Major Bowes Amateur Hour* and register a vote on the performers who had appeared on that evening's program.

On Sunday, March 12, 1933, only a few days after becoming the nation's 32nd president, Franklin Delano Roosevelt (FDR) launched his "fireside chats" over radio from the White House. The public listened—and approved. His wife, Eleanor, later had her own biweekly talk program, sponsored by Pond's cold cream and Sweetheart soap, among others.

The Emergence of Radio Commentary

But often more frequently heard that even FDR's popular chats or his wife's trilling broadcasts were two programs of commentary and opinion—Fr. Charles W. Coughlin's *The Golden Hour of the Little Flower* and *The Good Gulf Show,* hosted by the enormously influential and widely admired "cowboy entertainer," Will Rogers.

Why their enormous popularity? "For the first time, radio allowed Americans to get to know or at least feel they knew people like Coughlin and Rogers as genuinely human persons," says Harwood. "That was the power of radio."

In 1934, Coughlin, a Roman Catholic priest originally from Canada, was getting more mail than the president (or anyone else in the country), writes historian William Manchester in his narrative history of America from 1932 through 1972, *The Power and the Dream.* That meant about 80,000 letters every week, according to Manchester. But when the "Radio Priest" (as the press dubbed him) delivered an especially strong polemic—the program, broadcast from Coughlin's home church in Detroit and aired from 6 P.M. to 7 P.M., CST, on CBS—it meant as many as 1 million letters, requiring a staff of 150 clerks to sort them (and gather an average of $20,000 per week in contributions). Stating what perhaps was obvious to most, *Fortune* magazine in 1932 called Coughlin's program "just about the biggest thing that ever happened to radio."

Rogers, too, had a sizeable audience. He already was a national celebrity when he launched his program on NBC in 1933, a half-hour on Sunday evenings right after Coughlin's program. Ben Yagoda, one of Rogers' biographers, notes that the week after the program began Protestant ministers across the country complained about a 50 percent decline in attendance at Sunday-evening services. It was a problem solved by one clergyman who brought a radio to church, placed it in the sanctuary and allowed his congregation to listen to the program during prayer breaks, according to Yagoda.

On at least one occasion Coughlin and Rogers joined in a common effort. It was to urge the American people to reject Roosevelt's appeal to the Senate for the United States to adhere to decisions handed down by the World Court. Neither man liked the idea and both said so loudly enough that FDR's appeal was rejected. Coughlin, pointing to his 45 million regular listeners, claimed to have been the decisive voice in turning public opinion against the president.

Two Unique Men with Different Opinions

But in style and in their opinions on most issues Rogers and Coughlin stood very far apart, and their radio shows were as unalike as they possibly could be. The grandiloquent, sonorous Coughlin was passionate, intense and a chain-smoker. Rogers was so laid back, plainspoken and homespun that despite his wealth and success on Broadway and in Hollywood, most people were convinced he'd never really left his home in east Oklahoma where he'd been raised in Indian territory in the humblest of backgrounds.

Coughlin—whom historian Manchester calls "a natural television talkshow host"—got his start in radio in 1926 after the Ku Klux Klan burned down his parish church in the Detroit suburb of Royal Oak. The director of a local station took pity and offered the priest time on the air to raise funds to rebuild the church. By 1930 *The Golden Hour of the Little Flower* was reaching millions of Americans nationwide via 17 CBS stations. When CBS dropped Coughlin in 1932 as too controversial, the priest immediately organized a radio network of more than 60 stations to carry his program.

During the early years of the Great Depression, Coughlin denounced capitalism as evil. Often, his talks were written to order by students at Washington's Brookings Institution, according to historian Arthur Schlesinger Jr. in his book *The Politics of Upheaval*.

Coughlin was an early supporter of Roosevelt and the New Deal, arguing in his radio sermons that the choice for America was "Roosevelt or Ruin," a slogan he changed in the mid-1930s, after he had become virulently anti-FDR, to read "Roosevelt and Ruin." At the same time, his anti-Semitism coming to the fore, Coughlin began calling the New Deal the "Jew Deal" and to urge listeners to invest (as Coughlin did himself) in silver, the "Gentile metal."

In the late 1930s, Coughlin went so far as publicly to denounce people who criticized Adolf Hitler. By criticizing the German dictator, Coughlin said, Americans were "breeding international bad feeling." Such statements won him denunciations from the Roman Catholic hierarchy in the United States. "We do not like to hear almost hysterical addresses from ecclesiastics," said Cardinal O'Connell of Boston, where Coughlin was very popular. But by 1942, when his Church superiors ordered Coughlin to silence, most of his once enormous listening audience had abandoned him.

When Rogers began his radio show for Gulf Oil Co. in 1933, he already was a famous movie star and America's most widely read newspaper columnist. The $50,000 he received for his first seven half-hour programs Rogers divided between the Red Cross and the Salvation Army. Uncomfortable performing in an empty studio, he brought an audience to watch him before the microphone and respond to his comments, even though he complained on radio that the studio audience laughed in the wrong places, thinking they had to laugh everywhere so they'd get invited back.

Where Coughlin's sermons were laboriously prepared, Rogers was spontaneous and disorganized, "full of 'you know's' and 'well's,' rampaging non sequiturs, infectious giggles and mid-sentence changes of subject," according to Rogers biographer Yagoda. During the week, Rogers would make notes and practice his ideas before friends and family—then throw the notes away before he arrived at the studio.

Rogers was a conservative Democrat but liked the affable FDR, praising the president for his personal leadership during hard times. Interestingly, the Oklahoma cowboy advised the president to lay off radio for at least a year after coming to office—advice Roosevelt luckily didn't heed, since FDR's chats were immediately as popular as they were reassuring.

The Freedom of Radio

Yagoda says Rogers was freer on the air than anywhere else, censoring himself less than he did in his newspaper columns. Thus Rogers, who was part Cherokee, said on radio in one of his ironic and humorous rambles: "Our record with the Indians is going to go down in history. It is going to make us might' proud of it in the future when our children of 10 or more generations read of what we did to them. Every man in our history that killed the most Indians has got a statue built for him. . . ."

During one infamous program, Rogers used what today sometimes is called the "N-word," calling a song he was describing a "n***** spiritual." The studio was deluged by calls from across the nation objecting to Rogers' language—a protest that sounds very contemporary. The chastened and chagrined cowboy offered apologies on the air and in his column.

Rogers usually was good at reading the mood of the country. More so than any other radio figure of his time, and certainly more so than Coughlin, he was closest to the commonsensical and let's-get-real approach that characterizes the best of talk radio today.

In talking about Roosevelt, for example, Rogers explained the man's popularity in words that haven't been improved on: "The whole country is with him. Even if what he does is wrong they are with him. Just so he does something. If he burned down the Capitol we would cheer and say, 'Well, we at least got a fire started anyhow.'"

The early radio people were admired as much as they were because "they knew they had to rely on words, and words alone," Harwood says. "Listening to [recordings of] them today, you realize how much they were able to make themselves into artists."

CHAPTER 4

Events That
Shaped a Decade

AMERICA'S DECADES

The Crime of the Century: The Lindbergh Baby Kidnapping

James D. Horan

The American people idolized Colonel Charles A. Lindbergh after his solo flight across the Atlantic in 1927. When his son was kidnapped on March 1, 1932, the nation was shocked and angry, writes historian and novelist James D. Horan in the following excerpt from *The Desperate Years: A Pictorial History of the Thirties*, and the whole world watched during the investigation and trial that followed. Horan describes desperate searches, clandestine meetings, and cruel hoaxes. Once the money was delivered and the body was discovered, Horan writes, it was the perseverance of detectives and scientists that identified Bruno Hauptmann as the kidnapper. According to the author, it was the testimony of the wood expert, Arthur Koehler, who identified Hauptmann as the owner of the infamous kidnap ladder, that convicted Hauptmann of the kidnap-murder of the son of an American hero.

T he shabby, green-painted sedan chugged up a road in New Jersey's Sourland Mountains and stopped near the clapboard mansion, bone-white in the moonlight. A man carefully raised a homemade ladder, climbed it swiftly, and swung inside the window. The child in the nursery

---

whimpered sleepily as he was lifted from the crib. Then came the hurried descent, the fall from the ladder. A few minutes later the car was racing back down the dark roads.

A Shocking Crime

It was the night of March 1, 1932. Charles Augustus Lindbergh, Jr., twenty months old, had been kidnapped.

The crime was perhaps without parallel in the public shock, indignation, and fury it produced. The nation and all the civilized world was appalled. Tiny Charles was the son of an idol, the Lone Eagle who had flown all the way across the Atlantic in 1927, the first ever to do so.

The child's absence was discovered later that night by nurse Betty Gow. Anne Morrow Lindbergh, pregnant with her second child, was preparing for bed; Colonel Charles A. Lindbergh was in the downstairs library reading. Betty hurried from one to the other. Neither had the baby. Lindy rushed upstairs. Just inside the open window, its shutter warped so it could not be tightly closed, was an envelope containing a crudely written note. It read:

> Dear Sir
>
> Have 50000$ ready 25000$ in 20$ bills 15000$ in 10$ bills and 10000$ in 5$ bills After 2–4 days we will inform you were to deliver the money We warn you for making anyding public or for notify the pol [rest of the word was blurred] The child is in Gut care
>
> Indication for all letters are singnature and three holes

The letter ended with a design of interlocking circles and pierced holes.

Despair and fury shook Lindbergh as he read the note. But with the good sense of a man of fortitude, he told the police, who swarmed over the house within minutes, "Please be careful of fingerprints."

At first everyone expected that the kidnapper would be caught within hours. After all wasn't every road and bridge in New Jersey sealed off—every citizen, every policeman on the entire eastern seaboard watching for the car, for clues?

He must be caught soon. . . . No one foresaw the long, dreary, heart-breaking search that would follow.

There was one wild moment when police found Henry (Red) Johnson, Betty Gow's admirer, in Hartford after an all-night drive, a bottle of milk in his car. But Johnson was cleared quickly. Then Oliver Whateley, Lindbergh's butler, Mrs. Whateley, Betty Gow, and Violet Sharpe (who later committed suicide under the stress of police questioning), were also cleared.

Negotiating with the Kidnapper

On March 7, 1932, the *Bronx Home News* received a letter from Dr. John F. Condon, Bronx schoolteacher. There was nothing new in this; Dr. Condon had been writing the *Home News* for years on almost every conceivable subject. But in this letter Condon offered to pay one thousand dollars out of his small savings to the kidnapper if he would return the child.

The editors who knew Condon smiled when they read the letter, but someone decided that a brief story should be written on his offer. The letter lay on a rewriteman's desk for hours and was almost forgotten, but a news brief finally appeared in the March 8, 1932, edition.

The next day Condon received a letter bearing a cabalistic symbol of interlocking circles in red and blue. He was informed that he had been selected to act as negotiator between the Lindbergh family and the kidnapper. Condon contacted Lindbergh, who asked him to come to Hopewell, New Jersey, at once.

There police experts compared the symbols; they were found to be the same as were used in the original kidnap note. The Lindberghs authorized Dr. Condon to act in the matter, and several notes followed, including messages inserted in a newspaper "personal" column, setting up a meeting.

Today Dr. Condon's ransom negotiations with the famous "John" seem almost unbelievable. They met twice, both times near a cemetery. All the trappings of a badly written melodrama were present: the deep-voiced stranger "John," wisps of clouds trailing across the moon, the night wind moaning through the trees, gleaming tombstones nearby.

At one of their meetings, on April 2, 1932, Dr. Condon gave the stranger fifty thousand dollars and a note was turned over by John saying the child was aboard "boad Nelly" near Martha's Vineyard. Lindbergh took to the sky to search for the boat and his baby. He crossed and crisscrossed the area, scanning the fishing boats with powerful glasses.

There was nothing.

A Series of Hoaxes

But his cup of anguish was not yet filled. In April, 1932 Gaston Means, a former Department of Justice investigator who had spent two years in prison and had once been placed on trial for murder, persuaded Washington heiress Mrs. Evalyn Walsh McLean that he was in touch with the kidnappers. Mrs. McLean gave him $100,000 on his promise that the child would be turned over to a priest in Washington.

Again nothing.

When the child was not produced, Mrs. McLean went to her attorneys, who notified police. Means was arrested and indicted.

But there was still another cruel, heartrending hoax. John Hughes Curtis, a socialite shipbuilder whose fortune had been wiped out by the Depression, came to the Lindbergh home with a weird story.

As he told it, he had been driving in Norfolk when a stranger jumped on the running board of his car and asked if he would be the go-between in the payment of the ransom. Curtis agreed, and the stranger then told him the baby was aboard a two-masted fishing schooner. Again Lindbergh believed. He spent two days searching for the boat off the Virginia capes. He returned to learn that the body of his son had been found in the woods not far from his home.

When Curtis showed up at the Hopewell house, he was greeted by police. In the early hours of the morning he asked for a typewriter and began typing feverishly.

"At the present time," he wrote, "I am sane. But I honestly believe that for the past seven or eight months I have not been myself due to financial troubles. . . ."

Curtis was tried and fined a thousand dollars. Means was sent to prison for fifteen years.

Justice James M. Proctor, who presided over his trial, observed, "The Lindbergh case brought out all the best in the hearts of men, but also gave opportunity to some to display the weakness and wickedness of human nature. . . ."

The Perseverance of Detectives and Scientists

While state and federal police were methodically hunting for clues to the kidnap-murderer, a sharp-faced New York City detective was put at the head of a team of more than a hundred detectives who were assigned to the case. Lieutenant James J. Finn had been personally selected by Colonel Lindbergh, who remembered the soft-spoken police officer from the time of his hero's welcome in 1927, when Finn had been one of his bodyguards.

Finn's greatest attribute was an infinite patience. He had a theory, almost an obsession as he later called it, that the kidnapper would be caught passing the ransom money. He constructed a large chart of the metropolitan area and with other officers—federal, state and city—started to travel the more than 76,000 square miles on the trail of the bloody money.

The first note had appeared on April 4, in the East River Savings Bank at Ninety-Sixth Street and Amsterdam Avenue. Finn and Treasury agents hurried to the bank, but no one could recall who had handed in the bill. Hundreds of accounts, hundreds of deposits were checked. They yielded nothing.

Every month or so a bill trickled in—a five here, a ten there. In a confidential room at Police Headquarters, Finn carefully stuck colored pins into the map to show where the bills had turned up. A forest of pins began to grow, but like a forest, grew slowly.

While Finn studied his map, a federal expert named

Arthur Koehler was matching pieces of wood. Like Finn, Koehler had infinite patience.

The white-haired scientist practically lived with the ladder used by the kidnapper. It was in three sections, each seven feet long, expertly joined together but broken in the middle—apparently under the weight of the kidnapper and the child. The nails were cleanly driven, the saw cuts smooth and true. Every rung was even. The three sections fitted perfectly, round pins sliding easily into grooves drilled for that purpose.

Only a man skilled with tools could have made that ladder.

But the two rails caught Koehler's attention as the days passed. Both edges had been planed with a plane not in good condition which had left ridges. The microscope told him that the wood had passed through a planer at 93/100 inch for every revolution of the top and bottom cutter heads, and 86/100 inch per revolution on the side heads. This meant there were eight knives in the top and bottom cutter heads and six knives on the side head.

For the rest of the year Koehler checked every planing mill from Alabama to New York. Only twenty-five used such a planer. Two were ruled out because they did not dress lumber. Each of the twenty-three other firms supplied samples of dressed lumber; only one bore revolution marks identical to those found on the kidnapper's ladder. That company was in McCormick, South Carolina, and out of forty-five shipments made during the period before the crime, Koehler traced one to a Bronx lumber yard.

Finn's map, Koehler's wood . . . wood and dollars were building a bridge to the electric chair for a man who still remains one of the most enigmatic criminals of the twentieth century. . . .

A Search for Marked Ransom Bills

For twenty-eight months the colony of brightly colored pins on Lieutenant James J. Finn's map in New York City police headquarters had grown to a large, irregular patch covering parts of Yorkville and the upper Bronx area. Each pin represented a Lindbergh ransom bill passed in restaurants, filling stations, banks, and stores.

The theory that the kidnapper and killer of tiny Charles Augustus Lindbergh would eventually be trapped by passing the yellow-backed ransom bills had by this time almost become an obsession with Finn. By now, two years and five months after the fifty thousand dollars had been paid to the mysterious John, Finn headed a task force of over a hundred veteran detectives all dedicated to breaking what the press in the United States and abroad referred to as the crime of the century.

The first note was passed only two days after the ransom had been paid. It showed up at the East River Savings Bank, at Ninety-Sixth Street and Amsterdam Avenue. Treasury agents and Finn hurried there, but the tellers could not recall the persons who had passed the bill.

After that day the bills trickled into Finn's office by fives and tens. Each time Finn and his men hurried to the place where the bill had been passed only to be greeted with the disappointing news that the teller or clerk could not recall what the person looked like who had given the bill.

Finn would return to his office and carefully press another pin into his map.

Then the presidential order taking the United States off the gold standard gave impetus to the hunt. After May 1, 1933, the possession of gold notes would be illegal. On that last day a man carrying a bundle of certificates arrived at the Federal Reserve Bank. He waited patiently in line with the others and then tendered his bundle. The teller rapidly counted the bills; $2,980. Three days later bank officials checking the serial numbers were shocked to find they were all ransom bills. The name recorded was J.J. Faulkner of a West 149th Street address. As Finn suspected, the address was fictitious.

Then, on the evening of Nov. 26, 1933, a man passed a five-dollar note at the Loew's Sheridan Theatre in Greenwich Village. The cashier, Mrs. Cecilia M. Barr, recalled him because he "drew it from his watch pocket and tossed it through the window."

This time Finn got a description; five feet nine inches, high cheekbones, flat cheeks, a pointed chin, and a German accent. The man Dr. Condon had given the ransom to had had an accent.

By this time a pattern was emerging. The bills were creased lengthways and sideways so they could be carried in a man's watch pocket.

Trapping the Kidnap-Murderer

Finn also was sure the man drove a car and that he might be trapped through a filling station. Several had reported getting the bills. On this theory Finn concentrated his search directly on gas stations. He had a composite picture drawn by a police artist and sent out thousands of flyers asking station attendants to record the serial number of every five, ten and twenty received, and if possible who had paid it.

By mid-1934 the bills began to turn up almost weekly; the forest of pins on Finn's map now completely covered the Bronx and Yorkville.

On Saturday afternoon, September 15, 1934, a man with a German accent driving an old sedan swung into the Warner-Quinlan gas station at 2115 Lexington Avenue.

Walter Lyle, the attendant, later described the incident to a reporter. "He said he wanted five gallons of gas," Lyle said. "I noticed that he spoke with a decided German accent. Usually most people who come in at least smile and pass the time of day when you are giving them gas, but not this fellow. His face was flat and emotionless, his eyes were cold. When I hooked up the hose he gave me a five-dollar bill. I suddenly remembered the flyer asking us to watch for fives, tens, and twenties. Something told me to take down his license number. When I went in to get the change I grabbed a pencil, and when I came out I jotted down his license number—4U 13-14, New York—on the bill. Then I put the bill into the register. It went to the bank and that's how the case was finally broken."

In the Mount Morris Branch of the Corn Exchange Bank, 85 East 125th Street, William R. Strong, a teller, saw Lyle's notation and checked the bank's list of bills. With trembling hands he dialed the Treasury and got agent Thomas H. Sisk, who had been assigned to the investigation.

"We are holding a five-dollar bill, Serial Number A73976634A," Strong said. "Our records show that it is one of the Lindbergh ransom bills. Will you please confirm this?"

Sisk quickly checked and got back on the phone.

"It's one of the bills all right. Do you have any idea. . . ?"

Strong broke in excitedly, "Somebody has written a license number on the bill. Here it is."

Within minutes Sisk had phoned Lieutenant Finn and Colonel Schwarzkopf, head of the New Jersey State Police, who was directing the manhunt in that state.

Identifying Bruno Hauptmann

The license plate was quickly checked with the New York State Motor Vehicle Records, and the name and address of Bruno Hauptmann was now in Finn's hands. The bill was also traced back to the gas station, and Lyle identified the artist's drawing of the kidnapper as a good likeness of the man who had given him the bill.

Finn and his men now began tailing Hauptmann. On September 18, 1934, just three days after the bill was given to Lyle, Finn and a carload of detectives boxed Hauptmann's car against a curb at Tremont and Park Avenues in the Bronx and arrested him. As they searched him, Finn eagerly dug his fingers into Hauptmann's watch pocket. He silently held up a creased twenty-dollar gold certificate.

Hauptmann was quickly arraigned in the Bronx County Courthouse while hundreds of newsmen and newsreel photographers jammed the streets. He was held in $100,000 bail, which he did not raise, and later extradited to New Jersey to stand trial the following year.

Police and Treasury agents virtually tore Hauptmann's house and garage apart. Cleverly concealed in a hole drilled in a plank was $840, and an additional $13,750, all in ransom notes, were hidden in the garage.

Hauptmann stolidly insisted he was innocent. He told Finn that the money was given to him in January of 1934 "in a shoe box" by a friend, Isidor Fisch, who had gone back to Germany and died. Hauptmann insisted he didn't know what was in the box until months later.

"It was a nasty day. It had been raining and I went to the broom closet to get a broom. In some way I must have hit the box with the handle of the broom and I looked up and saw it was filled with money, all wet.

"I took the money into the garage to dry and even then I didn't bother to count it. I figured that Fisch was dead so it wouldn't hurt anyone if I spent some of it—so I did."

Police delving into Hauptmann's background found that he had been in the German Army in World War I and had jumped ship to get into this country. He was a carpenter and had one child, Manfred. His bewildered wife insisted to police she never knew anything about the kidnapping or the money. Police believed her.

Now that Hauptmann was in jail, Finn, his detectives, and New Jersey's attorney general David Wilentz began gathering the evidence that they hoped would someday send Bruno Hauptmann to the chair. . . .

The Trial of the Century

The trial of Bruno Richard Hauptmann opened on the first day of January, 1935, and the instant Judge Thomas W. Trenchard's gavel slammed down on his worn desk, the eyes of the civilized world turned to the rural village of Flemington, New Jersey, and its century-old courthouse, where Hauptmann was charged with the kidnap-murder of tiny Charles Augustus Lindbergh, son of the first man of the skies.

The trial lasted until February 15. There were more than 380 exhibits and approximately 1,500,000 words of testimony. At the time of the kidnapping, there had been no law about summoning the FBI into a kidnapping case after twenty-four hours had passed. Hauptmann was tried for causing the baby's death while in the commission of a felony; that is, breaking into the nursery and stealing something of value—not the boy, but the nightclothes in which he slept.

Such evil, as cited in the indictment, "offended the peace of this state, the government and dignity of the same."

There were many preliminary witnesses who testified primarily to lay the groundwork of the State's case, but the star witness for the prosecution was Colonel Lindbergh. To millions of newspaper readers and radio listeners, Lindbergh was no longer the Lone Eagle, but a tight-faced, bereaved father describing how he had done everything possible to recover his infant son. The highlight of his testimony came when he told how Dr. John Condon paid the $50,000 ransom. Lindbergh had been only a few feet from Condon when the money was passed to the kidnapper.

He told a hushed courtroom that he had heard the shadowy figure in the wind-tossed night call out to Condon, "Over here, doctor."

Attorney General David Wilentz asked Lindbergh if he had heard that voice since.

Lindbergh nodded. "I have."

"Whose voice was that?"

Lindbergh said without hesitation, "It was the voice of Bruno Hauptmann."

Dramatic Testimony

Another unforgettable witness was old Amandus Hockmuth, a gnarled farmer of eighty-seven, long a resident of the back country of Hopewell. As with many old men, his principal occupation was watching the long and lonely road that stretched past his farmhouse, hoping that something would happen—anything—to break the monotony of the dragging days. Something did happen, he said, at about noon on March 1, 1932, ten hours before the discovery of the kidnapping.

"I saw a car coming around the corner, pretty good

speed—and I expected it to turn over," he said. "And when it got to be about twenty-five feet away from me the driver looked out at me like this—" the old man looked startled, then scowled. "The driver looked like he had seen a ghost."

"And that man you saw, is he in this courtroom?" Wilentz asked.

The old man slowly peered about the courtroom. "Yes, alongside that trooper there."

"Point him out," Wilentz snapped.

The old man with trembling movements rose from his chair and, head thrust forward like a hound on the scent, picked his way through the forest of chairs and desks until he paused in front of Hauptmann. Then slowly, dramatically, he touched him.

"Right here," he called out.

Hauptmann snarled in German, "The old man is crazy!"

But it was obvious the drama was not lost on the jury.

Hauptmann finally took the stand, and the Western Union telegraph keys clattered all day delivering his testimony to the remote points of the globe.

"I saved a lot of money," he said, and went into a detailed explanation of how he had dabbled with small accounts in Wall Street. He also repeated on the stand the story he had told police of how Isidor Fisch had given him the money police had found in his garage.

"He threw a party when he left for Germany; it was at his request we held it in our house. We invited a couple of friends, and about nine o'clock Fisch came out and got a little bundle in his hand. My wife was in the baby's room. We went into the kitchen and he said, 'I leave it, don't mind, keep care of it and put it in a tight place.' I didn't ask what it was; I put it in the broom closet on the upper shelf."

When he had finished his direct testimony Wilentz launched a savage cross-examination, at one point pounding with fury as he shouted, "You lied to police, didn't you? Didn't you lie? . . . They're all lies."

Hauptmann shouted back angrily, "No . . . no . . . you stop that!"

Fingerprints played no part, yet were forever cropping up because, for all the evidence against the defendant (physical evidence at that) not one fingerprint was discovered to accuse him. The State's explanation was, of course, that the kidnapper had worn gloves.

The Kidnapper's Ladder

Several witnesses testified about a plank or board that had disappeared from Hauptmann's attic, laying the groundwork for Koehler, the wood wizard, to give his testimony about the ladder.

Max Rauch, who owned the house in which Hauptmann lived, testified that in October, 1931, the attic floor was complete. Two weeks after Hauptmann's arrest, Rauch went into the attic and discovered that a strip of board was missing.

This was the board that Hauptmann was alleged to have used in making the ladder.

Detective Lewis J. Bornmann told of going into Hauptmann's attic and discovering that part of one of the floorboards had been removed. He also found a small pile of sawdust, indicating the spot where the board had been sawed. . . .

The stage was then set for Arthur Koehler, the wood expert of the U.S. Forest Service Laboratory at Madison, Wisconsin, who appeared that afternoon. It was his testimony—and the ladder—that really sent Hauptmann to the electric chair.

Nobody saw the ladder built. Nobody saw it used. But the story of its journey from a South Carolina mill to the Bronx lumberyard, to a floor in Hauptmann's attic to the ladder discarded outside the Lindbergh home in Hopewell, was an amazing tale of scientific detection.

Koehler told his story with a cool, calm, calculated manner, beginning with the homemade ladder police had found fifty feet from the house.

Koehler told how for eighteen months he had canvassed the mills of the East until he traced the wood to a ten-dollar purchase the carpenter had made in the Bronx—some of it to replace a floorboard in the attic of his house at 1279 East 222nd Street.

Koehler explained his microscopic examination of machine-plane marks on the surface of famous Rail 16—the one he matched with lumber stripped from the attic floor.

He showed that "someone" had sawed the attic board into almost equal lengths—and that in grain, distortion caused by knots, texture, and rings there was proof that "Rail 16" was once part of the attic board.

He pointed to four nail holes in the rail and matched them, to a minute fraction of an inch, against four nail holes found in a joist in the Hauptmann attic. He demonstrated how nails driven through the rail and into the joist "fitted perfectly, though one of them had been driven in slantingly."

"The ladder rail and the attic board were originally one piece." Koehler testified.

"In examining this ladder rail," he said, "I noticed that both edges had been planed with a hand plane. The plane was not in very good condition and left little ridges. . . .

"The ridges are of different size, and when I plane a piece of wood with that plane (taken from Hauptmann's tool chest), it makes similar ridges, of the same size and the same distance apart as those found on the ladder rail."

Connecting Hauptmann to the Ladder

Then he gave an amazing demonstration.

"I learned to do this with coins when I was a boy," he said, and placed a piece of paper over the edge of the rail and rubbed it with heavy crayon.

The ridges made by the defective plane showed in bold relief.

Koehler then affixed a piece of wood to the bench where judge Thomas W. Trenchard presided, clamped it tightly, marked it with a blue pencil to show the depth he would shave it and went to work with Hauptmann's plane. Discarding the shaving, he took more paper, placed it on the scraped surface and applied the crayon.

The markings on the two papers, one from the wood he had planed, the other from the ladder, were identical.

But Koehler was not finished. He returned to a discussion of machine-plane marks on the rail and told how the work was done by eight knives in revolving "cutter heads" and how one was not set properly and had left a ridge—visible only under a microscope.

"This lumber," he testified, "passed through the planer at 93/100ths of an inch for every revolution of the top and bottom cutter heads, and 86/100ths of an inch per revolution of the side heads. This meant there were eight knives in the top and bottom cutter heads and six knives in the side heads.

"Now from an investigation of planers used in this section of the country on Carolina pine, I found that comparatively few planers have eight knives in the top and bottom heads and six in the side heads.

"The fact is, I made a thorough canvass of all planing mills from New York to Alabama. There are 1,598 all together and I found only twenty-five firms that had such a planer. Two of these I could rule out because they did not dress this kind of lumber.

"I got samples from the other twenty-three firms and I found that only one of those firms made revolution marks of the same spacing as on the ladder rail. All the others made wider or narrower revolution marks."

That company was in McCormick, South Carolina, and out of forty-six shipments during the period in question, Koehler had traced one with the distinguishing plane marks to the National Lumber and Millwork Company in the Bronx. Hauptmann had bought ten dollars worth of it in December, 1931.

The hunt was over.

The jury began deliberating at 11:23 A.M., February 13. The verdict was announced at 10:44 that night. The routine of automatic appeals took months. Then at the last minute Governor Harold G. Hoffman gave Hauptmann a two-day stay of execution. But after the flurry of headlines was over, the stolid, impassive German carpenter finally walked into the death house of the New Jersey State Prison at Trenton, on the night of April 3, 1936, and was electrocuted.

The horror, the false hopes, the heartbreaks, the hoaxes are now only faded clippings or excerpts in anthologies. But the memory of Charles Augustus Lindbergh, age twenty months, is perpetuated in the law that bears his name—the Lindbergh kidnapping law.

The Trials of the Scottsboro Boys

Douglas O. Linder

The following article tells the story of nine black teenagers arrested and tried in Scottsboro, Alabama, for the alleged rape of two white women on a freight train to Memphis in 1931. Law professor Douglas O. Linder describes the trials, reversals, and retrials as well as the controversial personalities of those who sought to convict and those who came to the defense of "The Scottsboro Boys." The author explores in particular detail the examination and testimony of witnesses for the prosecution and defense in the retrials that began after the Supreme Court overturned the initial convictions. For example, Linder describes the testimony of alleged rape victim Ruby Bates, who recanted her original testimony, saying there had been no rape. After years in prison during their trials, appeals, and retrials, all of the Scottsboro Boys eventually found their way out of prison, Linder reports—the last in June 1950. According to Linder, the trial reflects the attitudes toward blacks in the Deep South of the 1930s and how these attitudes forever changed the lives of the Scottsboro Boys. Linder is an environmental and communications attorney who teaches at the University of Missouri School of Law in Kansas City, Missouri.

No crime in American history—let alone a crime that never occurred—produced as many trials, convic-

---

Excerpted from *Famous American Trials*, by Douglas O. Linder, from www.law. umkc.edu/faculty/projects/ftrials. Reprinted with permission.

tions, reversals, and retrials as did an alleged gang rape of two white girls by nine black teenagers on a Southern Railroad freight run on March 25, 1931. Over the course of the next two decades, the struggle for justice of the "Scottsboro Boys," as the black teens were called, made celebrities out of anonymities, launched and ended careers, wasted lives, produced heroes, opened southern juries to blacks, exacerbated sectional strife, and divided America's political left.

A Fight Aboard a Freight Train

Hoboeing was a common pastime in the Depression year of 1931. For some, riding freights was an appealing adventure compared to the drudgery and dreariness of their daily lives. For others, hopping rail cars was the available means to move from one fruitless job search to the next. On board the Southern Railroad's Chattanooga to Memphis run on March 25, 1931, were two dozen or so mainly male, and mainly young, whites and blacks. Among them were four black Chattanooga teenagers hoping to investigate a rumor of government jobs in Memphis hauling logs on the river and five other black teens from various parts of Georgia. Four young whites, two males and two females dressed in overalls, were also on the train, returning to Huntsville from unsuccessful job searches in the cotton mills of Chattanooga.

Sometime after the train crossed the Alabama border, a white youth walking across the top of a tank car intentionally stepped on the hand of a black youth named Haywood Patterson, who was hanging on to its side. Patterson had friends aboard the train and a stone-throwing fight erupted between white youths and a larger group of black youths. Eventually, the blacks succeeded in forcing all but one of the members of the white gang off the train. The one remaining white youth, Orville Gilley, was pulled back onto the train by Patterson after the train had accelerated to a life-endangering speed. Some of the whites forced off the train went to the stationmaster in Stevenson to report what they described as an assault by a gang of blacks. The stationmaster wired ahead and the train was stopped by a posse in Paint Rock, Alabama. Dozens of men with guns rushed at the train as it stopped, rounding up every black youth they could find. The nine captured blacks, soon to be called "The Scottsboro Boys," were tied together with plow line, loaded on a flatback truck, and taken to a jail in Scottsboro.

Also greeted by the posse in Paint Rock were two mill-workers from Huntsville, Victoria Price and Ruby Bates. One or the other of the girls, either in response to a question or on their own initiative, told one of the posse members that they had been raped by a gang of twelve blacks with pistols and knives. In the jail that March 25th, Price pointed out six of the nine boys and said that they were the ones who raped her. The guard reportedly replied, "If those six had Miss Price, it stands to reason that the others had Miss Bates." When one of the accused, Clarence Norris, called the girls liars he was struck by a bayonet. A crowd of several hundred "crackers" surrounded the Scottsboro jail the night of their arrest for rape, hoping for a good old-fashioned lynching. Their plans were foiled, however, when Alabama's governor ordered the National Guard to Scottsboro to protect the suspects.

The First Trials

Trials of the Scottsboro Boys began twelve days after their arrest in the courtroom of Judge A.E. Hawkins. Haywood Patterson described the scene as "one big smiling white face." Many local newspapers had made their conclusions about the defendants before the trials began. One headline read: "ALL NEGROES POSITIVELY IDENTIFIED BY GIRLS AND ONE WHITE BOY WHO WAS HELD PRISONER WITH PISTOL AND KNIVES WHILE NINE BLACK FIENDS COMMITTED REVOLTING CRIME." Representing the Boys in their uphill legal battle were Stephen Ruddy and Milo Moody. They were no "Dream Team [the team of lawyers led by Johnnie Cochran, who defended O.J. Simpson in his trial for the murder of his ex-wife Nicole and her friend, Ron Goldman]." Ruddy was an unpaid and unprepared Chattanooga real estate attorney who, on the first day of trial, was "so stewed he could hardly walk straight." Moody was a forgetful seventy-year old local attorney who hadn't tried a case in decades.

The defense lawyers demonstrated their incompetence in many ways. They expressed a willingness to have all nine defendants tried together, despite the prejudice such a trial might cause to Roy Wright, for example, who at age twelve was the youngest of the nine Scottsboro Boys. (The prosecution, fearing that a single trial might constitute reversible error, decided to try the defendants in groups of two or three.) The cross-examination of Victoria Price lasted only minutes, while examining doctors R.R. Bridges and John Lynch were not cross-examined at all. Ruby Bates was not asked about contradictions between her testimony and that of Price. The defense offered only the defendants themselves as witnesses, and their testimony was rambling, sometimes incoherent, and riddled with obvious misstatements. Six of the boys (Andy Wright, Willie Roberson, Charles Weems, Ozie Powell, Olen Montgomery, and Eugene Williams) denied raping or even having seen the two girls. But three others, all who later claimed they did so because of beatings and threats, said that a gang rape by other defendants did occur. Clarence Norris provided what one paper called "the highlight of the trial" when he said of the other blacks, "They all raped her, everyone of them." No closing argument was offered by defense attorneys. A local editorialist described the state's case as "so conclusive as to be almost perfect."

Guilty verdicts in the first trial were announced while the second trial was underway. The large crowd outside the courthouse let out a roar of approval that was clearly heard by the second jury inside. When the four trials were over, eight of the nine Scottsboro Boys had been convicted and sentenced to death. A mistrial was declared in the case of twelve-year old Roy Wright, when eleven of the jurors held out for death despite the request of the prosecution for only a life sentence in view of his tender age.

Finding Help from the Communist Party

The National Association for the Advancement of Colored People (NAACP), which might have been expected to rush to the defense of the Scottsboro Boys, did not. Rape was a politically explosive charge in the South, and the NAACP was concerned about damage to its effectiveness that might result if it turned out some or all of the Boys were guilty. Instead, it was the Communist Party that moved aggressively to make the Scottsboro case their own. The Party saw the case as providing a great recruiting tool among southern blacks and northern liberals. The Communist Party, through its legal arm the International Labor Defense (ILD), pronounced the case against the Boys a "murderous frame-up" and began efforts, ultimately successful, to be named as their attorneys. The NAACP, a slow-moving bureaucracy, finally came to the realization that the Scottsboro Boys were most likely innocent and that leadership in the case would have large public relations benefits. As a last-ditch effort to beat back the ILD in the battle over representation, NAACP officials persuaded renowned defense attorney Clarence Darrow to take their case to Alabama. But it was by then too late. The Scottsboro Boys, for better or worse, cast their lots with the Communists who, in the South, were "treated with only slightly more courtesy than a gang of rapists."

In January, 1932, the Alabama Supreme Court, by a 6-1 vote, affirmed all but one of the eight convictions and death sentences. (The court ruled that Eugene Williams, age thirteen, should have not been tried as an adult.) The cases were appealed to the United States Supreme Court which overturned the convictions in the landmark case of *Powell vs Alabama*. The Court, 7–2, ruled that the right of the defendants under the Fourteenth Amendment's due process clause to competent legal counsel had been denied by Alabama. There would have to be new trials.

The prosecutor in the retrials was Alabama's newly elected attorney general, Thomas Knight, Jr. Knight's father, Thomas Knight, Sr., had authored the Alabama Supreme Court decision upholding the original convictions.

The ILD selected two attorneys to represent the Scottsboro Boys in the retrials. The ILD quieted skeptics who
saw the organization caring more about the benefits it
could derive from the case than the Boys' welfare by asking Samuel Liebowitz to serve as the lead defense attorney.
Liebowitz was a New York criminal attorney who had secured an astonishing record of seventy-seven acquittals and
one hung jury in seventy-eight murder trials. Liebowitz was
often described as "the next Clarence Darrow." Liebowitz
was a mainline Democrat with no connections with or
sympathies toward the Communist Party. Joseph Brodsky,
the ILD's chief attorney, was selected to assist Liebowitz.

The Scottsboro Boys spent the two years between their
first trials and the second round, scheduled to begin in
March, 1933 in Decatur, in the deplorable conditions of
Depression-era Alabama prisons. While on death row at
Kilby prison, on the very date originally set for their own ex-
ecutions, they watched as another inmate was carried off to
unsoundproofed death chamber adjacent to their cells, then
listened to the sounds of his electrocution. Once or twice a
week they were allowed to leave their tiny cells, as they were
handcuffed and walked a few yards down the hall to a
shower. An early visitor found them "terrified, bewildered"
like "scared little mice, caught in a trap." They fought, they
wrote letters if they could write at all, they thought about
girls and life on the outside, they dreamed of their execu-
tions. As their trial date approached, they were moved to the
Decatur jail, a rat-infested facility that two years earlier had
been condemned as "unfit for white prisoners."

A Second Trial

The second trial of Haywood Patterson opened on March
30, 1933, in the courtroom of Judge James Horton.
Liebowitz moved to quash the indictments on the ground
that Negroes had been systematically excluded from jury
rolls. He raised some eyebrows by questioning the veracity
of local jury commissioners and many more when he insisted that prosecutor Knight stop his practice of calling

black witnesses, who Liebowitz had called to show had never served on juries, by their first names. To many local observers it was one thing to defend rapists—that, after all, is part of the American justice system—, but it was another, unforgiveable thing to come to Alabama and attack their social order and way of life. Unsurprisingly, the motion to quash the indictment was denied.

On April 3, Victoria ("Big Leg") Price was called to the stand. Direct examination was brief, only sixteen minutes. Price recounted her job-hunting trip to Chattanooga, the fight on the train between whites and blacks, and the gang rape in which Haywood Patterson was one of her attackers. Prosecutor Knight's strategy on direct was to cover the essential facts in a condensed, unadorned way that would provide few opportunities for defense attorneys to expose contradictions with the more detailed (and implausible) story she told in the first trials. Liebowitz's cross-examination was merciless. His questions suggested his answers. There was no Callie Brochie's boardinghouse in Chattanooga, as Price claimed. She was an adulterer who had consorted with Jack Tiller in the Huntsville freight yards two days before the alleged rape, and it was his semen (or that of Orville Gilley) that was found in her vagina. She was a person of low repute, a prostitute. She was neither crying, bleeding, or seriously bruised after the alleged gang rape. She was fearful of being arrested for a Mann Act violation (crossing state lines for immoral purposes) when she met the posse in Paint Rock, so she and Bates made groundless accusations of rape to deflect attention from their own sins. Throughout the four-hour cross, Price remained sarcastic, evasive, and venomous. She used her ignorance and poor memory to her advantage and proved to be a difficult witness to corner. On re-direct, Price added a new dramatic and inflammatory elaboration to her previous account: while she was being penetrated, she said, her attacker told her that when he pulled his "thing" out, "you will have a black baby."

Dr. R.R. Bridges, the Scottsboro doctor who examined the girls less than two hours after the alleged rapes, was the next prosecution witness to take the stand. He turned out to be a better witness for the defense. He did confirm that semen was found in the vaginas of the two girls (more in the case of Bates than of Price). Liebowitz, however, was able to show on cross-examination that the girls were both calm, composed, and free of bleeding and vaginal damage. Moreover, the semen that Bridges examined was non-motile, even though sperm generally live from twelve to forty-eight hours after intercourse.

The prosecution's best moment came when Arthur Woodall, a member of the posse who searched the defendants at Paint Rock, was on the stand. Woodall testified that he had found a knife on one of the defendants, though he couldn't remember which one. Liebowitz asked Woodall if he had asked the boy whether it was his knife. Woodall said that he had, and that the boy said he had taken it "off the white girl, Victoria Price." The surprised look on Liebowitz's face caused Knight to clap his hands and then dash out of the courtroom to hide his glee. Liebowitz moved for a mistrial, but Judge Horton denied the motion and instead told jurors they should ignore Knight's reaction.

The prosecution's only eyewitness to the crime was a farmer named Ory Dobbins who said he saw the defendants grab Price and Bates as they were about to leap from the train. The credibility of the farmer's testimony was seriously damaged by Liebowitz on cross, when he asked how it was that Dobbins could even be sure, given the speed of the train and his considerable distance from it, that it was a woman that he saw. Dobbins answered, "She was wearing women's clothes." Everyone who had followed the case knew that Bates and Price both were wearing overalls. "Are you sure it wasn't overalls or a coat?," Judge Horton asked. "No sir, a dress," Dobbins said.

The Defense

Defense witnesses were all called to serve a single purpose: to prove Price a liar and convince the jury that no rape had occurred aboard the Southern Railroad freight. Dallas

Ramsey, a Chattanooga resident, testified that he saw Price in the hobo jungle she denied ever having visited. George Chamlee, a Chattanooga attorney, testified that his investigation could turn up no evidence of a Callie Brochie or the boardinghouse that Price said she owned, and in which Price and Bates allegedly spent the night prior to her return train trip to Alabama. Six of the accused testified, including Willie Roberson, who testified that on the day of the alleged rape he was suffering from a serious case of venereal disease and was so weak that he could not walk without a cane, let alone leap from boxcar to boxcar as Price had claimed. Ozie Powell proved the weakest of the accused on the stand, confused and bewildered when asked by Knight on cross to affirm or disaffirm answers he had given to prosecution questions at the first trial. In an attempt to minimize the damage, Liebowitz asked only, when Knight's barrage was finished, "Ozie tell us about how much schooling you have had in your life?" Powell answered, "about three months." Knight had considerably less luck with Haywood Patterson. In desperation Knight asked Patterson, "Were you tried in Scottsboro?" Patterson replied, "I was framed in Scottsboro." An angry Knight shot back, "Who told you to say that?" Patterson answered, "I told myself to say it."

Lester Carter, the twenty-three-year-old travelling companion of Bates and Price, was one of the defense's most spectacular witnesses. Carter, who Price had denied having known until the day of the alleged crime, testified that he had met Bates, Price, and Price's boyfriend Jack Tiller in a Huntsville hobo jungle the night before he would travel with the two girls to Chattanooga. He told the jury that the night the four were together in the hobo jungle, and he began making love to Ruby Bates while Price did the same with Tiller. Carter testified that two days later, on the return trip to Hunstville from Chattanooga, he jumped off the freight train when fighting broke out between blacks and the outnumbered whites.

The appearance of the defense's final and most dramatic witness, Ruby Bates, might have been taken from the script of a hokey Hollywood movie. In the months before the trial, Bates' whereabouts were a mystery. Liebowitz announced that he was resting his case, then approached the bench and asked for a short recess. Minutes later National Guardsmen opened the back doors of the courtroom, and—to the astonished gasps of spectators and the dismay of Knight—in walked Ruby Bates. Under direct examination, Bates said a troubled conscience and the advice of famous New York minister Harry Emerson Fosdick prompted her to return to Alabama to tell the truth about what happened on March 25, 1931. Bates said that there was no rape, that none of the defendants touched her or even spoke to her, and that the accusations of rape were made after Price told her "to frame up a story" to avoid morals charges. On cross-examination, Knight ripped into Bates, confronting her both with her conflicting testimony in the first trials and accusations that her new versions of events had been bought with new clothes and other Communist Party gifts. He demanded to know whether he hadn't told her months before in his office that he would "punish anyone who made her swear falsely" and that he "did not want to burn any person that wasn't guilty." "I think you did," Bates answered.

In the summations that followed, none was more controversial than that of Wade Wright, Solicitor of Morgan County, who was assisting Attorney General Knight in the prosecution. In a line that would move thousands of Jews around the country to protest, Wright asked the Patterson jurors "whether justice in this case is going to be bought and sold with Jew money from New York?" Liebowitz jumped up and demanded a mistrial, which Judge Horton refused to declare. Knight seemed to be embarrassed by his colleague's blatantly anti-Semitic appeal and in his own summation told the jurors, "I do not want a verdict based on racial prejudice or religious creed." Knight, however, was himself no model of decorum, referring to Patterson as "that thing."

Liebowitz, in his summation, called the accusations of Price the "foul, contemptible, outrageous lie" of an "abandoned" woman. He closed with the Lord's Prayer and an all-or-nothing appeal to the jury: acquit them or give them the chair.

Another Guilty Verdict

At one o'clock on April 8, 1933, the jury was sent out to deliberate the fate of Haywood Patterson after Judge Horton reminded the jury that "You are not trying lawyers; you are not trying state lines." The next day the jury emerged from the juryroom laughing, leading some in the defense camp to think that they must have won an acquittal. They were wrong. The jury pronounced Patterson guilty and sentenced him to death. The decision on guilt took only five minutes. The testimony of Bates wasn't even considered. Liebowitz was stunned. Safely back in New York after the trial Liebowitz said of the jury that had just found his client guilty: "If you ever saw those creatures, those bigots whose mouths are slits in their faces, whose eyes popped out at you like frogs, whose chins dripped tobacco juice, be-whiskered and filthy, you would not ask how they could do it." Ruby Bates returned East with Liebowitz, then became the leading lady at ILD-sponsored Scottsboro rallies, where she would beg forgiveness, plead for justice for "The Boys," and join in singing The Internationale.

On June 22, 1933, Judge James Horton, described as looking like "Lincoln without the beard," convened court in his hometown of Athens, Alabama to hear a defense motion for a new trial. Hardly anyone held out hope that the motion would be granted. Horton, however, had become convinced that Price was lying. Not only was her story full of inconsistencies, but it was not corroborated by other witnesses or the medical evidence. Judge Horton had one additional reason to believe that Patterson was innocent that remained a secret until years after the trial. After Dr. Bridges presented his medical testimony, the prosecution had requested that Dr. John Lynch, originally listed as a prosecution witness, be excused from testifying. His testimony would only be redundant, according to Knight. After Horton excused the young doctor, he was approached by

Lynch who said he wanted to talk privately. Horton and Lynch talked in the courthouse men's bathroom while armed guards stood outside the door. Lynch told Horton he was convinced that the girls were lying, had told them so to their faces, and that they merely laughed at him. Horton urged Lynch to testify, but Lynch, only a few years out of medical school and just building a practice in Scottsboro, resisted, saying that to do so would ruin his career. Sympathizing with Lynch's predicament, Horton withdrew his demand. Judge Horton, who had to face re-election the next year, had been warned that setting aside the jury's verdict in this case would be political suicide. Horton, however, believed one should "let justice be done, though the heavens may fall." To a stunned courtroom, he announced that he was setting aside the verdict and death sentence, and ordering a new trial. (Horton, who was unopposed the previous time he ran, lost his judgeship in the next election.)

Attorney General Knight wasted no time in announcing that the state was convinced of the Scottsboro Boys' guilt and would press ahead with prosecutions. At the next trial, Knight promised, there would be corroboration for Price's story. Orville Gilley, the one white boy left on the train when the alleged rapes took place, had agreed to testify for the prosecution. The prosecution had one additional ground for optimism. Pressure in the right places had succeeded in getting the new trials transferred out of Judge Horton's courtroom. William Callahan, a septuagenarian, no nonsense judge, would preside at Haywood Patterson's next trial, scheduled for November, 1933. . . .

Convictions, Appeals, and Reversals

Guilty verdicts were quickly returned by juries in both the Patterson and Norris trials. Both defendants were sentenced to death. Liebowitz angrily promised to appeal the verdicts "to Hell and back." Judge Callahan, in the interest of judicial economy, agreed to postpone the trials of the remaining seven Scottsboro Boys until the appeals of the first two had run their course.

On February 15, 1935, the United States Supreme Court heard arguments in the Patterson and Norris cases. Liebowitz argued that the convictions should be overturned because Alabama excluded blacks from its jury rolls in violation of the equal protection clause of the Constitution. The names of blacks that appeared on the jury rolls introduced in Judge Callahan's courtroom were, Liebowitz told the justices, forged sometime after the start of Patterson's trial. Chief Justice Charles Evans Hughes asked Liebowitz if he could prove that allegation. Liebowitz had a page bring in the actual jury rolls and a magnifying glass. Hughes looked at the rolls, then passed it to the next seated justice, who then passed it to the next. Looks of disgust appeared on their faces. Six weeks later the Supreme Court announced their decision in *Norris vs. Alabama*, unanimously holding that the Alabama system of jury selection unconstitutional and reversing the convictions of Norris and Patterson. Liebowitz said, "I am thrilled beyond words." He hoped that the Court's decision would convince Alabama that the Scottsboro cases were no longer worth their economic and political cost.

The state decided to press ahead with prosecutions as the defense tried to deal with its own eternal problems. Two ILD lawyers in Nashville were arrested and charged with trying to bribe Victoria Price to change her testimony, infuriating Liebowitz, who said the ILD was "assassinating" the Scottsboro Boys. Liebowitz, meanwhile, was under criticism himself for having through his actions at previous trials alienated potential jurors. As Haywood Patterson's fourth trial began in January, 1936, in Judge Callahan's courtroom, Liebowitz agreed to let a local attorney named Charles Watts play the more visible role while he coached from a seat behind.

No surprise to anyone, Patterson was again convicted of rape. What was surprising, however, was that the jury sentenced him to seventy-five years in prison rather than giving him the death sentence the prosecution requested. One determined Methodist on the jury succeeded in persuading the other eleven to go along with his "compromise." The verdict represented the first time in the history of Alabama that a black man convicted of raping a white woman had not been sentenced to death. . . .

Seven of the nine Scottsboro Boys had been held in jail for over six years without trial by the time jury selection began in the third trial of Clarence Norris on Monday, July 12, 1937. Trying to beat the hundred degree heat, Judge Callahan rushed the trial even more than usual, and by Wednesday morning the prosecution had a death sentence. Andy Wright's trial was next; he got ninety-nine years. On Saturday, July 24 at eleven o'clock, Charlie Weem's jury returned and gave him seventy-five years. Moments later, Ozie Powell was brought into court and the new prosecutor, Thomas Lawson, announced that the state was dropping rape charges against Powell and that he was pleading guilty to assaulting a deputy. Then came the big news. Lawson announced that all charges were being dropped against the remaining four defendants: Willie Roberson, Olen Montgomery, Eugene Williams, and Roy Wright. He said that after "careful consideration" every prosecutor was "convinced" that Roberson and Montgomery were "not guilty." Wright and Williams, regardless of their guilt or innocence, were twelve and thirteen at the time and, in view of the jail time they had already served, justice required that they also be released. Liebowitz led the four from the jail to an awaiting car, and with an escort of state troopers they were driven to the Tennessee border. Free of Alabama, but not of the label "Scottsboro Boy" or from the wounds inflicted by six years in prison, they went on with their separate lives: to marriage, to alcoholism, to jobs, to fatherhood, to hope, to disillusionment, to disease, or to suicide. . . .

Either through paroles or escapes all of the Scottsboro Boys eventually found their way out of Alabama. Charles Weems was paroled in 1943, Ozie Powell and Clarence Norris in 1946, and Andy Wright, the last to leave Alabama for good (Wright had been paroled earlier, then returned because of a parole violation) in June, 1950. Haywood Patterson managed a dramatic escape in 1948. Patterson and

Norris each went on to participate in the writing of books about their lives. Patterson's book, *Scottsboro Boy,* was published in 1950 while he was a fugitive. Shortly after its publication, Patterson was arrested by the FBI, but Governor G. Mennen Williams of Michigan refused Alabama's extradition request. Norris published his book, *The Last of the Scottsboro Boys*, in 1979. Ten years later, on January 23, 1989, the last of the Scottsboro Boys was dead. . . .

The story of the Scottsboro Boys is one of the most shameful examples of injustice in our nation's history. It makes clear that in the Deep South of the 1930s, jurors were not willing to accord a black charged with raping a white woman the usual presumption of innocence. In fact, one may argue that the presumption seemed reversed: a black was presumed guilty unless he could establish his innocence beyond a reasonable doubt. The cases show that to jurors, black lives didn't count for much. The jurors that in April, 1933 had just voted to sentence Haywood Patterson to death were seen laughing as they emerged from the jury-room. Hannah Arendt wrote of "the banality of evil." Evil rarely comes in the form of monsters, but rather in the form of relatively normal people who, for reasons of careers, ideology, or a desire for society's approval, are indifferent to the human consequences of their actions. Because of indifferent jurors and career-motivated prosecutors, the self-serving and groundless accusations of a single woman were allowed to change forever the lives of nine black teenagers who found themselves in the wrong place at the wrong time.

It is easy, especially for a Minnesota native like myself, to look at the story of the Scottsboro Boys and to condemn a whole region of the country. That, however, is unfair. There were good people of the South—courageous newspaper editors, attorneys, ministers, and others—who fought for justice for the Scottsboro Boys. One southerner's actions stand out above all others. The decision of Judge James Horton to set aside the conviction of Haywood Patterson, despite the dire consequences that decision would have for his own career, was heroism, pure and simple.

Gangsters and G-Men: Fighting Crime in the Thirties

Frederick Lewis Allen

Americans in the thirties were concerned about the increasing influence of gangsters and racketeers and looked to the government for a solution, writes noted historian and journalist Frederick Lewis Allen in this excerpt from his book *Since Yesterday, the Nineteen-Thirties in America*. J. Edgar Hoover and his FBI agents, known as G-men, captured or eliminated "public enemies" like John Dillinger, becoming heroes who were memorialized in the movies of the day, Allen reveals. To further demonstrate the commitment to eliminating organized crime, Allen explains, special prosecutors like Thomas E. Dewey indicted and convicted racketeers like Lucky Luciano and corrupt city officials like those in New York's Tammany Hall.

Early in the evening of July 22, 1934, a group of agents of the Department of Justice, armed with pistols, gathered unobtrusively about a movie theatre on Lincoln Avenue, Chicago, Illinois. The leader of the group, Melvin H. Purvis, parked his car near the theatre door and carefully scanned the faces of the men and women who entered. At length Purvis recognized the man he wanted—though this man had dyed his hair, had had his face lifted, had grown a mustache, and had put on gold-rimmed glasses.

For two hours Purvis waited in his car, until the man came out of the theatre. Then Purvis signaled to his aides by thrusting an arm out of the car, dropping his hand, and closing it. The aides closed in on the movie-goer, and when he started to draw an automatic they shot him down. The next morning the headlines shouted that John Dillinger, Public Enemy No. 1, had been destroyed.

Another offensive of the reform spirit against things-as-they-had-been was well under way.

During the early years of the decade, there had been immense indignation at the prevalence of crime in America and the inability of the police to cope with it. This indignation had been sharpened by the Lindbergh kidnapping early in 1932. From that time on, every kidnapping case leaped into such prominence in the newspaper dispatches that most Americans imagined that a wave of kidnapping was sweeping the country. The public indignation took an ugly form at San Jose, California, late in 1933, when two men who had kidnapped young Brooke Hart, and had shot him, weighted his body, and thrown it into San Francisco Bay, were taken out of the San Jose jail by an angry mob and hanged on trees near by—whereupon the Governor of California, who had a curious notion of law and order, commented that the lynchers had done "a good job."

The Emergence of the FBI

Proceeding upon the theory that the states could not be sure of catching criminals (any more than they could be sure of stopping undesirable business practices) without Federal aid, Congress had passed laws giving the Federal authorities a limited jurisdiction over crimes which had hitherto been wholly under state jurisdiction. J. Edgar Hoover, the resourceful head of the Bureau of Investigation of the Department of Justice, saw his chance. When John Dillinger, a bank robber and hold-up man of the Middle West, proved to have a remarkable ability to shoot his way out of difficulty, Hoover sent his Federal men on the trail—though Dillinger's only Federal offense up to that time was said to have been the interstate transportation of a stolen car. Dillinger was labeled "Public Enemy No. 1" (now that Al Capone was in prison), and the public began to take notice.

The Federal agents caught up to Dillinger at St. Paul but he escaped, wounded. A few days later he appeared in a surgeon's office, leveled a gun, compelled the surgeon to give him treatment for his wound, and got away safely. Again he was found, at a summer resort in Northern Wisconsin; but although agents surrounded the building where he was staying, he escaped after a battle in which two men were killed and two were wounded. At last Purvis caught him in Chicago, as we have seen, and the story of John Dillinger came to an end.

But not the story of J. Edgar Hoover and his Federal agents. For these Federal sleuths now proceeded to capture, dead or alive, "Pretty Boy" Floyd, "Baby Face" Nelson, and so many other public enemies, one after another, that after Alvin Karpis was taken alive in 1936 the public quite lost track of the promotions in the Public Enemy class.

Hoover and his men became heroes of the day. The movies took them up, taught people to call them G-men, and presented James Cagney in the rôle of a bounding young G-man, trained in the law, in scientific detection, in target practice, and incidentally in wrestling. Presently mothers who had been noting with alarm that their small sons liked to play gangster on the street corner were relieved to observe that the favored part in these juvenile dramas was now that of the intrepid G-man, whose machine gun mowed down kidnappers and bank robbers by the score. The real G-men—with the not-quite-so-heavily-advertised aid of state and local police—continued to follow up their triumphs until by the end of 1936 they could claim that every kidnapping case in the country since the passage of the Lindbergh law in 1932 had been closed.

The Gangsters and Racketeers

But kidnapping and bank robbery, sensational as they were, were hardly the most menacing of crimes. The depredations of professional gangster-racketeers were more far-reaching and infinitely more difficult to combat. During the nineteen-twenties various gangster mobs, the most notorious of which was Al Capone's in Chicago, had built up larger, better organized, and more profitable systems of business-by-intimidation than the country had ever seen before. The foundation of these rackets was usually beer-running, but a successful beer-runner could readily handle most of the bootlegging trade in whisky and gin as a side-

Who Was the Public Enemy?

Elizabeth Klungness recalls her brief encounter with John Dillinger, pointing out that some journalists, like her father, questioned the zeal of the G-men.

When the name John Dillinger is mentioned, most people think of a notorious bank robber. My memory is of an unshaven shadowy man who stood behind a dirty screen door and motioned to my father.

Daddy was a feature writer for an Indianapolis newspaper in 1933. His articles were almost always controversial. When you read a Robert A. Butler by-line, you knew the story would contain the unexpected and a bias toward the underdog. . . .

When my father came out, he tipped his gray felt hat to old Mr. Dillinger and motioned for me to go to the car. I remember that he was very quiet on the way home, smoking his usual tipped cigarette in its amber-colored holder. I asked him why he would talk to a bad man instead of calling the police. Wasn't he scared?

"If I thought Dillinger was as dangerous as the police make him out to be, I would not have taken you with me," he replied. "The young man wants to surrender."

Dillinger was bad, but not nearly as bad as the police made him out to be, my father explained. Then he gave me one of those moral lessons that parents of the day were wont to offer. "When you are older, you'll realize that no one is all good or all bad.

line, branch out to take over the gambling and prostitution rackets, and also develop systems of terrorization in otherwise legitimate businesses, by using what purported to be an employer's association or a labor union but was really a scheme for extortion backed by threats to destroy the members' business—or kill them—if they did not pay. The pattern was different in every city and usually there were many rival gangs at work, muscling in on one another's territory from time to time to the accompaniment of machine-gun battles.

Sometimes people are accused of things they haven't done. It's up to newspapermen like me to try to point that out."

I could certainly understand what he was saying. My brother was always getting in trouble for things I did.

"If the police catch Dillinger," he said, "he'll probably be gunned down. John knows that. It's a simple way to close the files on many crimes."

Daddy was to meet Dillinger at a Chicago drugstore in a week's time and take him to the police. The outlaw had told him it was the only way he could be arrested without incident, that they wouldn't dare kill him as long as a well-known reporter was by his side. . . .

One week later what he feared most happened. He was set up, this time by a woman, and he was gunned down just as he had anticipated he would be.

My father was sad about his failure to accomplish the surrender. He went to see John's father and came home a bit poorer after financing a new shirt and haircut for the old man. I've often wondered what would have happened if the police had come by the Mooresville farmhouse that day. Would it have mattered that a little girl, her legs too short to touch the floor, was sitting on a porch swing outside the outlaw's hiding place? Would it make a difference today if there were more old-time writers dedicated to reporting truths even if they are less sensational?

Elizabeth Klungness, "The Lookout," *American Heritage*, April 1997.

During the early nineteen-thirties the racketeers—like legitimate business men—found business bad. The coming of the Repeal of the Prohibition of liquor, by breaking the back of the illicit liquor business, deprived these gentry of a vital source of revenue. But the technique of politically protected intimidation had been so well learned that racketeering went right on in many cities. Even in New York—a city which had never been so racket-ridden as Chicago and had elected in 1933 an honest and effective mayor, Fiorello LaGuardia—dozens of businesses were in the grip of rackets and their victims were too terrified to testify to what was going on.

But New York was to provide a classic demonstration of what the new reform spirit, properly directed, could do.

Fighting Corruption

The story of the demonstration really began on November 21, 1933—when Franklin D. Roosevelt was engaged in his breakfast-in-bed gold-buying plan, and General Johnson was approving National Recovery Administration (NRA) codes, and Mae West was appearing on the screen in "I'm No Angel," and Katharine Hepburn in "Little Women," and copies of *Anthony Adverse* were everywhere, and the first bad dust storm had just raged in the Dust Bowl, and the Century of Progress Fair at Chicago had just ended its first year, and the Civil Works Administration (CWA) had just been organized, and the United States had just recognized Soviet Russia. On that day the New York papers had carried on their inside pages an item of local news: the appointment as local Federal Attorney of one Thomas E. Dewey, who was only thirty-one years old. During the next year and a half young Dewey did well at this job. In the spring of 1935 a grand jury in New York, investigating racketeering, became so dissatisfied with the way in which the evidence was presented to it by the Tammany District Attorney that it rose up in wrath and asked Governor Lehman to appoint a special prosecutor. Governor Lehman appointed the valiant Dewey and on July 29, 1935, he set to work.

There followed one of the most extraordinary performances in the history of criminal detection and prosecution. Dewey mobilized an able staff of young lawyers and accountants in a highly protected office in the Woolworth Building, sent them out to get the evidence about racketeering, and to everybody's amazement got it, despite the terrified insistence of the very people whom he was trying to protect that they knew nothing at all. This evidence Dewey marshaled so brilliantly that presently he began a series of monotonously successful prosecutions. He put out of business the restaurant racket, to which at least 240 restaurants had paid tribute. He sent to prison Toots Herbert, who in the guise of a labor leader, head of Local 167, had collected large sums from the poultry business. He convicted Lucky Luciano, who had levied toll upon the prostitutes and madams of New York (with such smooth-running political protection that although during 1935 no less than 147 girls who worked for this combination had been arrested, not one of them had got a jail sentence). Within two years Dewey had indicted 73 racketeers and convicted 71 of them: and all this despite the unwillingness of witnesses to talk, the constant need of protecting against violence those who agreed to talk, and constant attempts at bribery and intimidation. Elected District Attorney in 1937, Dewey continued his onslaught, and in 1939 he secured the conviction of an important Tammany leader, James J. Hines. (Hines appealed, and at the end of the decade his case was still pending.)

The intimidation industry was not destroyed, of course, any more than kidnapping and bank robbery had been ended; but Dewey, like the G-men, had shown that crime could be successfully combated, and the lesson was widely noted. When the worthy members of the National Economic League, who in 1930 and 1931, as we have previously seen, voted that "Administration of Justice" and "Crime" and "Lawlessness" were—along with Prohibition—the important issues before the country, voted again in 1937, they decided that "Crime" offered a less important problem than "Labor," "Efficiency and Economy in Government," "Taxation," or "The Federal Constitution."

The drive against crime had won at least a temporary victory.

Labor Unrest During the Depression

Howard Zinn

Howard Zinn, a noted author and lecturer, claims that the acts of everyday Americans have shaped the country's history. In the following excerpt from his book *The Twentieth Century: A People's History*, Zinn explains that although the power of labor unions would increase during the 1940s, it was the general and sit-down strikes by workers in the 1930s that opened the door to unionization and labor legislation. Zinn argues that strikes were better tools for effecting change than union organizing, and like "buddies" in war, when fellow workers were fired or wages were cut, workers rallied around their fellows, often bringing business to a halt. Zinn is professor emeritus at Boston University, in Boston, Massachusetts.

A million and a half workers in different industries went on strike in 1934. That spring and summer, longshoremen on the West Coast, in a rank-and-file insurrection against their own union leadership as well as against the shippers, held a convention, demanded the abolition of the shape-up (a kind of early-morning slave market where work gangs were chosen for the day), and went out on strike.

Two thousand miles of Pacific coastline were quickly tied up. The teamsters cooperated, refusing to truck cargo

---

to the piers, and maritime workers joined the strike. When the police moved in to open the piers, the strikers resisted en masse, and two were killed by police gunfire. A mass funeral procession for the strikers brought together tens of thousands of supporters. And then a general strike was called in San Francisco, with 130,000 workers out, the city immobilized.

Five hundred special police were sworn in and 4,500 National Guardsmen assembled, with infantry, machine gun, tank and artillery units. The Los Angeles *Times* wrote:

> The situation in San Francisco is not correctly described by the phrase "general strike." What is actually in progress there is an insurrection, a Communist-inspired and -led revolt against organized government. There is but one thing to be done—put down the revolt with any force necessary.

The pressure became too strong. There were the troops. There was the American Federation of Labor (AFL) pushing to end the strike. The longshoremen accepted a compromise settlement. But they had shown the potential of a general strike.

That same summer of 1934, a strike of teamsters in Minneapolis was supported by other working people, and soon nothing was moving in the city except milk, ice, and coal trucks given exemptions by the strikers. Farmers drove their products into town and sold them directly to the people in the city. The police attacked and two strikers were killed. Fifty thousand people attended a mass funeral. There was an enormous protest meeting and a march on City Hall. After a month, the employers gave in to the teamsters' demands.

In the fall of that same year, 1934, came the largest strike of all—325,000 textile workers in the South. They left the mills and set up flying squadrons in trucks and autos to move through the strike areas, picketing, battling guards, entering the mills, unbelting machinery. Here too, as in the other cases, the strike impetus came from the rank and file, against a reluctant union leadership at the top. The *New*

York Times said: "The grave danger of the situation is that it will get completely out of the hands of the leaders."

Again, the machinery of the state was set in motion. Deputies and armed strikebreakers in South Carolina fired on pickets, killing seven, wounding twenty others. But the strike was spreading to New England. In Lowell, Massachusetts, 2,500 textile workers rioted; in Saylesville, Rhode Island, a crowd of five thousand people defied state troopers who were armed with machine guns, and shut down the textile mill. In Woonsocket, Rhode Island, two thousand people, aroused because someone had been shot and killed by the National Guard, stormed through the town and closed the mill.

By September 18, 421,000 textile workers were on strike throughout the country. There were mass arrests, organizers were beaten, and the death toll rose to thirteen. Roosevelt now stepped in and set up a board of mediation, and the union called off the strike.

Organizing the Sharecroppers

In the rural South, too, organizing took place, often stimulated by Communists, but nourished by the grievances of poor whites and blacks who were tenant farmers or farm laborers, always in economic difficulties but hit even harder by the Depression. The Southern Tenant Farmers Union started in Arkansas, with black and white sharecroppers, and spread to other areas. Roosevelt's Agricultural Adjustment Administration (AAA) was not helping the poorest of farmers; in fact by encouraging farmers to plant less, it forced tenants and sharecroppers to leave the land. By 1935, of 6,800,000 farmers, 2,800,000 were tenants. The average income of a sharecropper was $312 a year. Farm laborers, moving from farm to farm, area to area, no land of their own, in 1933 were earning about $300 a year.

Black farmers were the worst off, and some were attracted to the strangers who began appearing in their area during the Depression, suggesting they organize. Nate

Shaw recalls, in Theodore Rosengarten's remarkable interview (*All God's Dangers*):

> And durin of the pressure years, a union begin to operate in this country, called it the Sharecroppers Union—that was a nice name, I thought . . . and I knowed what was goin on was a turnabout on the southern man, white and colored; it was somethin unusual. And I heard about it bein a organization for the poor class of people—that's just what I wanted to get into, too. I wanted to know the secrets of it enough that I could become in the knowledge of it. . . .
>
> Mac Sloane, white man, said "You stay out of it. These niggers runnin around here carryin on some kind of meetin—you better stay out of it."
>
> I said to myself, "You a fool if you think you can keep me from joinin". I went right on and joined it, just as quick as the next meetin come. . . . And he done just the thing to push me into it—gived me orders not to join.
>
> The teachers of this organization begin to drive through this country—they couldn't let what they was doin be known. One of em was a colored fella; I disremember his name but he did a whole lot of time, holdin meetins with us—that was part of this job. . . .
>
> Had the meetins at our houses or anywhere we could keep a look and a watch-out that nobody was comin in on us. Small meetins, sometimes there'd be a dozen . . . niggers was scared, niggers was scared, that's tellin the truth.

Nate Shaw told of what happened when a black farmer who hadn't paid his debts was about to be dispossessed:

> The deputy said, "I'm goin to take all old Virgil Jones got this mornin.". . . .
>
> I begged him not to do it, begged him. "You'll dispossess him of bein able to feed his family."

An Issue of Class, Not Color

Nate Shaw then told the deputy he was not going to allow it. The deputy came back with more men, and one of them shot and wounded Shaw, who then got his gun and fired back. He was arrested in late 1932, and served twelve years in an Alabama prison. His story is a tiny piece of the great unrecorded drama of the southern poor in those years of the Sharecroppers Union. Years after his release from prison, Nate Shaw spoke his mind on color and class:

O, it's plain as your hand. The poor white man and the poor black man is sittin in the same saddle today—big dudes done branched em off that way. The control of a man, the controllin power, is in the hands of the rich man. . . . That class is standin together and the poor white man is out there on the colored list—I've caught that: ways and actions a heap of times speaks louder than words. . . .

Hosea Hudson, a black man from rural Georgia, at the age of ten a plowhand, later an iron worker in Birmingham, was aroused by the case of the Scottsboro Boys in 1931 (nine black youths accused of raping two white girls and convicted on flimsy evidence by all-white juries). That year he joined the Communist party. In 1932 and 1933, he organized unemployed blacks in Birmingham. He recalls:

Deep in the winter of 1932 we Party members organized a unemployed mass meeting to be held on the old courthouse steps, on 3rd Avenue, North Birmingham. . . . It was about 7000 or more people turned out . . . Negroes and whites. . . .

In 1932 and '33 we began to organize these unemployed block committees in the various communities of Birmingham. . . . If someone get out of food. . . . We wouldn't go around and just say, "That's too bad". We make it our business to go see this person. . . . And if the person was willing . . . we'd work with them. . . .

Block committees would meet every week, had a regular meeting. We talked about the welfare question, what was happening, we read the *Daily Worker* and the *Southern Worker* to see what was going on about unemployed relief, what people doing in Cleveland . . . struggles in Chicago . . . or we talk about the latest developments in the Scottsboro case. We kept up, we was on top, so people always wanted to come cause we had something different to tell them every time.

The Sit-Down Strike

In 1934 and 1935 hundreds of thousands of workers, left out of the tightly controlled, exclusive unions of the American Federation of Labor, began organizing in the new mass production industries—auto, rubber, packinghouse. The AFL could not ignore them; it set up a Committee for Industrial Organization to organize these workers outside of craft lines, by industry, all workers in a plant belonging to one union. This Committee, headed by John Lewis, then broke away and became the CIO—the Congress of Industrial Organizations.

But it was rank-and-file strikes and insurgencies that pushed the union leadership, AFL and CIO, into action. Jeremy Brecher tells the story in his book *Strike!* A new kind of tactic began among rubber workers in Akron, Ohio, in the early thirties—the sit-down strike. The workers stayed in the plant instead of walking out, and this had clear advantages: they were directly blocking the use of strikebreakers; they did not have to act through union officials but were in direct control of the situation themselves; they did not have to walk outside in the cold and rain, but had shelter; they were not isolated, as in their work, or on the picket line; they were thousands under one roof, free to talk to one another, to form a community of struggle. Louis Adamic, a labor writer, describes one of the early sit-downs:

> Sitting by their machines, cauldrons, boilers and work benches, they talked. Some realized for the first time how important they were in the process of rubber production. Twelve men had practically stopped the works! . . . Superintendents, foremen, and straw bosses were dashing about. . . . In less than an hour the dispute was settled, full victory for the men.

In early 1936, at the Firestone rubber plant in Akron,

makers of truck tires, their wages already too low to pay for food and rent, were faced with a wage cut. When several union men were fired, others began to stop work, to sit down on the job. In one day the whole of plant #1 was sitting down. In two days, plant #2 was sitting down, and management gave in. In the next ten days there was a sit-down at Goodyear. A court issued an injunction against mass picketing. It was ignored, and 150 deputies were sworn in. But they soon faced ten thousand workers from all over Akron. In a month the strike was won.

"It Was Like War"

The idea spread through 1936. In December of that year began the longest sit-down strike of all, at Fisher Body plant #1 in Flint, Michigan. It started when two brothers were fired, and it lasted until February 1937. For forty days there was a community of two thousand strikers. "It was like war," one said. "The guys with me became my buddies." Sidney Fine in *Sit-Down* describes what happened. Committees organized recreation, information, classes, a postal service, sanitation. Courts were set up to deal with those who didn't take their turn washing dishes or who threw rubbish or smoked where it was prohibited or brought in liquor. The "punishment" consisted of extra duties; the ultimate punishment was expulsion from the plant. A restaurant owner across the street prepared three meals a day for two thousand strikers. There were classes in parliamentary procedure, public speaking, history of the labor movement. Graduate students at the University of Michigan gave courses in journalism and creative writing.

There were injunctions, but a procession of five thousand armed workers encircled the plant and there was no attempt to enforce the injunction. Police attacked with tear gas and the workers fought back with firehoses. Thirteen strikers were wounded by gunfire, but the police were driven back. The governor called out the National Guard. By this time the strike had spread to other General Motors plants. Finally there was a settlement, a six-month contract, leaving many questions unsettled but recognizing that from now on, the company would have to deal not with individuals but with a union.

In 1936 there were forty-eight sit-down strikes. In 1937 there were 477: electrical workers in St. Louis; shirt workers in Pulaski, Tennessee; broom workers in Pueblo, Colorado; trash collectors in Bridgeport, Connecticut; gravediggers in New Jersey; seventeen blind workers at the New York Guild for the Jewish Blind; prisoners in an Illinois penitentiary; and even thirty members of a National Guard Company who had served in the Fisher Body sit-down, and now sat down themselves because they had not been paid.

The sit-downs were especially dangerous to the system because they were not controlled by the regular union leadership. An AFL business agent for the Hotel and Restaurant Employees said:

> You'd be sitting in the office any March day of 1937, and the phone would ring and the voice at the other end would say: "My name is Mary Jones; I'm a soda clerk at Liggett's; we've thrown the manager out and we've got the keys. What do we do now?" And you'd hurry over to the company to negotiate and over there they'd say, "I think it's the height of irresponsibility to call a strike before you've ever asked for a contract" and all you could answer was, "You're so right."

Legislating Labor Unrest

It was to stabilize the system in the face of labor unrest that the Wagner Act of 1935, setting up a National Labor Relations Board (NLRB), had been passed. The wave of strikes in 1936, 1937, 1938, made the need even more pressing. In Chicago, on Memorial Day, 1937, a strike at Republic Steel brought the police out, firing at a mass picket line of strikers, killing ten of them. Autopsies showed the bullets had hit the workers in the back as they were running away: this was the Memorial Day Massacre. But Republic Steel was organized, and so was Ford Motor

Company, and the other huge plants in steel, auto, rubber, meatpacking, the electrical industry.

The Wagner Act was challenged by a steel corporation in the courts, but the Supreme Court found it constitutional—that the government could regulate interstate commerce, and that strikes hurt interstate commerce. From the trade unions' point of view, the new law was an aid to union organizing. From the government's point of view it was an aid to the stability of commerce.

Unions were not wanted by employers, but they were more controllable—more stabilizing for the system than the wildcat strikes, the factory occupations of the rank and file. In the spring of 1937, a *New York Times* article carried the headline "Unauthorized Sit-Downs Fought by CIO Unions." The story read: "Strict orders have been issued to all organizers and representatives that they will be dismissed if they authorize any stoppages of work without the consent of the international officers. . . ." The *Times* quoted John L. Lewis, dynamic leader of the CIO: "A CIO contract is adequate protection against sit-downs, lie-downs, or any other kind of strike."

The Communist party, some of whose members played critical roles in organizing CIO unions, seemed to take the same position. One Communist leader in Akron was reported to have said at a party strategy meeting after the sit-downs: "Now we must work for regular relations between the union and the employers—and strict observance of union procedure on the part of the workers."

Thus, two sophisticated ways of controlling direct labor action developed in the mid-thirties. First, the National Labor Relations Board would give unions legal status, listen to them, settling certain of their grievances. Thus it could moderate labor rebellion by channeling energy into elections—just as the constitutional system channeled possibly troublesome energy into voting. The NLRB would set limits in economic conflict as voting did in political conflict. And second, the workers' organization itself, the union, even a militant and aggressive union like the CIO, would channel the workers' insurrectionary energy into contracts, negotiations, union meetings, and try to minimize strikes, in order to build large, influential, even respectable organizations.

The history of those years seems to support the argument of Richard Cloward and Frances Piven, in their book *Poor People's Movements*, that labor won most during its spontaneous uprisings, before the unions were recognized or well organized: "Factory workers had their greatest influence, and were able to exact their most substantial concessions from government, during the Great Depression, in the years before they were organized into unions. Their power during the Depression was not rooted in organization, but in disruption."

CHAPTER 5

Entertainment, Expression, and Escape in the Thirties

AMERICA'S DECADES

The Hollywood Studio System Adapts to Sound

Frank E. Beaver

In the following excerpt taken from his book *On Film: A History of the Motion Picture*, film historian Frank E. Beaver explores the new film styles that emerged in 1930s Hollywood as the major studios reacted to the depression and the introduction of sound technology. Some movie styles, such as backstage musicals and dance-films, were a direct product of the development of sound, Beaver writes, while gunshots and screeching tires added excitement to the already popular gangster film. Hard hit by the depression, Beaver explains, the Fox studio turned to the double-feature to entice audiences to their theaters, producing "B pictures"—low budget films with formulaic plots and lesser-known stars. To avoid bankruptcy, Universal Studios took advantage of the talent of Boris Karloff and its earlier success at the horror film to produce the successful *Frankenstein*. Although each studio had a different philosophy and style in the thirties, the author concludes that the studios met their goal of producing escapist entertainment for the depression-weary public. Beaver is a professor of film and video studies at the University of Michigan, at Ann Arbor.

Excerpted from *On Film: A History of the Motion Picture*, by Frank E. Beaver (New York: McGraw-Hill, 1983). Copyright ©1983 by McGraw-Hill, Inc. Reprinted with permission.

B y 1932 film directors in America had come to realize that sound was more than a technological intrusion. It was a valuable tool for intensifying the screen image while also offering rich opportunities for expressive sound-image arrangements.

The path to the successful coupling of sound and image had its rudimentary beginnings, as Eisenstein had noted, in the United States where the first sound synchronization systems were introduced in the late 1920s. Warner Brothers led the way with its Vitaphone sound-disc system in 1926, followed by the superior Case-Western sound-on-film method at Fox which was first demonstrated early in 1927.

As these two studios and, shortly thereafter, their competitors adapted to sound, new film genres and styles emerged. The major Hollywood producing organizations continued on their path toward individual personalities through a variety of responses to the "talking" picture. . . .

Warner Brothers profited from its leading role in the introduction of sound films. Its first all-talking pictures, *Lights of New York* and *The Singing Fool,* both released in 1928, were so successful at the box office that the studio was suddenly catapulted into a top position within the highly competitive industry. By the 1930s the studio also owned nearly 500 theaters in its expanding exhibition chain.

Tough Gangster Films

With the release of *Lights of New York* Warners discovered the appeal of the gangster story, popular to a degree during the silent era, but a genre which would be nurtured and exploited with unparalleled success after the introduction of sound. *Lights of New York* recounted a big-city tale of prohibition-era gangsterism in which an innocent young man is drawn into the illegal activities of bootleggers.

Despite its static, talky quality, Bryan Foy's film suggested the screen environment that eventually characterized the genre: the backrooms of night clubs and speakeasies where clandestine activities are carried out by con artists. Chorus girls, of which one is invariably allied with and often betrayed by her gangster boyfriend, stand on the periphery of the big-city underworld.

Missing from the fifty-seven minute film, however, was the automobile which later became a familiar element of the genre. The sound of screeching tires was soon introduced to add a new thrill to the motion-picture chase.

With the development of microphone follow-booms, camera silencers, and sound mixers for blending and dubbing aural elements (achieved as early as 1929), the studios were free to add such sensational sound effects as screeching tires and gunshots, and to keep their screen characters on the move. Warner Brothers continued to explore the narrative possibilities of the crime film and achieved renown in the early thirties with several classic illustrations of the genre. Most notable were *Little Caesar* (1930) with Edward G. Robinson, *The Public Enemy* (1931) with James Cagney, and *I Am a Fugitive from a Chain Gang* (1932) with Paul Muni. The tough, active quality of these pictures exhilarated a country in which real-life gangsterism had also captured public attention.

W.R. Burnett's novel about a gangster who progresses from a ruthless murderer to a victim of his own violent world provided the story material for Mervyn LeRoy's *Little Caesar*. Edward G. Robinson, portraying the leading character, Rico, is eventually shot to death in a vacant lot by policemen. Robinson's ability to project toughness and at the same time an almost boyish quality made the actor a major star. . . .

James Cagney appeared in his first Warners' film, *Sinners' Holiday*, in 1930, but it was *The Public Enemy*, his fifth picture, which established the actor as a virile and dynamic star. His portrayal of a lower-class boy who rises from simple surliness to gangster status is grimly drawn on the screen by director William Wellman. . . .

Warners' realistic crime cycle reached a peak with *I Am a Fugitive from a Chain Gang* in 1932. This film, starring Paul Muni, moved away from the standardized mythology of gangster stories and presented a vivid picture of prison life.

Muni was Jim Allen, a veteran who has been unjustly convicted of a crime and sent to a southern prison. The script by Sheridan Gibney, Howard J. Green, and Brown Holmes, and based on the true experiences of a former prisoner, exposed brutalities and injustices existent at the time in the American penal system. . . .

Social Dramas and "G-Men"

With *I Am a Fugitive from a Chain Gang*, Warner Brothers enhanced its growing reputation as a studio with a social conscience. Other important social dramas followed: *Wild Boys of the Road* (1933), a film about the plight of unemployed youth during the Depression; *Massacre* (1933), a study of the insensitivity of government agents in dealing with American Indians; *Black Fury* (1935), a story of conflict between management and labor in a Pennsylvania coal mining community; *The Black Legion* (1936), a film about mob violence and the organized hatred of foreigners; *They Won't Forget* (1937), a Mervyn LeRoy picture which exposed the evils of mob violence and retaliation.

The prominent role of Warner Brothers in the production of social message films was earned as pressure against such "editorial" films was increasing. In the early 1930s, Hollywood's self-regulatory Production Code Office stepped up its criticism of scripts which questioned the practices of American society, government, or industry. Warners was required, for example, in 1933 to delete scenes from two pictures which showed policemen in a less than favorable light. Efforts were also made to lighten the treatment of coal industry management in the script for *Black Fury*.

The Production Code's criticism was also often aimed at the studio's realistic crime films. Public protest from concerned civic groups about the effects of violence in gangster pictures forced the Code Office to monitor scripts which might continue to popularize societal misfits.

By 1935 Warners had for the most part left behind the antihero gangster story for crime films that presented law-enforcement characters as the protagonists. G-Men replaced "public enemies" as the tough guys at Warners; this reversal of emphasis projected a clear-cut conflict between good and evil and was, therefore, considered more acceptable to the censors.

Backstage Musicals and Screen Biographies

Faced with public pressure and industry censorship, Warner Brothers turned to other types of film entertainment. Two genres, the musical extravaganza and the biographical film, achieved particular success as Warner-styled products.

The Hollywood studios had persistently turned out unimaginative musical revues and operettas between 1929 and 1932. Warners' musical directors, with Busby Berkeley leading the group, injected new life into the genre with a backstage plotting device.

The backstage story line, as it evolved at Warners, centered on a plot about the efforts of a group of entertainers to produce a musical show. Setbacks and character conflicts in the struggle to get the musical on the stage provided dramatic interest. The musical numbers, usually irrelevant to the plot, appeared at various points throughout the film, and reached an extravagant, lavish peak near the film's conclusion.

Berkeley's success as choreographer in *Forty-Second Street* (1933), the "Gold Diggers" series (1933–1937), and *Footlight Parade* (1933) resulted from an impressive visual display of carefully synchronized, highly stylized musical numbers. Beginning with *Forty-Second Street* he had begun to separate the story from the musical elements in order to provide more interesting drama and more visually exciting music and dance segments. His ability to utilize editing and a fluid camera also added to the cinematic quality of his unusual film choreography.

Warners' many film biographies included: *Alexander Hamilton* (1931); *Voltaire* (1933); *The Story of Louis Pasteur* (1936); and *The Life of Emile Zola* (1937). These pictures provided suitable vehicles for Warners' male-dominated stock company which was led by Paul Muni, George Arliss, Spencer Tracy, Edward G. Robinson, James Cagney, Humphrey Bogart, and Errol Flynn. In the latter half of the 1930s Flynn's appearance in a series of adventure films, including *Captain Blood* (1935) and *The Adventures of Robin Hood* (1938), gave Warners some of its most successful pictures.

The studio's small group of female stars was headed by Bette Davis and Barbara Stanwyck, both of whom portrayed strong, independently willed screen characters. Davis, in particular, possessed at times a hardened, unscrupulous quality that matched that of Warners' many tough male characters.

The bold, forward-looking social stance of the Warners studios, its hard-hitting action pictures, escapist musicals, adventure stories, and biographical films sustained the studio through the uncertain 1930s. . . .

William Fox, early in 1929, sought to gain even more power by purchasing a controlling interest in the Loew's theater chain. Fox also closed deals that year for the purchase of additional theaters in Europe, further increasing the corporation's holdings and its outstanding debts.

B-Pictures and a Child Star

As one of the largest film conglomerates in the world, the Fox organization suffered more than others from the devastating consequences of the October 1929 stock market crash. The studio lost more than $3 million in 1930—a loss which resulted from a $12 million drop in company revenues during the twelve-month period. Because of continuing financial woes William Fox was forced to resign control of the corporation in 1932 and Sidney Kent, temporary studio head, made valiant efforts to keep the organization afloat.

Fox, like other plagued Hollywood companies, turned to the newly introduced exhibition practice of double-feature programming. The enticement of two motion pictures for the price of one was a Depression-inspired gimmick that had originated in New England in 1931.

The Fox organization proved particularly successful in turning out B-pictures of good quality. B-pictures were the less expensive films which appeared on double-feature bills. Characteristically lower in budget expenditure, populated by lesser-known stars, and often formulaic in design, B-pictures, nevertheless, became a specialized commodity at Fox with the guidance of Sol Wurtzel, a producer of considerable ability.

In 1934 a precocious child actress named Shirley Temple signed a contract with Fox and throughout the thirties was responsible for one low-budget hit film after another. Her first film at Fox was a musical revue with Warner Baxter, *Stand Up and Cheer* (1934). Temple's popularity soon surpassed that of Greta Garbo and other female luminaries of the decade. Her seven years and twenty-three films at Fox established Shirley Temple as the indisputable child star of motion pictures, a reputation which has yet to be seriously challenged.

When Fox films merged with Twentieth Century Pictures in 1935 to become Twentieth Century–Fox, Darryl Zanuck (1902–1979) of Twentieth stepped into the amalgamated studio as vice-president in charge of production. Zanuck earned a reputation as an energetic and efficient supervisor of studio operations. Like his counterparts elsewhere in Hollywood, he immersed himself totally in production activities and significantly influenced film quality and style. . . .

Metro-Goldwyn-Mayer: Producers, Prestige, and Glamorous Entertainment

As Metro-Goldwyn-Mayer moved into the sound era, the studio's efficient assembly-line system of making films was tightened to keep the corporation running smoothly. Working under Irving Thalberg's supervision were teams of creative producers, contract directors, writers, talented set designers, sound technicians, costumers, and, indispensably, an ever-growing number of glamorous stock players.

Many of the creative producers at M-G-M were individuals of taste and artistic judgment, whose presence was often more strongly felt in films they supervised than that of the contract directors. Albert Lewin headed production of M-G-M's "prestige" films, an innovative sound-era concept introduced by Thalberg that brought to the screen adaptations of popular literary works: *Anna Christie* (1930), *Strange Interlude* (1932), *What Every Woman Knows* (1934), *Mutiny on the Bounty* (1935), *The Good Earth* (1937). As supervisor of this specialized prestige category and as head of M-G-M's story department, Lewin earned a reputation as a cultured, stylish filmmaker.

David O. Selznick, a creative producer at M-G-M until 1936, personified the production supervisor who left a stamp on every film he produced. During the thirties his creative position was topped only by Thalberg's. In *Dinner at Eight* (1933), *Night Flight* (1933), *Dancing Lady* (1933), *Viva Villa!* (1934), *David Copperfield* (1935), *Anna Karenina* (1935), and *A Tale of Two Cities* (1935) Selznick produced one hit picture after another.

Selznick (also at that time Louis B. Mayer's son-in-law) participated fully in all facets of his filmmaking projects—choosing actors, doctoring scripts, and making final decisions on sets and costumes. In a significant move to improve film sound, he permitted musical composers to become involved in the making of films during production rather than afterward in the postproduction stage, maintaining that the early involvement of composers resulted in more appropriate and inspired scores.

Among the notable 1930s contract directors at M-G-M were Victor Fleming *(Captains Courageous),* Clarence Brown *(Idiot's Delight),* W. S. Van Dyke *(San Francisco),* Sam Wood *(A Night at the Opera),* Sydney Franklin *(The Good Earth),* and Robert Z. Leonard *(The Great Ziegfeld).* These individuals functioned efficiently within a studio system where coordination was more important than individual directing styles.

Yet, the versatility of the M-G-M directors showed in a

diverse collection of sound films made in the thirties for the family trade. These included the large assortment of literary adaptations, musical operettas with Jeanette MacDonald and Nelson Eddy, and numerous series films: *Tarzan, Andy Hardy, Dr. Kildare, Boston Blackie, The Thin Man,* and *Maisie.*

The goal at M-G-M of producing entertaining star-studded films of high technical quality resulted in recognizably distinctive products. Production values (set design, costumes, artistic lighting) assumed great importance in products which displayed the "studio look" to its fullest advantage. Glamorous stars were photographed in high-key lighting in costumes and settings that were designed to transmit luminous images. In close-up shots, Rembrandt back-lighting added additional glamour and romance to screen visages. A similar meticulous attention was paid by costume and set designers to pictorial details.

The accumulative visual effect of an M-G-M picture was that of a perfectly controlled, artificial environment. Stars such as Norma Shearer, Greta Garbo, Jean Harlow, Jeanette MacDonald, and Joan Crawford glowed in the hands of M-G-M's skillful cinematographers and technicians. And it would be an omission not to add that so too did male stars. Robert Taylor, John Gilbert, Cary Grant, Nelson Eddy, Franchot Tone, Robert Young, among a host of other leading men, were given a similar "prettified" treatment.

To provide stories for its stars and the eager technical staff, M-G-M assembled a prestigious group of writers that included Moss Hart, Frances Marion, Anita Loos, Charles MacArthur, and William Faulkner. By the time, however, that scripts by these high-caliber writers went through an assembly-line translation to the screen they had been shaped to fit the management's preference for escapist entertainment.

The principal challenge for writers at M-G-M came in trying to find new ways of supplying emotional fervor to romance-filled screen stories. The M-G-M style remained even after Thalberg's death in 1936 and Selznick's departure the same year to head his own production company and to make the greatest of all screen romances, *Gone with the Wind* (1939).

Universal: Monsters, Ingenues, and War

The advent of sound and the economic plunge brought on by the Depression reinforced Universal's symbiotic relationship with the major production-distribution organizations (Warner Brothers, M-G-M, Paramount, Fox). Carl Laemmle sold the sixty-odd theaters owned by Universal in the early 1930s and the studio settled down to its principal position as a supplier of films for the growing double-feature market.

The horror film, following the example of Universal's earlier silent success, Lon Chaney's *Phantom of the Opera* (1925), remained an important studio staple. In 1931 *Frankenstein,* starring Boris Karloff, helped Universal avert bankruptcy while establishing Karloff as a suitable replacement for Chaney who had died in 1930. Karloff was so successful in imitating Chaney's skillful and grotesque use of makeup that Universal followed *Frankenstein* with a number of spin-offs, including *The Bride of Frankenstein* (1935) and *The Son of Frankenstein* (1939).

During the latter part of the 1930s, the studio found a popular star in the teenage actress Deanna Durbin, whose pure soprano singing voice (*100 Men and a Girl,* 1937) and adolescent charm made her Universal's most successful and profitable contract performer.

All Quiet on the Western Front

The most important film produced at Universal during the 1930s, *All Quiet on the Western Front* (1930), managed to give the studio the distinction of having created one of the greatest war pictures of any period and also of having produced one of the first great sound motion pictures. Carl Laemmle, Jr., supervised the screen adaptation of Erich Maria Remarque's pacifist novel shortly after Laemmle's father appointed him head of studio operations at age 21.

All Quiet on the Western Front was a significant achievement for several reasons. It courageously presented German soldiers from a sympathetic point of view, and thereby offered a larger, more tragic understanding of war than that provided by the many anti-German pictures made in the United States after World War I. . . .

RKO: Technicolor, Special Effects, and Dance

The emergence of the Radio-Keith-Orpheum (RKO) studio occurred as a direct result of the advent of sound motion pictures. RKO was incorporated in 1929 as a subsidiary of the Radio Corporation of America (RCA). RCA had profited from its introduction of the Photophone Sound System in 1928 and with the incorporation of RKO expanded its business interests into the areas of film production, distribution, and exhibition.

Because of its late arrival in a well-formed industry, the stylistic identity of the RKO studios was not as apparent in the 1930s as that of the older, more established production companies. In the early years of its existence, RKO was unable to realize a profit despite a surprisingly impressive number of quality films.

Among RKO's early successes was *A Bill of Divorcement* (1932), a film in which Katharine Hepburn first brought her unique physical and vocal qualities before the attention of the filmgoing public. Another soon-to-be star, Leslie Howard, appeared about the same time in RKO's adaptation of Philip Barry's *The Animal Kingdom* (1932). Dolores Del Rio achieved star status in *The Bird of Paradise* (1932), one of RKO's many successful screen versions of well-known stage plays.

Also among RKO's early achievements were *Little Women* (1933) and the first feature-length three-color Technicolor film *Becky Sharp* (1935).

The Technicolor process used in *Becky Sharp*, an adaptation of Thackeray's *Vanity Fair,* culminated a lengthy period of experimentation with methods of supplying color to screen images. The progression led from hand-tinted frames (as early as 1896) to the unwieldy three-color Kinemacolor process (1906) to the improved Technicolor efforts of Herbert Kalmus and Robert Comstock in 1916–1917. Kalmus Technicolor, as the process came to be called, used a double negative lamination system in which red-orange-yellow colors were photographed on one negative and blue-green-purple on the other.

This system was first fully introduced in Douglas Fairbanks' costume-action picture *The Black Pirate* (1926). *The Phantom of the Opera,* made the year before, had contained color sequences, but Fairbanks' film was the first to apply Technicolor throughout. Color values in *The Black Pirate*, because of the two-color double-negative system, were not always precisely accurate. By 1932 Kalmus had perfected his process so that a full color range could be photographed on a single celluloid emulsion.

The improved Kalmus process, although expensive, was adopted with great success by Walt Disney in his cartoon *Flowers and Trees* (1932). Disney held the exclusive rights to the process until 1934. When the Disney contract expired and Technicolor became available for general use, RKO, before embarking on *Becky Sharp,* successfully produced a Technicolor short, *La Cucaracha* (1934). Experimentation with the Technicolor process was essential because of the bulky camera and special technicians (provided by Kalmus) required for filming.

Becky Sharp represented a major step toward acceptance of color for other than novelty films. Final acceptance came with *Gone with the Wind* and *The Wizard of Oz* in 1939, although color would continue to be seen by producers primarily as a romantic embellishment until the mid-1950s.

King Kong and the Astaire-Rogers Team

In its first decade RKO achieved additional significance with Willis O'Brien's clever special-effects film *King Kong* (1933), and with a series of dance-films with the talented Fred Astaire and Ginger Rogers.

King Kong employed stop-motion photography to animate the impassioned jungle creature (in actuality only 18 inches tall) who falls for lovely Fay Wray. Masterful miniature settings and trick photography (matte-screen processing) added to the film's illusory qualities. Most notably, however, *King Kong* managed to create dramatic involvement in addition to impressing audiences with its advanced technical achievements.

Beginning with *Flying Down to Rio* (1934), RKO provided filmgoers with a total of nine stylish, delightful dance films starring Astaire and Rogers. By contrast with dance pictures being produced at competing studios, emphasis was placed not on camera choreography and rhythmic editing but on the dancing performances themselves. Astaire and Rogers' dance numbers were photographed for the most part in long shot with minimal cutting. While the approach was clearly more theatrical than Busby Berkeley's dynamic spectacles, the graceful dancing style was extraordinary enough to require no technical embellishments. *Flying Down to Rio, The Gay Divorcee* (1934), *Top Hat* (1935), *Swing Time* (1936), and *Shall We Dance* (1937), all with Astaire and Rogers, ranked among the top box office successes of the thirties. These pictures were vital to RKO's first decade.

With the successful integration of sound into the American motion picture the studio system was at its top form in providing efficiently produced, escapist entertainment. Each studio by the mid-thirties had developed its own business philosophy and creative personality and these in turn were reflected back in the special qualities of its products. Emphasis ranged from the lavish, star-oriented films produced at M-G-M to the unadorned, workaday products from Harry Cohn's Columbia Pictures. Adolph Zukor's good, clean family products at Paramount stood in sharp contrast to the Warner Brothers' more sensationalized, tough character pictures.

Yet the Hollywood system with its varied emphases had one interest in common: each studio sought to avoid failure in a high-cost industry. To avoid failure the studio chieftains often narrowed their vision to their own under-standing of the kinds of motion pictures that would best match public tastes. The goal of the American film in the height of the studio years, above all else, was to satisfy the entertainment needs of a large, anonymous public. And that it did!

Fighting Crime in the Comics

Herb Galewitz

In the 1920s, law-abiding citizens were not affected by the activities of gangsters and criminals, but in the 1930s, when these same citizens were desperate to hold on to their jobs, if they still had them, they began to resent the gangster who thrived from illegal profits, writes Herb Galewitz in his foreword to *Dick Tracy the Thirties: Tommyguns and Hard Times*. According to Galewitz, comic strip creator Chester Gould, a Chicago resident, took out his frustrations with crime and the economy in a new comic strip featuring a hook-nosed crime fighter named Dick Tracy. Tracy was an effective cop who gunned down crooks like Big Boy, Broadway Bates, Steve the Tramp, and Stooge Viller and, according to the author, Dick Tracy also had a soft heart he reveals in his relationship with Tess Trueheart and a young boy named Junior. Galewitz notes that Dick Tracy was one of the few comics with an element of realism and the first action comic of its day. Galewitz is an editor and fan of early comic strips.

In the early thirties, machine guns rattled, illicit beer trucks roared down dark streets, and the hooch gangs were giving Chicago coppers a bad time. The country needed a super-sleuth—and got him in DICK TRACY by Chester Gould. The hook-nosed nemesis of the hoods launched his career of shooting down crooks and shooting up newspaper circulation.

A Time of Uncertainty

1931–33 was an era in American history that was so devastating to so many people and to such a degree that it is hard to comprehend at a distance of almost half a century.

The newspapers were filled with horror stories: men living in the streets under a viaduct in Brooklyn; a 28-year-old man dropping dead of starvation on the sidewalks of midtown Manhattan; a sanitation man committing suicide by jumping into an incinerator because his salary was too meagre to support his family. (Can you imagine the despair of those who had no jobs?)

The President for most of this period was Herbert Hoover, who had earned a reputation as a relief savior of war-torn Belgium. But when the economic bottom fell out of his own country, Hoover had no panacea for its recovery. At least none that worked.

All sorts of nostrums were tried. Local self-help organizations were formed and some had promotional tie-ins with show biz personalities like Georgie Jessel and Mary Pickford. The media stressed the need for people to keep buying to pump-prime the economy. Soothsayers and seers were asking the populace to put their shoulders to the wheel and all would be well.

Nothing worked. A New York *News* list of the 12 best stocks of the week showed a decline in value for all. The private philanthropic organizations were overwhelmed, while the mayors of the major cities were pleading with Washington to get federal and state welfare programs in operation before thousands would starve or freeze to death. Some newspaper editorials were also wondering where governmental welfare, if it came, was going to lead, but all agreed that the situation was serious.

Back in the 1920s, with the advent of Prohibition, new modes of criminal activity were spawned. Beer barons, rumrunners and speakeasies were added to the American

scene. Paved roads, faster cars, and the Thompson subma-
chine gun were all put to use by the underworld in a quest
for the quick buck.

During the relatively good economic times of the 1920s,
the hoodlum capers were viewed almost with detachment
by the general population. W.R. Burnett, author of the
seminal *Little Caesar*, recalled two incidents from a stay in
Chicago in the late 1920s. In what might today be called
"snuff" radio, Burnett remembers listening to a broadcast
from a local cafe, and hearing gunshots interrupt the dance
music. It was a gang rub-out.

Another time, the sound of explosions awoke Burnett in
his hotel room. Hurrying downstairs, he learned that a gang
war was in progress between garage owners, and one of the
rivals had thrown a few "pineapples" at his adversary's
building across the street. Neither the hotel manager nor
the garage workers were upset. It was "business as usual."

As Chester Gould states, if you were a law-abiding citizen and didn't get involved, these criminal antics wouldn't
really affect your day-to-day life.

A New Attitude Toward Crime

But after that fateful day in October, 1929, when the stock
market crashed, there was a decided change in the public's
attitude toward crime.

Now law-abiding citizens were without jobs or prospects,
and they deeply resented the gangster who was making large
illegal profits and thumbing his nose at the law while those
with jobs were desperate to hold on to them.

In the early 1930s, the depression continued to deepen
and kidnapping reached its all-time high (or low), to be climaxed in 1932 by the "crime of the century," the Lindbergh case. With the country in an uproar, and passions
fanned by the sensationalist and mostly misleading stories
in the newspapers, there was a demand for extreme penalties for all criminals. Curiously enough, the underworld
was called in to aid in the capture of the Lindbergh kidnappers and the return of the baby. The "boys" failed in

their efforts but they made a few bucks in the deal. (Recently in New York several Mafia types declared that they would find the "Son of Sam" murderer, [later identified as David Berkowitz, who killed six people in New York City during 1976 and 1977]. They too were unsuccessful, much to the chagrin of the tabloid newspapers.)

Chester Gould, a Chicago resident at the time, was no exception. He was just as fed up with the antics of the Capones and the Roger Touhys as were most of the citizens. Perhaps even more so. For almost a decade, he had been trying to get a comic strip into the Chicago *Tribune* and national newspaper syndication. His submissions had been mainly variations on then-popular comic strips. "Fillum Fables" was his most successful strip to date, but even Gould admits that it was a weak imitation of Ed Wheelan's "Minute Movies" and didn't last too long.

A Crimefighter in the Comics

By then Gould's resentment at not becoming a success, at the worsening economic situation and the burgeoning crime rate, came to a boil. Gould took out his frustrations in a new comic feature, "Plainclothes Tracy," that he sent to Captain Joseph Patterson in New York. Tracy was a cop who believed in "an eye for an eye" and fortunately Patterson, the head of the Chicago Tribune Syndicate, had the same philosophy and took Gould on. Patterson changed the name of the strip to DICK TRACY, directed Gould to "show the bullets going into the body," which became a trademark of the strip, suggested the bare bones of the first story, and DICK TRACY was off and running.

Gould threw himself into the work with enthusiasm, but it wasn't easy, and some days he worked around the clock. Inspiration came in spurts as it does for most artists. Gould relied heavily on melodrama, and such literary devices as chance encounters, the fortuitous overhearing of important conversations, liberal use of slang and dialect speech.

We must bear in mind that there had never been anything like DICK TRACY in comic strips. The vast majority were literally "funnies," such as "Captain and the Kids," "Bringing Up Father," "Smitty," "Toonerville Trolley," "Harold Teen," and others. The only New York *News* comics with any element of realism were "Winnie Winkle," "Little Orphan Annie," "Gasoline Alley," and "The Gumps." Though some had action sequences, they were minute compared to the almost continuous gunfights and sluggings in early DICK TRACY. "The Gumps," the most popular comic strip of the Chicago Tribune Syndicate, was to go into a head-to-head battle with DICK TRACY for the front page of the New York *Sunday News*. Within two years the two comics were alternating for that vaunted position. By the time Sidney Smith (creator of "The Gumps") died in 1935, DICK TRACY moved into permanent possession of that celebrated spot.

In the very first story Gould had introduced three "good-guy" characters that were to be mainstays for over a decade: Chief Brandon, Tess Trueheart, and Pat Patton. It was a great beginning, and it was strong enough to carry him through most of the very important first year.

"The Texie Garcia Caper," is the second story to appear in the strip. It begins as a straightforward pursuit of mobster Big Boy, but we are soon sidetracked by the attractive Texie, who is a far more interesting character, and we are into a fairly sophisticated tale of crooked lawyers and politicians.

"The Demotion of Dick Tracy" gives us a titillating view of the love life of Dick and Tess, and in reflection, a glimpse of the social mores of the early 1930s. The sight of Tracy in a bulky police overcoat nonchalantly shooting tin cans out in the sticks emphasizes how times have changed.

Broadway Bates' main claim to fame is that he bears a marked physical resemblance to the character Penguin in the Batman comic books of almost a decade later. Alas, Bates and his bob-haired girl friend, Belle, are not otherwise memorable, though Tracy will long remember the case after having a suitcase full of bricks dropped on his head. Mrs. Trueheart and Heinie, the kindly deli man, give the story some human interest, while Gould's use of silhouettes dramatically enhances the artwork.

"The Buddy Waldorf Kidnapping" was obviously inspired by the Lindbergh affair, and Tracy's beating of Big Boy is a wish fulfillment of an otherwise frustrated America.

With the "Alec Penn" and "Devil's Island" episodes Gould's inventiveness seemed to show signs of strain, as seen in plots dealing with secret rooms in a zoo, and a father who supposedly loves his daughter, but stands idly by while her life is threatened.

A Sidekick for Dick Tracy

At best these episodes were "pauses that refreshed," for on September 8, 1932, a new character was introduced that was to give the strip the impetus to carry it to the very top of the comic world. The new arrival was a nine-year-old nameless boy. Ostensibly Dick Tracy rescues the boy and gives him his own name, but in reality Junior rescued DICK TRACY. Not only did the stories get better and far more believable, but the artwork started to improve strikingly. Appropriately enough, accompanying Junior was the first of Gould's great villains, Steve the Tramp. Forty-six years later, old-time fans like Gil Kane, the popular comic book artist, fondly remember collecting one of the first DICK TRACY tie-ins, the Johnson caramel cards which reprinted the Steve the Tramp and "Stooge" Viller sequence. The introduction a little later of "Stooge" Viller, another great Gould creation, emphasized the fact that the author was now in full control.

Junior, always appealing in his checkered knickers, attracted the young, the old and all in between. The comic now became a must in the homes of millions of youngsters who badgered their parents to get the paper with DICK TRACY. Without a doubt, the comics were vital in maintaining the New York *News* as the largest circulating newspaper in the U.S. for a long time.

The number of newspapers carrying DICK TRACY never approached the massive syndication of such features as "Bringing Up Father" and "Blondie." The Chicago Tribune Syndicate believed that if a paper wanted to run DICK TRACY it had better be prepared to pay for it. There were no $5-per-week prices or package deals, as was common with other syndicates. The Chicago Tribune-New York News Syndicate, to give the full name, liked to call their comics operation a "Tiffany" affair, since they only handled some twenty-odd strips and almost every one was a winner. DICK TRACY went to the top of their list within a couple of years.

In intensity of readership, I doubt if there was any newspaper comic that approached DICK TRACY in the 1930s and 1940s. Kids were enthralled by it and soon were engulfed in a wave of Dick Tracy toys, games, and miscellany. By the end of the decade, there were Dick Tracy movies and radio shows to thrill his legion of fans.

The strip was still the main thing and it kept getting better. Characters to come in the immediate future included: "Confidence" Dolan; Jean Penfield, the Claudette Colbert look-alike in the memorable fight with Tess Trueheart; Ben Spaldoni, the crooked lawyer; J. Scotland Bumstead; the evil Doc Hump; Junior's mother; and the frizzy-haired cutie Toby Townley.

Gangsters, Bums, and Heroes in Baseball

Robert T. Smith

In the 1934 World Series, the St. Louis Cardinals, known as the "Gashouse Gang," introduced fans to "bench jockeying": verbal assaults on the personal sore spots of members of the opposing team, writes author and baseball fan Robert T. Smith. In the following article, Smith describes the antics of the Cardinals during the 1934 World Series, noting that other teams during and since the 1930s have made these verbal and physical assaults part of the allure of baseball. However, the author notes, the fans of the 1930s needed not only an outlet for their frustrations, but champions, and their heroes, like Joe DiMaggio and Lou Gehrig, fortified their belief that hard work and determination could conquer adversity.

The Gashouse Gang, the 1934 St. Louis Cardinals of which the Dean brothers [Paul and Dizzy], were important members, was almost a reincarnation of the 1894 Baltimore Orioles. There was the same fiery team spirit, the same reliance on craft, teamwork, and aggressive play, the same unified determination to keep umpires and opponents in their places.

Frank Frisch, the manager of the crew, was a graduate of the New York Giants, where he had been inoculated with

Excerpted from *Baseball: A Historical Narrative of the Game, the Men Who Have Played It, and Its Place in American Life,* by Robert T. Smith. Copyright ©1947, 1970 by Robert Smith. Reprinted with permission from Simon & Schuster, Inc.

the very virus of McGrawism [named for Giant manager John McGraw, known as a master tactician]. Leo Durocher, the shortstop, had earned the nickname Lippy from his own teammates when he was with Miller Huggins' New York Yankees; and he had got himself waived right out of the American League after two seasons. Dizzy Dean, of course, was no man to pull out of any sort of encounter, be it vocal or physical. Then there were Pepper Martin, the human torpedo; Muscles Joe Medwick, who did his arguing with his fists; Tex Carleton, who once took a swing at the great Dizzy Dean himself; Showboat Ernie Orsatti; Wild Bill Hallahan; and K.O. DeLancey.

Their doings during the championship season of 1934, and particularly in Detroit in the World's Series, sharpened the public taste for vocal and physical aggressiveness on the ball diamond to such an extent that the results have never been properly measured.

The Gashouse Gang set upon umpires and upon fans with a ferocity and a unanimity that had not been seen since McGraw was still playing third. In squads of four and five they used to march out to shout into an umpire's face, unmindful of the fact that Commissioner Landis, following Ban Johnson's lead, was ever ready to back the dignity and security of league umpires with the full strength of his office. It cannot be said that their verbal assaults upon umpires were as well motivated as were those of the old-time "kickers." There were two and often three umpires in even the most ordinary game nowadays, and they were all men who had been trained for their positions by years of major-league baseball or of minor-league umpiring. They were alert, quick-witted, and thoroughly honest members of an honorable profession. But Frisch knew that it helped team spirit and enraptured the customers if his gang yelled for every extra inch.

In the 1934 World's Series, the Gashouse Gang introduced to the whole nation an adjunct of professional ball which casual fans had never noticed—the art of bench jockeying, that is, digging vocal spurs into the personal sore spots of individual members of the opposing team. By their scholarly application of this talent they heated up opponents and fans until they finally boiled right over.

Detroit, that fall, when the World's Series began, was like an army camp. All normal commerce, all social activity, even the operations of the great newspapers, were either stalled or utterly unraveled. Clerks deserted their counters, mothers carried their hungering children to the ball park, workingmen stood idle in the street, trolleys neglected their schedules, salesmen forgot to make their rounds, businessmen shushed their customers, and office girls allowed correspondence to turn yellow in the sun. For the first time in twenty-five years Detroit had a World's Series in its home park, and the natives could not have been more stirred had they been called to repel an invasion from Mars. Every avenue and byway echoed with the blasts of street radios which promised great doings in the offing, reported the current play at the park, or repeated over and over again what had taken place just a few hours before.

Bench Jockeying in Detroit

There were three great heroes in the city then: Schoolboy Rowe, the enormous young hurler ("With a wind behind him," said Dizzy Dean, "he's pretty near as fast as Paul"); Manager Mickey Cochrane (Black Mike), a graduate of Connie Mack's Philadelphia Athletics, where he had become the greatest catcher of the day; and Hank Greenberg, the breathtakingly handsome first baseman who was threatening to push Babe Ruth right off the home-run throne.

Upon these three the brash St. Louis bench jockeys concentrated all their genius. Schoolboy Rowe, delighted to find himself able to face a radio microphone without swallowing his tongue, had concluded a broadcast with a gray little murmur to his wife, who was listening at home: "How'm I doing, Edna?" How many hundred times he must have wished he could have taken a broom and wiped those words away! For he could not make a move upon the diamond after that without a brassy chorus of "How'm I doing, Edna!" arising from the St. Louis bench amid hoarse cackles of sardonic merriment.

Some overwrought caption writer had seen fit to print a picture of Mickey Cochrane under the line OUR STRICKEN LEADER on a day when Mickey had been only mildly bruised. That particular phrase provided the St. Louis bench with a needle they must have stuck under Cochrane's skin a couple of thousand times.

Hank Greenberg reacted to his first World's Series with the tense excitement of most young and suddenly famous ballplayers. And the cries of the St. Louis players did not case his tension. "Boy," yelled Dizzy Dean, "what makes you so white? You're trembling like a leaf! Must be you heard Old Diz is going to pin your ears back!"

On the field of play the Gashouse Gang implemented their vocal needling with plenty of rough base running; and they finally hit the jackpot when Joe Medwick, who is put together like a small brick building, slammed into Marvin Owen, the Detroit third baseman, and Owen retaliated by tagging him with force enough to leave a mark. The two men almost simultaneously began to slug at each other. And when, after the row had been quelled and the St. Louis inning completed, Medwick took his position in the out-field, the near-by fans greeted him with a shower of veg-etables, worn-out fruit, sandwiches, boxes, pieces of chairs, and bottles—in fact, anything bruising they could set their hands to. Judge Landis, in the stands, finally decided that Medwick would have to be withdrawn.

It must not be thought that the Gashouse Gang was the first, the last, or the only team to instigate this wholesale participation by fans in the side issues of the game. In St. Louis there had been several instances of bottle throwing— one almost fatal injury to Umpire Billy Evans. In the twen-ties, Whitey Witt, then New York outfielder, had been struck on the head and seriously hurt by a thrown bottle. McGraw's Giants, too, had undergone a shower of bottles in the same St. Louis park. Detroit fans in the twenties, stirred to action by an exchange of obscenities, bean balls, and fisticuffs on the diamond, piled down into the fight to the number of many hundreds, bringing clubs made out of chairs to give the New York Yankees' Murderers' Row a little of their own medicine. And in the Yankee Stadium, not too long ago, fans heaved a gross or two of bottles at Umpire Rue because he had called a ball foul which might possibly have been fair.

But it was the Gashouse Gang and its eager publicists who began to make it clear that "color" in the form of rough talk and violence was as salable a commodity as eccentricity. In St. Louis, coupled with aggressive and winning baseball, it pulled in throngs so deep they had to sit on the grass. . . .

A Need for Heroes

But the public attitude toward baseball, through the Roosevelt era, was not entirely one of vaunting the loudmouth, the name-caller, and the picker of fights. Much was left of the sophisticated sentimentality of the late twenties, when hero-worship, both gay and solemn, colored the published annals of the game. As the thirties grew older, however, and people in increasing numbers participated in the great mass movements—the NRA, the sit-down strikes, the new unions of employed and unemployed, the petitionings of Congress—they became less likely to be moved to tears by the story of the man who silently bled to death because "the show must go on" or so that fellow crooks rather than "coppers" should privately avenge his murder. Heroes now had to be of truly heroic size: not men who owed allegiance to a team, a private ethic, or the College Militant, but men who faced a whole world of enemies, with a town, a county, or even half a nation at their backs. . . .

In the seasons just preceding the Second World War, fans in many parts of the country used to lend themselves quite honestly to the delusion that the Browns, the Dodgers, the Pirates, or the Reds were championing them and their city against all who had conspired to keep the milk, the honey, and the gold forever from them. And there is more than mere comedy in the wild hysteria of the Brooklyn fans when, in 1941, the abused and underrated Dodgers, representing the most ridiculed and least appreciated community in the state, finally won their first championship since 1920. Nor was there much to laugh at in their weeping despair when Yankee sluggers found a chink in the gate large enough to insert their dangerous bats and storm through to victory in the World's Series. . . .

Other towns . . . had their own heroes in this age. In Boston, I know, many boys felt about Wesley Ferrell—who used to throw his "nothing" ball down to his brother Rick while batter after batter waved vainly at it—the way they should have felt about their fathers. In the early part of the depression period, the Braves' pitchers, Lou Fette and Jim Turner, two "old men" (they were rookies, though in their thirties), brought solace to many a young fellow who was watching for the first gray whisker on his temple.

In Cincinnati young Johnny Vander Meer became the man most kids wanted to be when they grew up: he pitched two no-hit games in succession. Pitcher Bobo Newsom (called Bobo because he called everybody else Bobo) had a following in nearly every city in the country, for he played in almost every one shuttling from majors to minors, from National to American Leagues, and from team to team in a manner never equaled. A few of the better folk found baseball reasonably attractive after blue-blooded young Charlie Devens, a star at Harvard, had put in a spell with the Yankees. In Washington and Chicago, Joe Kuhel was known as the ablest first baseman in the business; and Bill Jurges was another man who could have had a free drink in almost any Chicago bar when beer came back. New York kids grew to manhood and womanhood blindly admiring a quiet lad who had been a major leaguer since he was sixteen—Mell Ott, who finally became manager of the Giants.

For the fans who missed Babe Ruth—who had left baseball before the 1930's were out—the Yankees offered Joe Dimaggio, a lean, long-nosed center fielder from Califor-

306

nia. Joe, compared to Ruth, was like a ballplaying machine. He never seemed to excite himself at the bat. He swung smoothly and gracefully, with great precision and a tremendous follow-through. He was what is known as a wrist hitter, for he held his swing until the final instant, took almost no forward stride (his stance was nearly as widely spread as Harry Hooper's) and then snapped the bat at the ball in a short swift arc. He was not a bad-ball hitter, was not given to striking out, and never offered the appearance of either gaiety, or anger, or tremendous effort. His smile was self-conscious, his manner withdrawn to the point of chill. He was interested in money—his own and other men's. He preferred the company of those who "counted" and had little time for small boys who wanted autographs. Like the majority of modern ballplayers, he was of a saving nature, never upset anyone with the size of his tips or the abandon of his spending, and sought out many devices for boosting his income off the field and on.

A Synthetic Hero

He was as accomplished on defense as he was at bat. He sped gracefully and easily across the green outfield, hardly seeming to lift his feet higher than the grasstops. Until he injured a shoulder, he sent long, low, almost geometrically perfect throws into the diamond. He was soft-spoken on and around the ball field and created no exciting stories for the press—except the wonders he worked at bat. His marriage to a showgirl and the subsequent rumors of divorce made a scattering of items for the Broadway columnists, but these were nothing to the fans. He held out frequently for higher pay, once hired a Broadway character to "manage" him, and made himself unpopular early in his career, with some fans and teammates, by missing, for one reason or another, part of the training and playing season. . . .

An Authentic Hero

The only really authentic hero of modern baseball is Lou Gehrig, the solid young man from Columbia, who dogged

Babe Ruth's steps in almost every home-run race for several seasons.

Lou, like Babe, Dizzy Dean and so many others, had to grow up in baseball—although, because he said very little when he was new in the game, his adolescent personality was never thrust upon the public. But newspaper reporters who met him in the 1920's, when he was just a big strong boy with a mighty bat and a rudimentary knowledge of how to play first base, were often repelled by him. Lou was a boy who had been made much of by devoted parents (all their other children had died). Perhaps in consequence of this he was driven, as many such boys are, by an excruciating sense of inadequacy, into painful self-consciousness. Scared speechless by the great men who gathered to interview him, he could only grunt and growl at them like a sulky child.

He was driven, too, by a grim ambition and by dogged thrift. He was determined to succeed at baseball, in spite of the devil. And he was consumed by a desire to keep himself secure with all the money he could save. It was Gehrig's smoking ambition that kept him playing ball day in and day out, season after season, in spite of colds, headaches, broken thumbs, and Charley horses; that turned him from an awkward kid who, one coach thought, was too pigheaded to learn, into a finished infielder. Lou did not miss a ball game for fourteen years. And it was his thrift that caused him to walk all the way from his hotel to the training park and thus save the fare, to save on expense money, to avoid having to give a tip. These were things that made a poor impression on many writers who knew him as a recruit.

Success brought a gradual loosening up to Lou. Not that he ever let up on himself. He was a man who could never stop trying no matter how black the outlook or how long the road. If he seemed to be weakening, he knew only that he needed to deal more harshly with himself and thus get back into physical trim. He never wore a hat except when he had a baseball cap on. He often went out in winter without an overcoat or vest.

It was not his home-run records (he twice led the league and once tied for the leadership) or his incredible string of consecutive games (2130) that made Lou truly great. He became a hero off the diamond by the quiet and courageous way he faced the fact that he was dying of an incurable disease, by his utter sincerity when, after his enforced retirement from the game, he accepted a tumultuous tribute from fans, political leaders, peanut sellers, ushers, ballplayers, sports writers, and umpires, by modestly disclaiming any virtue except that he was "the luckiest man in the world." He meant that to have a devoted wife, as he had, good friends, a fine record, financial success, and to have been able to provide handsomely for his beloved parents were more to him than the fact that, at the age of thirty-six, he was the victim of a crippling disease with only an even chance to live. Gehrig died in 1941, just before his thirty-eighth birthday. He is the only ballplayer ever to have had a New York street named after him. The blue street signs just outside the Yankee Stadium now carry the inscription: Lou Gehrig Plaza.

Depression Jazz: From Swing to Hot Jazz Revival

Burton W. Peretti

In the following excerpt from his book *The Creation of Jazz: Music, Race, and Culture in Urban America*, Burton W. Peretti, an amateur musician and professor of history at the University of Kansas and the University of California at Berkeley, explores the evolution of jazz during the depression. When Prohibition was repealed, Peretti writes, jazz musicians were no longer needed to draw people into speakeasies and nightclubs, and to support themselves, many jazz musicians chose to join swing dance-bands, where jazz became popularized. Big band leaders like Benny Goodman, Woody Herman, Duke Ellington, and Artie Shaw became stars, Peretti explains, but the trend toward marketing forced the dance-bands to select music not for its artistic merit but what was popular. However, once these big dance-bands became established, Peretti reveals, they were able to form small improvisational groups that revived the "hot" jazz of the twenties, allowing jazz musicians to explore their art.

As a subclass of the occupation, jazz musicians suffered further when Prohibition was repealed in 1933 and their music was no longer needed to attract customers into speakeasies and bootleggers' nightclubs. When the liquor racket lost its reason for being, it took such gangland figures as Joe Glaser a few years to adapt to the "legitimate" world of music management. During these difficult times musicians could not look to recording for any kind of income opportunities. After 1930, as wary Americans virtually abandoned their demand for durable items, the recording and phonograph industries were crippled with unique severity. Record sales fell from 104 million in 1927 to a mere six million in 1932, every small company closed, and as Roland Gelatt has written, "by January 1933 the record business in America was practically extinct." In addition, jobs in radio at that time paid poorly; for example, the Ellington band was not paid at all for its broadcasting from Los Angeles' Cotton Club in 1932. From 1926 to 1930 union scale had been set at weekly minimums ranging from thirty to seventy-five dollars, and the best players often earned comfortable salaries exceeding one hundred dollars a week. After 1931 New York and Los Angeles musicians only infrequently worked more than three nights per week, and perhaps earned ten dollars a night in wages and tips. As late as 1935 the AFM's level-C pay scale, in effect in Harlem, was set at only thirty-five dollars a week for band members and twice that for leaders. . . .

Some musicians had to find new and unusual ways to support themselves. In the mid-1930s, Sidney Bechet and the trumpeter Tommy Ladnier ran a dry-cleaning shop in Harlem, one of the few nonmusical ventures entered into by leading players at that time. The trumpeters George Mitchell and William Samuels, the arranger Zilner Randolph, and others joined the WPA's musical organizations. In Chicago Samuels carried ninety-four dollars a month in a forty-piece, all-black WPA orchestra at a time when he paid thirty-five dollars monthly in rent and supported a wife and three children. Samuels also "really got deeply involved with the union in the '30s to survive the Depression," and eventually spent "half of the time with the union, and the other half playing music." The Federal

Music Project of the WPA established four music schools in Manhattan and three in Harlem, and hired more than one hundred musicians as part-time instructors. In some instances musicians were able to obtain good jobs; for example, the expiring Capone nightclub chain in Chicago lingered into the 1930s, and in 1931 Milt Hinton held onto a sixty-dollar weekly job in a speakeasy.

The Commercialization of Jazz

The most lucrative alternative facing the impoverished musician in the thirties—entering the commercial dance-band market—was also for some the most artistically problematic. To commercialize, jazz musicians had to travel to New York City, where most of the depression-ravaged, streamlined popular music industry was located. Very few accomplished jazz players remained in Chicago, New Orleans, and other cities during the Depression, and those in New York attempted to sign on with dance bands, radio studios, Broadway pit orchestras, and even the Muzak Corporation and other producers of "musical environments." In 1934 nearly one-fifth of all AFM members belonged to New York's Local 802. . . .

Art Hodes wrote that "it was New York that taught me that the customer is always right and you have to please the people, but darn it, that's one lesson I haven't learned well." Some black musicians, who may have found a greater variety of benefits in the commercial activity and sheer density of Manhattan, did not demonize New York so intensely in the 1930s. Scoville Browne of Chicago, foreshadowing Ralph Ellison's antihero, "saw New York as being better. . . . I guess it's because you could hide more in New York . . . a person can lose his identity in New York," especially a black person, in a society where whites "don't like to be seen talking to too many black people."

Perhaps as a result of such a willingness to find strength in numbers (at the risk of invisibility), black musicians were not inclined to criticize the market-oriented nature of commercial music. Duke Ellington let his manager, Irving

Mills, add lyrics to his pieces, and he had his band play popular radio ballads. The numbers prostituted the group's talents, but were essential to its commercial success. By 1938, band members were making over one hundred dollars a week, and Barney Bigard recalled that "we worked clean through the Depression without even knowing there was one. I guess we were one of the best-paid, best-known bands in the U.S.A." In 1937 Cab Calloway's band members made the same weekly salary. The fraternal and communal nature of large bands had appealed to black musicians since the first years of the jazz era, and in the early thirties these groups were not reluctant to offer a commercial product that might help to sustain them. . . .

Justifying Going Commercial

The process of "becoming commercial," like the search for a steady income during the Depression, was not always this atavistic. Such a devotee of pure jazz music as John Hammond, who promoted Count Basie's band in the late 1930s because it was a fresh, rhythmically exciting group, still thought it necessary to counsel Basie on "refining" the least urbane musical qualities of his band, "the places where people could jump on it" (as Hammond's contemporary Helen Oakley Dance recalled). Like [Joseph "Wingy"] Manone, Hammond realized that commercial success would come to those musicians who presented a particular kind of showmanship that would appeal to the largest audience. Earl Hines learned to become a master of ceremonies in the thirties, studying "stage deportment, and I paid a lot of attention to vocalizing" and to maintaining a big grin onstage. "But one day, up at the Apollo Theatre, I smiled so much that when I got offstage I couldn't get a smile off my face. . . . It was as though my muscles froze. . . . I was really giving them the ivory!". . .

The Emergence of Swing Bands

In general, though, the uneasy mating of jazz and the mass market led to the unexpected and explosive "Big Band Era" of 1935–47. In early 1935, to the surprise of musicians and promoters, young audiences began to attend and cheer concerts by the Benny Goodman, Tommy Dorsey, Bob Crosby and other large bands, and buy their records and listen to their radio programs, in rapidly growing numbers. Black bands and audiences were not immune to the growth of what was now being marketed as swing music. As the bassist Quinn Wilson recalled, "we changed to swing" in 1935, "started playing Benny Goodman type of music . . .

What Were Women Wearing in the Thirties?

In this brief excerpt, John Peacock reviews changes and innovations in women's fashion during the decade.

The holiday mood of the hectic and emancipated 1920s, with its dramatic rejection of womanly curves and feminine flounces, faded with the dawn of the 1930s, a decade plagued by worldwide economic depression.

The fashionable clothes of the previous period, which had been drawn with bold outlines, no waist, abbreviated hemlines and a denial of feminine curves, gave way to a longer, leaner and more figure-hugging silhouette which defined the waist, accentuated the shoulders and narrowed the hips. The fashionable thirties woman emerged mature, understated, cautious and, above all, sophisticated. Her wardrobe contained specialist outfits for every occasion: day, afternoon, sport, spectator sport, informal evening, formal evening, dinner, theatre and more.

Until the middle of the decade, women's fashion moved comparatively slowly. By 1935 the look which had emerged was epitomized by the suit, either crisply tailored or more softly structured. A sleek, fitted jacket, with square, padded shoulders and a tiny waist in its proper place, was teamed with a skirt or dress in matching fabric. This outfit was considered the ultimate in elegance and chic.

it was a more subdued type of jazz. . . . Instead of playing oom-pah, oom-pah, I just made it flow from one note to another." In Benny Carter's view, New York had for a decade been the "melting pot" of jazz, and the highly homogenized swing music of the Goodman band may have been the end result. The record and touring industries revived, and the profits were extraordinary. In 1939, after trying a number of different musical approaches, Artie Shaw became a major swing bandleader and earned a personal net income of twenty thousand dollars for every week of touring. . . .

The introduction of washable, easy-care luxury fabrics, such as silk, crepe-de-chine and satin, revolutionized garments of all kinds, from nightdresses to underwear to day dresses and blouses. In addition, the development of man-made fabrics, such as rayon, viscose rayon and tricot, and the improved methods of manufacturing and mass-production techniques meant that well-made and well-cut clothes became available to a wider range of women.

From 1930 evening dresses were a fashion unto themselves. Long or ankle-length, often with a short train, they were moulded onto the body like wet cloth by means of bias-cutting. As much flesh as possible was revealed: for example, halter necklines left the shoulders and most of the back exposed. As the decade progressed, evening dresses became increasingly more extravagant and varied in style, ranging from sleek and figure-hugging crepes and silk satins, to ruffled diaphanous silk-organdie dresses with puffed sleeves, to multi-layered embroidered net crinolines with tightly fitted, boned, strapless bodices.

Fur—both of the expensive and the cheap varieties—was worn extensively throughout the 1930s in the form of coats, capes, stoles, wraps, accessories and trimmings. The most popular furs were sable, mink, chinchilla, Persian lamb and silver fox, all worn both for day and evening.

John Peacock, "Introduction," *Fashion Sourcebooks: The 1930s*, London: Thames and Hudson, 1997.

In general, the big bands were expected to duplicate their commercial hits with the frequency and precision of a phonograph record; individual soloists, as well as bands, earned livings by playing the same "spontaneous improvisations" countless times. In 1939, after making his famed recording of "Body and Soul," the saxophonist Coleman Hawkins would never be able to escape listeners who asked him to play exact renditions of that solo.

The big bands usually stifled solo and collective improvisation, dissatisfying those musicians who cherished the spontaneity and diversity of jam sessions. Bud Freeman, who had pursued jazz in the 1920s because it presented "an escape" from social restrictions, found that playing in the Goodman and Tommy Dorsey bands—which gave as many as nine performances a day—was a new, musical restriction he had to flee. "You were, in a sense, almost in jail, and the music—if I had not been a player of improvised jazz, I couldn't take it. I loathe the idea of having to do what somebody wants me to do." Milt Hinton, who played with the Cab Calloway band at the new Cotton Club in downtown Manhattan in 1937, perceived harmful psychosocial consequences of a long, repetitious residence. While it was pleasant at first to "be with your family" since "the guys had been on the road, . . . you get sick of that show, man. The same crap every night. . . . After six months it gets kind of dull to you, and maybe you're getting into some altercations with your old lady in town, and you get restless . . . everybody's anxious to go now.".. .

The big-band leaders were required by commercial demands to be disciplinarians. Benny Goodman and Tommy Dorsey, Freeman argued, "were hard men. They had to be." Freeman himself tried to lead a band, but found that "I could not be custodian over other people's lives. . . . I had all I could do to handle myself." Dorsey ruled his men with an explosive temper. Freeman, only briefly in his band, would "often wonder about the guys who had to just sit back and play and take Tommy's insults and all that." Benny Goodman, a greater musician and more complex man, mixed toughness with many other qualities and goals. Freeman noted that he "never saw a man work as hard as he did" to maintain both a band and his own superior clarinet playing. Goodman "knew what he was doing and he knew what he wanted and he was like a machine." Goodman's remoteness, egotism, and sternness were famous among jazz musicians, but they were leavened at times with kindnesses, humor, and a social conscience. Perhaps, as Freeman suggests, no one else strove as mightily as Goodman to maintain his musical and personal integrity while also working to conquer the commercial world. The respect Goodman earned from white and black, commercial and marginal, musicians indicates that he perhaps did manage to reconcile the contradictions of his career.

A "Hot" Jazz Revival

Goodman characteristically worked to preserve hot jazz by forming small improvisatory groups that performed and recorded along with the big band. Other bandleaders followed Goodman's lead and formed such combos as Artie Shaw's Gramercy Five, Woody Herman's Woodchoppers, Bob Crosby's Bobcats, Tommy Dorsey's Clambake Seven, and Duke Ellington's various small groups. Players who had gained anonymity in big-band sections thus were not always compelled to abandon their mastery of and dedication to improvisation, blues harmonies, working in small groups, and sophisticated syncopation.

This development was particularly significant because it indicated how the success of big bands produced an environment which nurtured and financed their antithesis. In the late 1930s, some white veterans of twenties hot jazz initiated a quasi-commercial movement to preserve small-group improvisation, which strove to remain separate from the big-band milieu. Spontaneous performances by small groups, or jam sessions, were supported financially by small groups of record collectors and musicians.

In New York, these individuals self-consciously sought to recapture the nightclub setting of the early twenties, in

which musicians mingled and played together with minimal intrusion from profit-minded promoters, programmed
audiences, and technological media. With the help of Columbia University students, the record store owner Milt
Gabler, and a group of club owners, the Chicagoans and
others virtually recreated their adolescence. Eddie Condon,
whom Max Kaminsky described as "a perennial youth of
the twenties," used publicists' connections in his wife's
family to develop regular concerts and jam sessions at a
few clubs on New York's 52nd and 56th Streets, and eventually opened a club himself in the 1940s. Gabler's Com-
modore Records label captured these musicians on disk;
Life magazine ran an approving pictorial article in 1938;
hot clubs formed across the country; and the twenties jazz
revival began.

The movement was an interesting mixture of new publicity techniques, an authentic folk-musical heritage (black
musicians were usually welcomed), and the self-conscious
portrayal of jazz as an art form. In the 1930s Milt Gabler
(as quoted by Condon) expressed a dual (and contradictory) desire both to popularize hot jazz and to maintain its
artistic elitism. "It's recognized now. . . . It's now just a
matter of spreading it to a larger number of people. Over
here we never think anything is recognized until the entire
population takes it up; then we get tired of it and call it
common and look for something else. You can't do that
with an art; in fact I don't think an art is ever popular;
there aren't enough people with taste and understanding to
make it popular. It's the cheap imitations of art that are
sold by the million.". . .

The white revivalist musicians did find an audience in the
52nd Street clubs. This group indulged in pre-Depression,
pre-World War Two nostalgia while they welcomed incre-
mental musical innovation, and the audience treated the musicians like artists who could also retain an urban-adolescent
brashness. This small community of artists and listeners presented an escape from some (but by no means all) of the
dilemmas presented by the growth of mass culture.

The literary critic Dwight Macdonald may have had the hot revival in mind when, in the late 1940s, he began to call for "a number of smaller, more specialized audiences that may still be commercially profitable" as an antidote to the hegemonic effect of mass marketing on folk and elite art. In fact, Macdonald concluded in 1962 that jazz was "the only art form that appeals to both the intelligentsia and the common people." This was a simplistic evaluation, but it reflected quite accurately the dual ambitions of the hot revivalists. The musicians who had spent their 1920s youths striving to incorporate useful aesthetic and musical notions into their new style were able by 1940 to produce an effective and stimulating institutional response—the commercial nightclub—to the dominance of the big bands and mass culture.

CHAPTER 6

Looking Toward the Future

AMERICA'S DECADES

The Legacy of the New Deal

Roger Biles

Although it failed to restore economic prosperity, the New Deal put into place policies that remain today, including safeguard agencies like the Securities and Exchange Commission (SEC), the Federal Deposit Insurance Corporation (FDIC), and the National Labor Relations Board (NLRB), writes historian Roger Biles in the following excerpt from his book *A New Deal for the American People*. According to Biles, not only did the New Deal establish a greater role for the government in American life through its social welfare legislation, but the struggle to develop effective legislation brought together Northern and Southern Democrats to create a national majority that lasted into the 1980s. Biles is professor of history at Oklahoma State University in Stillwater, Oklahoma.

A t the close of the Hundred Days, Franklin D. Roosevelt said, "All of the proposals and all of the legislation since the fourth day of March have not been just a collection of haphazard schemes, but rather the orderly component parts of a connected and logical whole." Yet the president later described his approach quite differently. "Take a method and try it. If it fails admit it frankly and try another. But above all, try something." The impetus for New Deal legislation came from a variety of sources, and Roosevelt relied heavily at various times on an ideologically diverse group of aides and allies. His initiatives reflected the contributions of, among others, Robert Wagner, Rexford Tugwell, Raymond Moley, George Norris, Robert LaFollette, Henry Morgenthau, Marriner Eccles, Felix Frankfurter, Henry Wallace, Harry Hopkins, and Eleanor Roosevelt. An initial emphasis on recovery for agriculture and industry gave way within two years to a broader-based program for social reform; entente with the business community yielded to populist rhetoric and a more ambiguous economic program. Roosevelt suffered the opprobrium of both the conservatives, who vilified "that man" in the White House who was leading the country down the sordid road to socialism, and the radicals, who saw the Hyde Park aristocrat as a confidence man peddling piecemeal reform to forestall capitalism's demise. Out of so many contradictory and confusing circumstances, how does one make sense of the five years of legislative reform known as the New Deal? And what has been its impact on a half century of American life?

The Not So New Deal

A better understanding begins with the recognition that little of the New Deal was new, including the use of federal power to effect change. Nor, for all of Roosevelt's famed willingness to experiment, did New Deal programs usually originate from vernal ideas. Governmental aid to increase farmers' income, propounded in the late nineteenth century by the Populists, surfaced in Woodrow Wilson's farm credit acts. The prolonged debates over McNary-Haugenism in the 1920s kept the issue alive, and Herbert Hoover's Agricultural Marketing Act set the stage for further federal involvement. Centralized economic planning, as embodied in the National Industrial Recovery Act, flowed directly from the experiences of Wilson's War Industries Board; not surprisingly, Roosevelt chose Hugh Johnson, a veteran of the board, to head the National Recovery Administration (NRA). Well established in England and Germany before the First World War, social insurance appeared in a handful of states—notably Wisconsin—before the federal government became involved. Similarly, New Deal labor reform took its cues from the path-breaking work of state legislatures. Virtually alone in its originality, compensatory fiscal policy seemed revolutionary in the 1930s. Significantly, however, Roosevelt embraced deficit spending quite late after other disappointing economic policies and never to the extent Keynesian economists advised. Congress and the public supported the New Deal, in part, because of its origins in successful initiatives attempted earlier under different conditions.

Innovative or not, the New Deal clearly failed to restore economic prosperity. As late as 1938 unemployment stood at 19.1 percent and two years later at 14.6 percent. Only the Second World War, which generated massive industrial production, put the majority of the American people back to work. To be sure, partial economic recovery occurred. From a high of 13 million unemployed in 1933, the number under Roosevelt's administration fell to 11.4 million in 1934, 10.6 million in 1935, and 9 million in 1936. Farm income and manufacturing wages also rose, and as limited as these achievements may seem in retrospect, they provided sustenance for millions of people and hope for many more. Yet Roosevelt's resistance to Keynesian formulas for pump priming placed immutable barriers in the way of recovery that only war could demolish. At a time calling for drastic inflationary methods, Roosevelt introduced programs effecting the opposite result. The NRA restricted production, elevated prices, and reduced purchasing power, all of which were deflationary in effect. The Social Security Act's payroll taxes took money from consumers and out of circulation. The federal government's $4.43 billion deficit in fiscal year 1936, impressive as it seemed, was not so much greater than Hoover's $2.6 billion shortfall during his last year in office. As economist Robert Lekachman noted, "The 'great spender' was in his heart a true descendant of thrifty Dutch Calvinist forebears." It is not certain that the application of Keynesian formulas would have sufficed by the mid–1930s to restore prosperity, but the president's cautious deflationary policies clearly retarded recovery.

Establishing Safeguards

Although New Deal economic policies came up short in the 1930s, they implanted several "stabilizers" that have been more successful in averting another such depression. The Securities and Exchange Act of 1934 established government supervision of the stock market, and the Wheeler-Rayburn Act allowed the Securities and Exchange Commission (SEC) to do the same with public utilities. Severely embroiled in controversy when adopted, these measures have become mainstays of the American financial system. The Glass-Steagall Banking Act forced the separation of commercial and investment banking and broadened the powers of the Federal Reserve Board to change interest rates and limit loans for speculation. The creation of the Federal Deposit Insurance Corporation (FDIC) increased government supervision of state banks and significantly lowered the number of bank failures. Such safeguards restored confidence in the discredited banking system and established a firm economic foundation that performed well for decades thereafter.

The New Deal was also responsible for numerous other notable changes in American life. Section 7(a) of the NIRA, the Wagner Act, and the Fair Labor Standards Act transformed the relationship between workers and business and breathed life into a troubled labor movement on the verge of total extinction. In the space of a decade government laws eliminated sweatshops, severely curtailed child labor, and established enforceable standards for hours, wages, and working conditions. Further, federal action eliminated the vast majority of company towns in such industries as coal mining. Although Robert Wagner and Frances Perkins dragged Roosevelt into labor's corner, the New Deal made the unions a dynamic force in American society. Moreover, as Nelson Lichtenstein has noted, "by giving so much of the working class an institutional voice, the union movement provided one of the main political bulwarks of the Roo-

sevelt Democratic party and became part of the social bed-
rock in which the New Deal welfare state was anchored."

A Greater Role for Government

Roosevelt's avowed goal of "cradle-to-grave" security for
the American people proved elusive, but his administration
achieved unprecedented advances in the field of social welfare. In 1938 the president told Congress: "Government
has a final responsibility for the well-being of its citizen-
ship. If private co-operative endeavor fails to provide work
for willing hands and relief for the unfortunate, those suffering hardship from no fault of their own have a right to
call upon the Government for aid; and a government worthy of its name must make fitting response." The New
Deal's safety net included low-cost housing; old-age pensions; unemployment insurance; and aid for dependent
mothers and children, the disabled, the blind, and public
health services. Sometimes disappointing because of limiting eligibility requirements and low benefit levels, these social welfare programs nevertheless firmly established the
principle that the government had an obligation to assist
the needy. As one scholar wrote of the New Deal, "More
progress was made in public welfare and relief than in the
three hundred years after this country was first settled."

More and more government programs, inevitably resulting in an enlarged administrative apparatus and requiring
additional revenue, added up to a much greater role for the
national government in American life. Coming at a time
when the only Washington bureaucracy most of the people
encountered with any frequency was the U.S. Postal Service, the change seemed all the more remarkable. Although
many New Deal programs were temporary emergency measures, others lingered long after the return of prosperity.
Suddenly, the national government was supporting farmers,
monitoring the economy, operating a welfare system, subsidizing housing, adjudicating labor disputes, managing
natural resources, and providing electricity to a growing
number of consumers. "What Roosevelt did in a period of

a little over 12 years was to change the form of government," argued journalist Richard L. Strout. "Washington had been largely run by big business, by Wall Street. He brought the government to Washington." Not surprisingly, popular attitudes toward government also changed. No longer willing to accept economic deprivation and social dislocation as the vagaries of an uncertain existence, Americans tolerated—indeed, came to expect—the national government's involvement in the problems of everyday life. No longer did "government" mean just "city hall."

The operation of the national government changed as well. For one thing, Roosevelt's strong leadership expanded presidential power, contributing to what historian Arthur Schlesinger, Jr., called the "imperial presidency." Whereas Americans had in previous years instinctively looked first to Capitol Hill, after Roosevelt the White House took center stage in Washington. At the same time, Congress and the president looked at the nation differently. Traditionally attentive only to one group (big business), policymakers in Washington began responding to other constituencies such as labor, farmers, the unemployed, the aged, and to a lesser extent, women, blacks, and other disadvantaged groups. This new "broker state" became more accessible and acted on a growing number of problems, but equity did not always result. The ablest, richest, and most experienced groups fared best during the New Deal. NRA codes favored big business, and Agricultural Adjustment Administration (AAA) benefits aided large landholders; blacks received relief and government jobs but not to the extent their circumstances merited. The long-term result, according to historian John Braeman, has been "a balkanized political system in which private interests scramble, largely successfully, to harness governmental authority and/or draw upon the public treasury to advance their private agendas."

Political Reorganization

Another legacy of the New Deal has been the Roosevelt revolution in politics. Urbanization and immigration changed the American electorate, and a new generation of voters who resided in the cities during the Great Depression opted for Franklin D. Roosevelt and his party. Before the 1930s the Democrats of the northern big-city machines and the solid South uneasily coexisted and surrendered primacy to the unified Republican party. The New Deal coalition that elected Roosevelt united behind common economic interests. Both urban northerners and rural southerners, as well as blacks, women, and ethnic immigrants, found common cause in government action to shield them from an economic system gone haywire. By the end of the decade the increasing importance of the urban North in the Democratic party had already become apparent. After the economy recovered from the disastrous depression, members of the Roosevelt coalition shared fewer compelling interests. Beginning in the 1960s, tensions mounted within the party as such issues as race, patriotism, and abortion loomed larger. Even so, the Roosevelt coalition retained enough commitment to New Deal principles to keep the Democrats the nation's majority party into the 1980s.

Yet for all the alterations in politics, government, and the economy, the New Deal fell far short of a revolution. The two-party system survived intact, and neither fascism, which attracted so many followers in European state's suffering from the same international depression, nor communism attracted much of a following in the United States. Vital government institutions functioned without interruption, and if the balance of powers shifted, the national branches of government maintained an essential equilibrium. The economy remained capitalistic; free enterprise and private ownership, not socialism, emerged from the 1930s. A limited welfare state changed the meld of the public and private but left them separate. Roosevelt could be likened to the British conservative Edmund Burke, who advocated measured change to offset drastic alterations—"reform to preserve." The New Deal's great achievement was the application of just enough change to preserve the American political economy.

Not Revolutionary, but Status Quo

Indications of Roosevelt's restraint emerged from the very beginning of the New Deal. Rather than assume extraordinary executive powers as Abraham Lincoln had done in the 1861 crisis, the president called Congress into special session. Whatever changes ensued would come through normal governmental activity. Roosevelt declined to assume direct control of the economy, leaving the nations resources in the hands of private enterprise. Resisting the blandishments of radicals calling for the nationalization of the banks, he provided the means for their rehabilitation and ignored the call for national health insurance and federal contributions to Social Security retirement benefits. The creation of such regulatory agencies as the SEC confirmed his intention to revitalize rather than remake economic institutions. Repeatedly during his presidency, Roosevelt responded to congressional pressure to enact bolder reforms, as in the case of the National Labor Relations Act, the Wagner-Steagall Housing Act, and the FDIC. The administration forwarded the NIRA only after Senator Hugo Black's recovery bill mandating 30-hour workweeks seemed on the verge of passage.

As impressive as New Deal relief and social welfare programs were, they never went as far as conditions demanded or many liberals recommended. Fluctuating congressional appropriations, oscillating economic conditions, and Roosevelt's own hesitancy to do too much violence to the federal budget left Harry Hopkins, Harold Ickes, and others only partially equipped to meet the staggering need. The president justified the creation of the costly Works Progress Administration (WPA) in 1935 by "ending this business of relief." Unskilled workers, who constituted the greatest number of WPA employees, obtained but 60 to 80 percent of the minimal family income as determined by the government. Roosevelt and Hopkins continued to emphasize work at less than existing wage scales so that the WPA or the Public Works Administration (PWA) never competed with free labor, and they allowed local authorities to modify pay rates. They also continued to make the critical distinction between the "deserving" and "undeserving" poor, making sure that government aided only the former. The New Deal never challenged the values underlying this distinction, instead seeking to provide for the growing number of "deserving" poor created by the Great Depression. Government assumed an expanded role in caring for the disadvantaged, but not at variance with existing societal norms regarding social welfare.

The New Deal effected no substantial redistribution of income. The Wealth Tax Act of 1935 (the famous soak-the-rich tax) produced scant revenue and affected very few tax-payers. Tax alterations in 1936 and 1937 imposed no additional burdens on the rich; the 1938 and 1939 tax laws actually removed a few. By the end of the 1930s less than 5 percent of Americans paid income taxes, and the share of taxes taken from personal and corporate income levies fell below the amount raised in the 1920s. The great change in American taxation policy came during World War II, when the number of income tax payers grew to 74 percent of the population. In 1942 Treasury Secretary Henry Morgenthau noted that "for the first time in our history, the income tax is becoming a people's tax." This the New Deal declined to do.

Finally, the increased importance of the national government exerted remarkably little influence on local institutions. The New Deal seldom dictated and almost always deferred to state and local governments—encouraging, cajoling, bargaining, and wheedling to bring parochial interests in line with national objectives. As Harry Hopkins discovered, governors and mayors angled to obtain as many federal dollars as possible for their constituents but with no strings attached. Community control and local autonomy, conditions thought to be central to American democracy, remained strong, and Roosevelt understood the need for firm ties with politicians at all levels. In his study of the New Deal's impact on federalism, James T. Patterson concludes: "For all the supposed power of the New Deal, it was unable to impose all its guidelines on the autonomous forty-eight states. . . . What could the Roosevelt administration have done to ensure a more profound and lasting impression on state policy and politics? Very little.

Choosing Freedom Before Equality

Liberal New Dealers longed for more sweeping change and lamented their inability to goad the president into additional action. They envisioned a wholesale purge of the Democratic party and the creation of a new organization embodying fully the principles of liberalism. They could not abide Roosevelt's toleration of the political conservatives and unethical bosses who composed part of the New Deal coalition. They sought racial equality, constraints upon the southern landholding class, and federal intrusion to curb the power of urban real estate interests on behalf of the inveterate poor. Yet to do these things would be to attempt changes well beyond the desires of most Americans. People pursuing remunerative jobs and the economic security of the middle class approved of government aiding the victims of an unfortunate economic crisis but had no interest in an economic system that would limit opportunity. The fear that the New Deal would lead to such thoroughgoing change explains the seemingly irrational hatred of Roosevelt by the economic elite. But, as historian Barry Karl has noted, "it was characteristic of Roosevelt's presidency that he never went as far as his detractors feared or his followers hoped."

The New Deal achieved much that was good and left much undone. Roosevelt's programs were defined by the confluence of forces that circumscribed his admittedly limited reform agenda—a hostile judiciary; powerful congressional opponents, some of whom entered into alliances of convenience with New Dealers and some of whom awaited the opportunity to build on their opposition; the political impotence of much of the populace; the pugnacious independence of local and state authorities; the strength of people's attachment to traditional values and institutions; and the basic conservatism of American culture. Obeisance to local custom and the decision to avoid tampering with the fabric of American society allowed much injustice to survive while shortchanging blacks, women, small farmers, and the "unworthy" poor. Those who criticized Franklin Roosevelt for an unwillingness to challenge racial, economic, and gender inequality misunderstood either the nature of his electoral mandate or the difference between reform and revolution—or both.

If the New Deal preserved more than it changed, that is understandable in a society whose people have consistently chosen freedom over equality. Americans traditionally have eschewed expanded government, no matter how efficiently managed or honestly administered, that imposed restraints on personal success—even though such limitations redressed legitimate grievances or righted imbalances. Parity, most Americans believed, should not be purchased with the loss of liberty. But although the American dream has always entailed individual success with a minimum of state interference, the profound shock of capitalism's near demise in the 1930s undermined numerous previously unquestioned beliefs. The inability of capitalism's "invisible hand" to stabilize the market and the failure of the private sector to restore prosperity enhanced the consideration of stronger executive leadership and centralized planning. Yet with the collapse of democratic governments and their replacement by totalitarian regimes, Americans were keenly sensitive to any threats to liberty. New Deal programs, frequently path breaking in their delivery of federal resources outside normal channels, also retained a strong commitment to local government and community control while promising only temporary disruptions prior to the return of economic stability. Reconciling the necessary authority at the federal level to meet nationwide crises with the local autonomy desirable to safeguard freedom has always been one of the salient challenges to American democracy. Even after New Deal refinements, the search for the proper balance continues.

"The World of Tomorrow": The 1939 New York World's Fair

Richard M. Ketchum

In the following excerpt from his book *The Borrowed Years, 1939–1941: America on the Way to War*, noted author, editor, and historian Richard M. Ketchum describes the transformation of a dump in Queens, New York, into "The World of Tomorrow," where 25 million Americans had an opportunity to glimpse General Motors' miniature City of Tomorrow and wear buttons that read "I have seen the future" at the New York World's Fair in 1939. Although the fair did not live up to critical and financial expectations, Ketchum writes, it still offered Americans hope that science and technology would find a way to solve social problems. According to Ketchum, the fair offered a variety of amusements, including precision swimming at the Aquacade and a 250-foot parachute jump from Life Savers tower. According to Ketchum, the fair provided a vision of peace, prosperity, and a General Motors automobile for all.

I n suggesting that Great Britain's royal couple include the New York World's Fair on their itinerary, Franklin Roosevelt was only echoing the absolute certainty of millions of Americans that the extravaganza on Long Island's Flushing Meadow was far and away the best show in town in 1939. . . .

Grouped around the Fair's Theme Centre—a seven-hundred-foot, needle-like obelisk known as the Trylon, and a two-hundred-foot, 4.2-million-pound globe called the Perisphere—was a mind-boggling array of technological wonders, promotional gimmicks, educational displays, and amusements calculated to suit just about every taste. (On instructions from Fair officials, the midway was never to be referred to as a midway; it was the "amusement loop.")

On April 30, when President Roosevelt opened the fair "to all mankind," he proclaimed to an audience of sixty thousand that "our wagon is hitched to a star of peace." During a day of parades, concerts, and fireworks, 206,000 people paid a 75-cent admission charge before the counting mechanism—which kept a running tally on a giant business machine revolving atop the National Cash Register building—broke down; an eight-year-old Wisconsin cow gave birth to a fifty-three pound bull calf; and Albert Einstein, the renowned German physicist who was now a refugee in America, threw a switch that lit up a myriad of fountains and floodlights "with cosmic ray impulses."

A Glimpse of the Future?

For only $7, it was said, the average family could have a dandy time at the Fair, and who could not, when the free exhibits included such marvels as General Electric's ten-million-volt man-made lightning; a twenty-two-foot transparent man; Westinghouse's robot named Elektro that had twenty-six different tricks, including walking, talking, and smoking a cigarette; a Children's World; a City of Tomorrow; a miniature rocket voyage to the moon; and, best of all, according to a poll of fairgoers taken by the Gallup organization a few weeks after opening day, General Motors' (GM) Futurama. This stunning glimpse of a vast cross section of the United States, all of it in miniature, for which GM had coughed up $7.5 million, was designer Norman Bel Geddes's vision of what the country was going to be like two decades hence. To behold what lay in store for 1960 America, you sat for fifteen minutes in an armchair on a moving conveyor belt, peering out over a gigantic scale model that contained 500,000 individually designed buildings, more than a million tiny trees, and fifty thousand scale-model automobiles scooting across an intricate network of superhighways and multideck bridges. As you progressed along this wondrous panorama, a sound device explained that happy-go-lucky Americans of the coming generation would spend a great deal of their time roving thither and yon about the countryside, thanks to express highways with separate fifty-, seventy-five-, and hundred-mile-per-hour lanes, in which speeds, lane changes, and periodic stops would be controlled by radio towers, facilitating accident-free trips from coast to coast in little more than a day's time. Raindrop-shaped, air-conditioned, diesel-powered cars, with a sticker price of only $200, would be the favorite mode of transportation for these mobile, fun-loving folk, who would be blessed with two-month vacations and a mere handful of possessions to tie them down. Interestingly, the most contented people in 1960, according to an article on the Futurama in *Life* magazine, would "live in one-factory farm villages producing one small industrial item and their own produce.". . .

If the Fair was not precisely the world of tomorrow it was certainly the hope of a better day ahead, an extension of the old American dream that if things didn't work out where you were, you could always move on to the next frontier. Implicit in the wonders of Flushing Meadow was the assurance that science and technology would provide that next frontier, and thousands of Americans who were deathly tired of the world of today, sporting GM Futurama buttons that read "I have seen the future," wandered hot and footsore through the fairgrounds, gawking with a sense of awe and excitement at the miracles of a promised land. They saw a rich amalgam of dreams—a streamlined General Motors car in every garage, an airport in every village, a world where cancer and infantile paralysis were diseases of the past, where agriculture was infinitely bountiful, where the nations of the world lived side by side in harmony. To show the folks of a distant future—fifty centuries hence—what the world of 1939 was really like, Westinghouse Electric's president and Grover Whalen lowered into the ground a gleaming metal time capsule, containing such items as an alarm clock, a can opener, a Mickey Mouse plastic cup, some of the latest fabrics, coins, the Lord's Prayer in three hundred languages, the alphabet, photographs, magazines, films, books, a speech by Franklin D. Roosevelt, and a gloomy message from the great Albert Einstein for anyone who might be lucky enough to find and disinter the time capsule in the year 6939.

The "Amusement Loop"

There was, of course, a less earnest side to this exhibition. "As an attraction for crowds, science does not seem to compete with an undressed woman," Charles Lindbergh commented wryly after touring the World of Tomorrow, and by the time the Fair closed in November, six months after opening day, it was a safe bet that the 26 million visitors had spent considerably more time on the "amusement loop" than at the more serious exhibits, uplifting though the latter might be. There were girlie shows and freaks, live monsters and a Laff in the Dark, a tank where you could watch Oscar the Obscene Octopus wrestle with an almost-naked maiden in "Twenty Thousand Legs Under the Sea," and the crowds' particular favorite, Billy Rose's Aquacade, starring the shapely Olympic medalist Eleanor Holm and several score "Aquafemmes"—precision swimmers who splashed around the pool in time to waltz music.

Equally successful was the 250-foot parachute jump from the Life Savers tower. Strapped in your seat, you were hoisted slowly into the air, up and up, to get a bird's-eye view of the restaurants and rides, the huge exhibition halls, the fountains playing in the Lagoon of Nations, the Japanese pavilion modeled after an ancient Shinto shrine, and beyond it the Soviet Union's monolithic marble tower, topped by a statue of a worker holding the red star and Lenin's uncompromising dictum: "The Russian Revolution must in its final result lead to the victory of Socialism." Off to one side, beyond the roller skating, beyond Gay New Orleans and the Aquacade, was the Lake of Liberty. Far in the distance, visible from the very top of the tower, you could see the United States building and the Court of Peace, surrounded by the pavilions of various nations. Farther to the north were the British pavilion with its gleaming gold imperial lion and the Coldstream Guards band, Italy's determinedly modernistic structure, the League of Nations building, and Poland's graceful tower, rising above a restaurant that served Polish vodka and forty different hors d'oeuvres, and that nation's pavilion, where officials urged visitors to enter an essay contest that began, "I would like to visit Poland

TV Debuts at the New York World's Fair

In this excerpt taken from the website The Television Archives, *Jim Von Schilling reports American reactions to RCA's first television broadcast at the New York World's Fair in 1939.*

John Pavlic was amazed on April 30, 1939, when he saw television for the first time. I can't believe it. I must be dreaming," the Navy sailor from Youngstown, Ohio, told a reporter for the *New York Herald Tribune*. Pavlic was among hundreds of Americans who watched television for the first time that day, when the New York World's Fair opened in Flushing Meadows, Queens. . . .

For Pavlic and nearly all Americans in 1939, seeing pictures in motion on a small screen was a novelty in the spring of 1939—and a source of wonderment. Pavlic's shipmate, James Vogt of Omaha, "just stared" at the screen of the TV set on display, wrote the *Herald Tribune* reporter. Beatrice Minn, also seeing TV for the first time that day, exclaimed, "I never thought it would be like this. Why, it's beyond conception, and here it is."

Jim Von Schilling, "Sixty Years Ago: April 1939, TV Debuts at the New York World's Fair," *The Television Archives,* http://ccs.compubell.com/~mweinber/nyfair.html.

because . . ." Then suddenly you had reached the top, the parachute was released, and your stomach dropped out from under you in that breathtaking instant before the chute filled with air and floated slowly to earth. . . .

A Peaceful Place in a Stormy World

By the time the Fair closed for the year on November 1, 1939, many of the international exhibitors that had assembled here a few months earlier as peaceful competitors had become mortal enemies of their neighbors across the Lagoon of Nations. By then, war had shattered the hopeful tomorrow that brought a community of nations and commercial enterprises together in Flushing Meadow. The Poles, whose homeland was overrun by the Germans and the Russians, continued in a daze to go through the motions of summer, urging those who visited the pavilion to enter the contest and write an essay about why they wanted to visit Poland. Before winter was out, the Soviet building would be torn down and the site landscaped, so that when the Fair reopened in 1940, groups in foreign costumes could perform folk dances and native songs on what would be called the "American common." Of the amusement concessions, only Billy Rose's Aquacade, the parachute jump, and Frank Buck's Jungleland made money the first season. New York's merchants and hotelkeepers were calling the Fair a flop, since their revenues for the year were below those of the non-Fair years 1937 and 1938. The New York World's Fair Corporation was broke, with an operating loss of $10 million and its bonds in default. Grover Whalen's projected fifty to sixty million paying customers proved to be exactly 25,817,625, and Whalen himself, in an effort to drum up business for 1940, was tiptoeing around the edges of Europe's battlefields looking for prospects. An embittered Joseph Shadgen, whose idea it had been in the first place, never went near the fairgrounds, lost his job with the corporation, sued for $1 million, and settled for $45,000. His daughter Jacqueline, however, whose offhand remark about what she had learned in school had started the whole thing, visited the Fair any number of times and loved it, as did almost everyone else who was fortunate enough to see the fantastic paradise in Flushing Meadow during that final summer of peace.

Maybe the Fair was merely an illusion or a conjurer's trick, but it enabled nearly 26 million visitors, mostly Americans, to broaden their painfully cramped horizons by exposure—never mind how superficially—to the cultures of scores of foreign nations, letting them see in the flesh who their true allies were, reassuring them with the physical presence and the rich accents of English and French, Canadians, Australians, and New Zealanders, Finns, Belgians, and Brazilians, even Czechs and Poles, as if to say that war was only a temporary aberration and that one day soon we friends would get together again. For four happy, shining months, the World of Tomorrow provided a bright vision of a world without poverty or war or hatred, a world of dreams where everyone had plenty to eat and a General Motors automobile, where nations lived side by side in peace, where bands played and strangers smiled at each other because they had nothing more important in mind than having a good time.

Changing Foreign Policy: From Isolation to Intervention

Gerald D. Nash

At the end of the 1930s, some consultants advised President Franklin Roosevelt that the United States needed to take a more active role in world affairs in order for the nation to take advantage of economic opportunities. Americans, however, still disillusioned by their experiences in World War I, believed that the United States should refrain from becoming involved in world politics, writes historian Gerald D. Nash in his book *The Great Depression and World War II: Organizing America, 1933–1945*. According to Nash, Roosevelt decided to follow the wishes of the American public, and so did not become involved when Germany steadily advanced into Europe and Japan into the Far East. However, as the decade drew to a close, Nash reveals, Roosevelt slowly tried to prepare the American public for U.S. intervention when he expressed concern about German and Japanese aggression in his Quarantine Address, comparing aggression to a disease that must not be allowed to spread. In 1938, Congress voted military appropriations to prepare the American military. By 1939, Nash remarks, the overriding interest in America was no longer the depression but the threat of Nazi aggression.

While Franklin D. Roosevelt struggled with domestic issues throughout his first two terms, foreign affairs took an increasingly greater portion of his time and energy in his later terms. During this period Americans were watching the collapse of the European order and the fall of democratic governments throughout the world.

The Depression and Foreign Policy

Understandably, the Great Depression itself created many diplomatic problems for Americans. Instability in the international economy contributed to the depressed economic conditions within the United States and to mass unemployment. The precipitous decline of American exports overseas cost thousands of jobs in the United States. Violent fluctuations in foreign currencies affected U.S. gold reserves and disrupted import and export trade. Withdrawal of foreign investments in 1929 and 1930 added to panic selling and the collapse of securities markets. The impact of the Depression, however, was not solely economic. A troubled economy worldwide led to the collapse of democratic governments in Europe and the rise of militarism, rearmament, and territorial expansion. These actions challenged Americans on two fronts. On the one hand they viewed the rise of dictatorships as a threat to American democratic values. On the other hand, disillusionment over American participation in World War I was widespread, and pacifist sentiment—particularly among young people—was strong. The seeming failure of President Wilson's plans for a stable world order left many Americans embittered and disappointed. They felt passionately that the United States should not immerse itself in the treacherous currents of world politics too deeply.

Isolation thus became the keynote of United States foreign policy during Roosevelt's first term in the White House. Historians such as William Appleman Williams who leaned toward a New Left view have argued that even in the Depression era, Americans were more involved in world affairs than they realized. Such involvement is relative, however. In comparison to Cold War diplomacy between 1945 and 1970, Roosevelt's policies in the 1930s appear to reflect the nation's desire for nonintervention. His policy was to steer clear of European and Asian embroilments while consolidating American influence in the Western Hemisphere. In Congress the desire to retreat into isolation was perhaps even stronger. Meanwhile, various antiwar organizations such as the Veterans of Future Wars and the Fellowship of Reconciliation sprang up and gained strength.

Soon after assuming the presidency, Roosevelt was forced to make a decision concerning American cooperation with other nations in respect to international tariff policies and currency stabilization. Months before he left office, the internationally minded Herbert Hoover had indicated American willingness to work with the British and French to solve the economic problems related to the Depression. In spring 1933 the major European industrial nations were planning a conference in London for July, at which their representatives were expected to work out detailed programs to help the world economy. Roosevelt was beset with conflicting advice concerning American involvement in the London Economic Conference. On the one hand Secretary of State Cordell Hull, long an advocate of free trade, urged him to lower tariff and other trade barriers. On the other hand, though, Brains Truster Raymond Moley [one of a collection of experts in various fields who advised Roosevelt], insisted that Roosevelt would jeopardize many of his domestic economic recovery measures if he made new international commitments. The choice seemed to be between a nationalist or an internationalist approach to economic recovery. Faced with this difficult choice, Roosevelt wavered. He sent Hull to head the official American delegation at the conference, but soon after Hull arrived in London, Roosevelt was persuaded by Moley's arguments, and on July 3, he sent his "Bombshell" message to the conference, in which he declared his opposition to American participation in international efforts to regulate currencies or trade. Hull was stunned, but abided by the decision. Roosevelt's message effectively wrecked the conference and further efforts to conclude international economic agreements in 1933. Without the cooperation of the United States, such attempts were futile.

To some extent the impression of many Europeans that the United States was retreating into greater isolation was mitigated by American recognition of the Soviet Union in November 1933. Disturbed by Japan's invasion of Manchuria, Roosevelt cast a more benevolent eye on the U.S.S.R. as a potential ally. Despite considerable criticism at home, the president extended official United States recognition to the Soviet Union, and in return, the Communist government promised to pay war debts owed to Americans and to abate its propaganda in the United States, two promises it did not keep.

Isolationist Sentiments Grow

During 1934 American isolationist sentiment was whipped into virtual hysteria by the investigations of the Nye Committee. Established by Congress to explore the causes of American entry into World War I, the committee, which was headed by isolationist Senator Gerald P. Nye of North Dakota, focused its attention on munitions manufacturers. Operating under the assumption that wars were caused by economic forces, the committee charged that the United States had been tricked into World War I by munitions makers. Although the evidence Nye and his staff collected hardly warranted such a conclusion, the committee's work had an enormous impact on the American public and stiffened isolationist resolve.

Partly because of the work of the Nye Committee, Congress responded aggressively to preclude further American involvement in European affairs. In 1935 it approved the Pitman Resolution, which prohibited exports of American arms to war-torn areas. The resolution also prohibited American merchant vessels from carrying munitions into such areas and withheld protection from Americans who travelled on ships belonging to belligerents. In 1936 and

1937 Congress enacted additional neutrality acts to strengthen its resolve of noninvolvement. The Neutrality Act of 1936 prohibited loans to belligerent parties; the act of 1937 introduced an arms embargo but contained a cash-and-carry clause whereby belligerents who could pay for arms and who could transport them would be permitted to make arms purchases in the United States. Unfortunately, the impact of these acts was not what Congress had hoped. They benefited aggressor nations by increasing the difficulty with which those attacked could secure necessary arms. In a sense the legislation only delayed the day of reckoning when Americans had to decide whether or not to join other democratic nations in opposing totalitarian expansion.

For the immediate time, however, the isolationist mood of Americans was also revealed in Roosevelt's diplomacy in the Far East. After more than a decade of discussion, Congress agreed to grant the Philippine Islands, ceded to the United States by Spain after the Spanish-American War, their independence. American sugar producers in particular strongly favored such a move since Philippine sugar competed with their own product. And as long as the Philippines were part of the United States, American tariff duties did not apply. The Tydings-McDuffie Act of 1934 provided for Philippine independence after a ten-year period of transition.

Refusing to Act

The disinclination of Americans to become too closely involved with European affairs was also reflected in the Administration's refugee policies. As the Nazis stepped up their persecution of Jews and other minorities, a steady trickle of German Jews sought refuge in countries around the world. Although many beseeched the United States to allow them entry, Congress refused to modify the existing quota, which allowed only 150,000 immigrants to enter the country each year. President Roosevelt was sympathetic to their plight but hesitant to take overt action. Furthermore, some State Department workers, such as Assistant Secretary Breckinridge Long, had anti-Semitic leanings. As a result, while about 120,000 German-Jewish refugees were permitted to enter the United States between 1933 and 1941, millions more found the doors closed and eventually perished in Nazi death camps.

Meanwhile, the continued Japanese invasion of China posed real problems for the United States. In 1933 Japanese armies marched into the rive northern provinces of China—in direct violation of the Open Door agreements, the Nine-Power Pact of 1921, and the Kellogg-Briand Pact of 1927. Like Hoover, Roosevelt felt constrained to watch helplessly. His own absorption in the problems of domestic depression as well as the strong prevailing mood of isolation severely limited his alternatives.

On July 7, 1937, the Japanese intensified and broadened their invasion, and in the midst of a full-scale military attack against China, Japanese war planes sank the American gunboat *Panay* off Shanghai. Even in the face of this action, the majority of Americans were still opposed to any overt action by their government. A Gallup poll reported that more than 70 percent of Americans opposed any intervention. And more than a two-thirds majority in Congress voted against imposing any sanctions against the Japanese. In fact, most Americans breathed easier when they learned that the Japanese government had apologized and offered to pay damages for the *Panay*.

A Good Neighbor Policy

Paradoxically, though, the desire to remain aloof from the problems of Europe and Asia led the United States to seek more collaboration with other countries in the Western Hemisphere. With his talent for appropriate phrases, Roosevelt called this new idea the Good Neighbor policy. American concern for national security and solidarity against communism was obviously one motivation, but another was the desire to expand foreign markets during the Depression years. To fulfill this policy, Roosevelt took on the role of diplomat as he sought to dampen strong anti-American feelings throughout South America that were in part a product of United States interventionist policies in the decade following the Spanish-American War.

Like so many of Roosevelt's programs, the Good Neighbor policy embraced a many-sided approach. Economic cooperation was one facet. Congressional action on tariffs was another facet. By 1934 Congress approved the Reciprocal Trade Agreements Act, which allowed the president to negotiate treaties to reduce American tariffs for nations that made reciprocal reductions in return. Within two years Roosevelt had concluded thirteen such agreements, many with South America. During the same period United States exports rose more than 14 percent. The Reciprocal Trade Agreements Act proved to be one of the more successful of the New Deal's foreign policies. Also in 1934 the United States established the Export-Import Bank, which made loans to South American countries seeking to stabilize their currencies.

At the same time Roosevelt took special care to impress Latin Americans with the desire of the United States not to intervene in their affairs. At the Inter-American Conference at Montevideo, Uruguay, in 1933, the United States supported a declaration pledging nonintervention among the Western Hemisphere states. The president underscored this policy by supporting the abrogation of the Platt Amendment, which had given the United States the right to intervene in the affairs of Cuba. In a treaty with Panama in 1936, American negotiators gave up similar privileges. The president withdrew Marines from Haiti in 1934 and joined with representatives of twenty other governments in South America to ratify a Protocol of Non-Intervention at the Inter-American Conference in Buenos Aires, Argentina, in 1936. Roosevelt's personal appearance at this meeting underscored the importance he attached to fostering close ties and goodwill with Latin American countries.

To embellish its image as the friendly giant in the north, the United States also played a positive role as mediator of conflicts in Latin America as, for example, when American officials played a role in settling strife between Peru and

Colombia in 1933. Roosevelt assiduously refrained from intervening in the Cuban revolution of 1933, and used great self-restraint in refusing to intervene when Mexico expropriated American oil companies during the 1930s. When Germany, Italy, and Japan entered into the Axis Alliance in 1936, nations of the Western Hemisphere adopted the Convention for Collective Security. This provided for mutual consultation in case of attack and brought the United States closer to its neighboring nations than it had been in many years.

The Gathering War Clouds

By 1937, however, Roosevelt began to doubt the effectiveness of American diplomacy in limiting Axis expansion. In 1935 Adolf Hitler marched his troops into the Rhineland, which had been declared a buffer zone at Versailles, [France, where the United States, Britain, France, and Italy negotiated a treaty with Germany after World War I]. In 1938 he occupied the Czech Sudetenland, and marched into Austria as well.

Two years earlier, Hitler's Axis partner, Benito Mussolini, had conquered Ethiopia. In Spain both Hitler and Mussolini provided active military support for their would-be fellow dictator, General Francisco Franco, who was fighting a civil war to overthrow the elected republican government. Fascist politicians were also influential in Hungary and Rumania.

Due mostly to the worsening international situation Roosevelt's second administration saw increasingly heated debate between noninterventionists and interventionists concerning the course of American foreign policy. A strong isolationist policy prevailed. If the president himself had doubts about isolationism, he was careful to keep them to himself. He proceeded with characteristic caution, seemingly anxious not to alienate public opinion, but between 1937 and 1940 Roosevelt took an increasingly firm stand against German and Japanese expansion in Europe and the Far East respectively.

This departure from nonintervention was first heralded in what became known as Roosevelt's Quarantine Address, given in Chicago on October 5, 1937. Prompted by the recently accelerated Japanese advance into China, Roosevelt called for the quarantining of aggressor nations by the international community. Possibly he was sounding out public opinion to determine whether or not isolationist sentiment was weakening, but certainly the tone of the address—and the fiery manner in which he delivered it— was firmer than any of his previous presidential foreign policy statements:

> The political situation in the world, which of late has been growing progressively worse, is such as to cause grave concern and anxiety to all the peoples and nations who wish to live in peace and amity with their neighbors . . . the peace, the freedom, the security of 90 percent of the population of the world is being jeopardized by the remaining 10 percent who are threatening a breakdown of all international order and law. Surely the 90 percent . . . must find some way to make their will prevail. . . . It seems to be unfortunately true that the epidemic of world lawlessness is spreading. And mark this well! When an epidemic of physical disease starts to spread, the community approves and joins in a quarantine of the patients in order to protect the health of the community against the spread of the disease.

Such a quarantine against aggressor nations was his prescription for maintaining peace in the increasingly precarious international order.

Preparing the Military

The worsening international situation also aroused alarm in Congress. In consultation with the president, the lawmakers reluctantly voted to embark on a military preparedness program. Throughout the Depression Congress had made only minimal appropriations for the armed forces. Between 1933 and 1937 appropriations had averaged only about $180 million annually. The navy—a favorite of Roosevelt's—fared much better than the army, which numbered no more than 110,000 officers and men. In fact, the army was so poverty stricken that its men were forced to drill with wooden rifles. The Military Appropriations Act of 1938 changed all this as Congress voted $1 billion to expand the armed forces. A strong America, Roosevelt declared, would be the best deterrent against a would-be aggressor:

> The American nation is committed to peace and the principal reason for the existence of our armed forces is to guarantee our peace. The army of the United States is one of the smallest in the world. However . . . its efficiency is steadily improving.

Amid American rearmament preparations in 1938 and 1939, the political situation in Europe worsened. At the Munich Conference of 1938 British Prime Minister Neville Chamberlain and French Premier Edward Daladier abjectly surrendered to Hitler's demand for the annexation of all of Czechoslovakia. In March 1939 German troops invaded Czechoslovakia while its British and French allies stood impotently by. In Spain Franco won a decisive victory over the Republicans and established a harsh fascist dictatorship. Mussolini was preparing to move Italian troops into Albania and Greece, to give himself a foothold in the Balkans. And in September 1939 Nazi troops attacked Poland, which they subdued and occupied within a month. The invasion of Poland left England and France little choice but to resist, and on September 1, 1939, World War II officially began.

Most Americans were still hopeful that the outbreak of World War II in Europe would not lead to significant changes in the Roosevelt Administration's policy of nonintervention. Only in later years did Americans come to realize that the war ended the isolationism in United States diplomacy. Throughout the 1930s the Depression was a major influence on foreign relations. Disillusionment after World War I had strengthened the isolationist mood, but the Depression led Americans to be even more concerned with domestic than foreign problems. Increasing helplessness of the League of Nations during the 1930s, as well as the outbreak of armed hostilities in Europe, Africa, and the Far East, only intensified the resolve for nonintervention. Involvement of the United States in international crises was considered to be as detrimental to the national interest in the 1930s as United States intervention supposedly had been in the First World War. As President Roosevelt often said, the great enemy which Americans had to right was the Depression. The year 1939 found the United States in a rapidly changing world. The Nazi menace to western civilization was replacing the Depression as the overriding issue in American public life. American policymakers found themselves increasingly devoting time to foreign affairs rather than to domestic issues.

Chronology

1929

March 4—Herbert Hoover is inaugurated as the thirty-first president of the United States.

October 24—The stock market crashes, wiping out 40 percent of the paper values on common stock.

November 19–27—Hoover convenes several conferences with the leading spokesmen of industry, finance, agriculture, the Federal Reserve system, and public utilities, asking them to pledge to maintain employment, wages, and prices.

1930

June—Congress passes the Smoot-Hawley Tariff to raise agricultural duties.

October—Hoover forms the President's Emergency Committee for Employment (PECE).

1931

May 1—President Hoover officially opens the world's tallest building, the Empire State Building; however, as a result of the depression, most of the office space is vacant.

November 7—The National Credit Corporation opens for business but fails to encourage investment.

Charlie Chaplin stars in *City Lights*.

1932

February/March—The Reconstruction Finance Corporation approves loans to banks, railroads, and lending institutions, but no industrial recovery follows.

March 1—The twenty-month-old son of aviator Charles A. Lindbergh is kidnapped.

June—Fifteen thousand depression-weary veterans and their families march on Washington, D.C., demanding that they be paid their World War I bonus; however, Hoover calls on General Douglas MacArthur to drive the veterans out, and the nation reacts with shock as troops drive unarmed men, women, and children out of the nation's capital.

July 1—The Justice Department establishes the U.S. Bureau of Investigation; to avoid confusion with the Bureau of Prohibition, the name permanently changes to the Federal Bureau of Investigation in 1935.

July 21—Hoover signs the Emergency Relief and Construction Act, providing $1.5 billion for public construction, $300 million in loans to states for direct relief, and $200 million for the liquidation of ruined banks, but funds fall short and delays keep programs from being implemented.

November 8—Franklin Delano Roosevelt defeats Herbert Hoover and becomes the thirty-second president of the United States.

1933

February 15—President-elect Roosevelt escapes an attempt on his life in Miami, Florida, when shots are fired by Giuseppe Zangara.

March 4—Roosevelt delivers his inaugural address that warns "the only thing we have to fear is fear itself," and begins what becomes known as the first hundred days of the New Deal.

March 9—Congress passes the Emergency Banking Relief Act, and Roosevelt closes U.S. banks until they can prove their solvency, which many did, reopening on March 12.

March 12—Roosevelt launches his "fireside chats" over the radio from the White House.

March 31—The Reforestation Relief Act creates the Civilian Conservation Corps with 250,000 immediate jobs for men aged eighteen to twenty-five.

May 12—Congress establishes the Federal Emergency Relief Administration and the Agricultural Adjustment Act.

May 18—Congress creates the Tennessee Valley Authority, which builds dams, generates and sells electricity, manufactures and sells fertilizers, establishes flood control, and develops navigation.

May 27—Congress passes the Federal Securities Act, which requires the government to register and approve all issue of stocks and bonds.

June 6—The Securities Exchange Act creates the Securities and Exchange Commission.

June 16—The Banking (Glass-Steagall) Act creates the Federal Deposit Insurance Corporation; Congress establishes the National Industrial Recovery Act (NIRA), which creates the National Recovery Administration, whose symbol is the blue eagle and its motto "We Do Our Part"; NIRA creates the Public Works Administration, headed by Harold L. Ickes.

December 5—Prohibition is repealed.

Fay Wray stars in the movie *King Kong*.

Walt Disney releases his *Silly Symphonies* cartoon the *Three Little Pigs*.

1934

Spring/Summer—More than a million and a half American workers go on strike, including San Francisco longshoremen, who bring the city's waterfront to a standstill.

June 19—The Communications Act of 1934 creates the Federal Communications Commission.

July 22—John Dillinger, Public Enemy No. 1, is gunned down by federal agents.

Summer—Hundreds of thousands of residents of the Dust Bowl states, including Oklahoma, Arkansas, and Texas, migrate to nearby states or to the Pacific Northwest and California.

1935

Winter—The Supreme Court declares NIRA unconstitutional in *Schecter v. United States*, arguing that Congress had no control over intrastate commerce.

May 6—By executive order, Roosevelt creates the Works Progress Administration headed by Harry Hopkins.

June—Babe Ruth retires with 714 home runs, a lifetime average of .342, and the highest slugging average in history (.690).

July 5—Congress establishes the National Labor Relations Act, also known as the Wagner Act.

August 13—The first Neutrality Act prohibits loans to belligerent parties but encourages noninvolvement in foreign affairs.

August 14—Congress passes the Social Security Act, which establishes old-age pensions, unemployment insurance, and welfare.

September 30—Roosevelt dedicates the Hoover Dam.

November 9—Labor leaders who support Roosevelt's policies, like John L. Lewis of the United Mine Workers, create the Committee for Industrial Organization.

The Marx Brothers star in *A Night at the Opera.*

1936

April 3—Bruno Richard Hauptmann is electrocuted for first-degree murder in the kidnap-death of Charles A. Lindbergh Jr., son of aviator Charles Lindbergh.

Summer—U.S. track superstar Jesse Owens, an African American, captures four gold medals at the Summer Olympics in Berlin in front of Adolf Hitler.

November 3—Roosevelt is reelected president, defeating Alfred M. Landon and giving Roosevelt the largest electoral victory ever recorded in an election, 523–8.

December 28—General Motors employees sit down at GM's Fisher Body Plant in Cleveland, Ohio; the strike ends forty-four days later.

1937

February 5—Roosevelt submits a proposal asking Congress to expand the number of Supreme Court justices, which opponents label Roosevelt's "court-packing plan"; Congress defeats the plan in July.

May 1—Roosevelt signs a second Neutrality Act that prohibits loans and arms to belligerent nations.

May 6—The crash of the zeppelin *Hindenburg* in Lakehurst, New Jersey, is broadcast coast to coast.

May 26—Press photographers capture the beating of four United Auto Worker union organizers by Ford Motor Company toughs; this event becomes known as the "Battle of the Overpass."

Walt Disney releases the first feature-length cartoon, *Snow White and the Seven Dwarfs*.

1938

May 17—The Vinson-Trammel Naval Expansion Act plans to bolster the Navy with new ships, carriers, and planes; expand naval bases in the United States; and fortify bases in Midway, Wake, and Guam.

June 22—Joe Louis defeats Max Schmeling in Yankee Stadium before seventy thousand people.

June 25—Congress passes the Fair Labor Standards Act, which establishes a national minimum wage and limits work hours.

October 31—Orson Welles's dramatization of H.G. Wells's story *War of the Worlds* broadcasts nationwide over CBS, causing widespread panic.

1939

January 12—Roosevelt asks Congress for $525 million more for defense, especially for airplanes.

January 25—Using a cyclotron, John Durning splits an atom in his lab at Columbia University, suggesting that nuclear fission is possible.

April 30—The New York World's Fair opens in Flushing Meadows, Queens, where RCA introduces television to the American people and begins the nation's first television broadcast.

May 1—*Batman* debuts as a comic strip hero by D.C. Comics.

July 4—New York Yankee Lou Gehrig, with a lifetime batting average of .340, retires after being struck by a fatal disease and tells a packed house, "I consider myself the luckiest man on the face of the earth."

August 2—Albert Einstein writes a letter to President Roosevelt warning him of Nazi efforts to purify Uranium-235, which might be used to build an atomic bomb.

September 3—England and France declare war on Germany.

November 4—Roosevelt signs a revised version of the Neutrality Act that repeals the arms embargo but prohibits travel and loans to belligerents.

Gone with the Wind attracts record-breaking crowds who clamor to see Clark Gable and Vivien Leigh in the Civil War–torn South.

Judy Garland stars in *The Wizard of Oz*.

1940
April 9—German armies subdue Norway and Denmark.

June 10—Roosevelt delivers a commencement speech at the University of Virginia that publicizes his position that the United States should extend aid to the Allies.

June 13—President Roosevelt signs a $1.3-billion defense bill.

June 22—France surrenders to Germany.

July 10—The German Luftwaffe begins the Battle of Britain, dropping thousands of bombs on British cities through March 1941.

November 5—Roosevelt is reelected president, defeating Wendell Wilkie.

December 17—Roosevelt submits a lend-lease proposal to Congress that is not passed until March 1941.

December 29—Roosevelt tells Americans in a fireside chat that the United States "must be the great arsenal of democracy."

For Further Reading

General Studies

William J. Barber, "FDR's Big Government Legacy," *Regional Review,* Summer 1997. Available from the Federal Reserve Bank of Boston, 600 Atlantic Avenue, Boston, MA 02106.

A. Scott Berg, *Lindbergh.* New York: Putnam, 1998.

George J. Church, "1929–1939: Despair," *Time,* March 9, 1998.

Terry A. Cooney, *Balancing Acts: American Thought and Culture in the 1930s.* New York: Twayne, 1995.

Robert Dallek, *Franklin D. Roosevelt and American Foreign Policy: 1932–1945.* New York: Oxford University Press, 1979.

Farrell Dobbes, *Teamster Rebellion: The 1930s Strike and Organizing Drive That Transformed the Labor Movement in the Midwest.* New York: Pathfinder Press, 1972.

Hugh Gregory Gallagher, *FDR's Splendid Deception.* New York: Dodd, Mead and Company, 1985.

Lorraine Glennon, "1930s," *Parents,* August 1996.

John Steele Gordon, "Farewell to Taft-Hartley," *American Heritage,* October 1994.

Juliet Haines Mofford, *Talkin' Union: The American Labor Movement.* Carlisle, MA: Discovery Enterprises, 1997.

Richard H. Pells, *Radical Visions and American Dreams: Culture and Social Thought in the Depression Years.* Chicago: University of Illinois Press, 1998.

David Plotke, *Building a Democratic Political Order: Reshaping American Liberalism in the 1930s and 1940s.* New York: Cambridge University Press, 1996.

Theodore J. St. Antoine, "How the Wagner Act Came to Be: A Prospectus," *Michigan Law Review,* August 1998.

Alan Singer, "The 1932 Veterans' Bonus March on Washington," *Social Education,* January 1990. Available from NCSS Publications, PO Box 2067, Waldorf, MD 20604-2067.

Susan Ware, *Holding Their Own: American Women in the 1930s.* Boston: Twayne, 1982.

The Depression and the New Deal

Alan Brinkley, *Voices of Protest: Huey Long, Father Coughlin, and the Great Depression*. New York: Random House, 1983.

Bruce I. Bustard, *A New Deal for the Arts*. Seattle: University of Washington Press, 1997.

James R. Chiles, "Bang! Went the Doors of Every Bank in America," *Smithsonian*, April 1997.

Wilbur J. Cohen, "A Salute to 25 Years of Social Security," *Public Welfare*, Winter 1993.

Phoebe Cutler, *The Public Landscape of the New Deal*. New Haven, CT: Yale University Press, 1985.

Kenneth S. Davis, *FDR: The New Deal Years 1933–1937*. New York: Random House, 1986.

Robert Eden, *The New Deal and Its Legacy*. Westport, CT: Greenwood, 1989.

Glen H. Elder Jr., *Children of the Great Depression*. Boulder, CO: Westview Press, 1998.

Robert C. Goldston, *The Great Depression: The United States in the Thirties*. Greenwich, CT: Fawcett Premier Books, 1970.

Laura Hapke, *Daughters of the Great Depression: Women, Work, and Fiction in the American 1930s*. Athens: University of Georgia Press, 1995.

Leslie Alexander Lacy, *The Soil Soldiers: The Civilian Conservation Corps in the Great Depression*. Radnor, PA: Chilton, 1976.

William Leuchtenburg, *Franklin D. Roosevelt and the New Deal, 1932–1940*. New York: Harper and Row, 1963.

Ernest W. May, "Charity During the Great Depression," *The American Enterprise*, May 1996.

Nancy E. Rose, "Discrimination Against Women in New Deal Work Programs," *Affilia: Journal of Women and Social Work*, Summer 1990. Available from SAGE Publications, Inc., 2455 Teller Road, Thousand Oaks, CA 91320.

Studs Terkel, *Hard Times: An Oral History of the Great Depression*. New York: Pantheon, 1970.

Errol Lincoln Uys, *Riding the Rails: Teenagers on the Move Dur-

ing the Great Depression. New York: Penguin, 1993.

Susan Ware, *Beyond Suffrage: Women in the New Deal*. Boston: Harvard University Press, 1981.

Harris Gaylord Warren, *Herbert Hoover and the Great Depression*. New York: Norton, 1967.

Susan Winslow, *Brother Can You Spare a Dime?* New York: Paddington, 1976.

Donald Worster, *Dust Bowl: The Southern Plains in the 1930s*. New York: Oxford University Press, 1979.

Radio

Bert Berdis, "A Brief History of Humor Radio," *Mediaweek*, September 4, 1995. Available from BPI Communications, Inc., 1515 Broadway, New York, NY 10036.

Edward Bliss, *Now the News: The Story of Broadcast Journalism*. New York: Columbia University Press, 1992.

Philip Collins, *Raised on Radio*. New York: Pantheon, 1998.

Norman H. Finkelstein, *Sounds in the Air: The Golden Age of Radio*. New York: Scribner/Macmillan, 1993.

J. Fred MacDonald, *Don't Touch That Dial! Radio Programming in American Life, 1920–1960*. Chicago: Nelson-Hall, 1979.

Robert W. McChesney, "Media and Democracy: The Emergence of Commercial Broadcasting in the United States, 1927–1935," *OAH Magazine of History*, Spring 1992. Available from the Organization of American Historians, 112 North Bryan Avenue, Bloomington, IN 47448-4199.

Robert L. Mott, *Radio Sound Effects: Who Did It, and How, in the Era of Live Broadcasting*. Jefferson, NC: McFarland, 1993.

Popular Culture

Jesse Berrett, "Diamonds for Sale: Promoting Baseball During the Great Depression," *Baseball History 4: An Annual of Original Baseball Research*. Westport, CT: Meckler, 1991.

Thomas Doherty, *Pre-Code Hollywood: Sex, Immorality, and Insurrection in American Cinema 1930–1934*. New York: Columbia University Press, 1999.

Thomas W. Gilbert, *The Good Old Days: Baseball in the 1930s.* Danbury, CT: Franklin Watts, 1996.

Brent P. Kelley, *Early All-Stars: Conversations with Standout Baseball Players of the 1930s and 1940s.* Jefferson, NC: McFarland, 1997.

Jack Kroll, "Monster Mash," *Newsweek,* June 22, 1998.

Carol Martin, *Dance Marathons: Performing American Culture of the 1920s and 1930s.* Jackson: University of Mississippi Press, 1994.

Richard Miniter, "Bad Economics Makes Bad Movies," *The American Enterprise,* September/October 1997.

Janet Montefiore, *Men and Women Writers of the 1930s: The Dangerous Flood of History.* New York: Routledge, 1996.

John Springhall, "Censoring Hollywood: Youth, Moral Panic and Crime/Gangster Movies of the 1930s," *Journal of Popular Culture,* Winter 1998. Available from Popular Press, Bowling Green State University, Bowling Green, OH 43403.

Mark A. Vierra, *Sin in Soft Focus: Pre-Code Hollywood.* New York: Harry N. Abrams, 1999.

Index

Index